# DISCOVERING LOST
# AUTOMOBILES
# AND THEIR STORIES

# DISCOVERING LOST
# AUTOMOBILES
## AND THEIR STORIES

## MICHAEL WARE

PEN & SWORD
TRANSPORT
AN IMPRINT OF PEN & SWORD BOOKS LTD.
YORKSHIRE – PHILADELPHIA

First published in Great Britain in 2022 by
Pen and Sword Transport
An imprint of
Pen & Sword Books Ltd.
Yorkshire - Philadelphia

ISBN 978 1 39901 900 2

Typeset in Minion Pro 10/12 by SJmagic DESIGN SERVICES, India.

Printed and bound in India by Replika Press Pvt. Ltd.

Pen & Sword Books Ltd incorporates the imprints of Pen & Sword Books Archaeology, Atlas, Aviation, Battleground, Discovery, Family History, History, Maritime, Military, Naval, Politics, Railways, Select, Transport, True Crime, Fiction, Frontline Books, Leo Cooper, Praetorian Press, Seaforth Publishing, Wharncliffe and White Owl.

For a complete list of Pen & Sword titles please contact

PEN & SWORD BOOKS LIMITED
47 Church Street, Barnsley, South Yorkshire, S70 2AS, England
E-mail: enquiries@pen-and-sword.co.uk
Website: www.pen-and-sword.co.uk

or

PEN AND SWORD BOOKS
1950 Lawrence Rd, Havertown, PA 19083, USA
E-mail: Uspen-and-sword@casematepublishers.com
Website: www.penandswordbooks.com

# CONTENTS

# DEDICATION

I dedicate this book to the work of the Federation of British Historic Vehicle Clubs. Without their vigilance many of the cars described in this book, once they have been restored, would not be able to be taxed and driven on the public highway.

The FBHVC exists to uphold the freedom to use historic vehicles on the road. It does this by representing the interests of owners of such vehicles to politicians, government officials and legislators both in the UK and Europe. There are over 540 subscribing organisations representing a total membership of over 250,000 in addition to individual and trade supporters. Full details from www.fbhvc.co.uk.

# FOREWORD

I am delighted to write the foreword for this fascinating book. Michael Ware is not only a noted author, journalist and researcher, but he's also a motoring legend. He organised the very first Beaulieu Autojumble in 1967. From its modest beginnings, not unlike Glastonbury which was started at a similar time, it has flowed into one of the most important motoring festivals in the world. The essence of the Beaulieu Autojumble is also the essence of this wonderful book. At Beaulieu, we enthusiasts don't see a rusty old spare part, but the potential it has in a future restoration. Whether that restoration becomes a reality or a dream is irrelevant, for the most important part is seeing the potential, and in our imagination turning lead into gold (or in my case metal into rust).

So many of us find great pleasure in discovering some magical hidden dream and this book is filled with them. The great gurus tell us that to find contentment in life we need to find something to love, something to do and something to look forward to. We motoring enthusiasts are fortunate in that our hobby will give us all three of these. Michael's book beautifully reminds me of this as the pages bring our hobby enchantingly to life.

Jools Holland OBE, DL

Jools Holland with one of the cars from his collection.

# INTRODUCTION

When I first became enthusiastic about the older car it was the late 1950s and classics were still on the road in everyday use and the vintage enthusiast looked to scrapyards for pre-war cars to rebuild. For example, my first trip to a scrapyard near Guildford, when I was an art student, produced a vintage Humber in running order. It was priced at £35 and I could not afford it. A trip to Cumberland in 1963 introduced me to two brothers who had run a scrapyard for many years. I was able to discern an early Austin 20 and a 509A Fiat, a 1926 Star. My friend David Skinner who had brought me on this trip was there to buy the remains of a 1919 Vulcan which he purchased for £15. He was also attracted to a c1920 Belsize that had been shortened into a tractor (but the cut off parts were still with it) and purchased that for £10. Later I went with Michael Sedgwick to do an article on Harold Goodey's Yard at Twyford. This was the real thing with tractors, traction engines and 1930s cars literally piled three high on top of one another. Sadly, all these interesting yards are now long gone and those on the hunt have had to look elsewhere. Soon the phrase we are now very familiar with, 'barn find', came into being. So, what is a 'barn find'? Wikipedia sums them up as follows:

A barn find is a classic car, aircraft or motorcycle that has been re-discovered after being stored, often in a derelict condition. The term comes from their tendency to be found in places such as barns, sheds, car ports, and outbuildings, where they have been stored for many years. The term usually applies to vehicles that are rare and valuable and which are consequently of great interest to collectors and enthusiasts despite their poor condition. In the past barn find vehicles were typically subjected to exhaustive restoration, to return them to a condition close to that when they were built. However, the current trend is to treat the cars more sympathetically, to avoid restoration that removed evidence of the cars' history and to place greater value on any original features the car retains even if they are in poor condition.

This book is about barn finds, though I tend not to use those words too often. I have often wondered who coined the phrase. I suspected the late Michael Worthington-Williams who had been writing about such things for far longer than I, but when asked he did not claim to have been the first to use the words, though I suspect he may have been. I also cannot find out from contacts in the USA if the words were first used over there. I suppose it does not matter who used them first. Some people do not like the term as it seems to be specific when in fact it is used to cover a very wide range of locations. Let's just accept it as a generic term and move on!

What I find so fascinating is the history behind the find, why was the vehicle left unused for so many years, often in poor storage? In many cases the owners are as interesting as the cars! I am just as happy to write about ordinary everyday cars as I am about an exotic sports car, and for me the value does not matter. Most of the cars in this book have been off the road for 20 or more years, some over 50 years. The majority of the accounts were published in my 'Lost and Found' column in *Classic and Sports Car* magazine over the last 12 or so years. A book gives one a chance to expand on the relatively short piece used in the magazine. I am grateful to *Classic and Sports Car* for allowing these items to be re-worked and presented here.

I drifted into writing about long lost cars quite by accident. I was a photographer by profession and after three years training at the Guildford School of Art Photographic department I started my own business in 1959 and by a stroke of luck got drawn into motor sport photography for the next five years. Nothing posh like Grand Prix racing but mainly ordinary club racing, hill climbs and sprints. In 1963 I took up the post of Photographic Librarian (and photographer) at the Montagu

Motor Museum at Beaulieu. In 1966 the Museum's Curator 'the late, great Michael Sedgwick' decided to go out on his own as a freelance motoring writer. Lord Montagu asked if I would like to become the Museum's curator – a career change I had never envisaged. In 1972 the present Museum building was opened and the Museum became a Charitable Trust and I remained as curator and manager of the Trust until retirement in 2001.

In 1983 Tony Dron had become editor of *Thoroughbred and Classic Cars* (later just *Classic Cars*) and had asked a friend of mine, Nick Baldwin, if he would write a monthly column entitled 'Discovered'. He also suggested to Tony that I be allowed to help him! Looking back on those early articles I see that we were referred to as motoring sleuths and it was not until 1985 that our names were actually divulged and included on the page. In the first appearance of the column a story which fascinated me concerned the remains of a c1927 Brocklebank, a Birmingham built car. I just loved the name and the fact that it was owned by the Thunderstorm Census Organisation. Why

they had the remains is not recorded. I wrote at the time, 'The chassis has been exposed to the weather, for many years, but one or two other bits and pieces are apparently under cover. There is no mention of the car having been struck by lightning!' Since that time, even though I have written over 3,100 such articles I have not written about another Brocklebank or in fact heard of another one. No doubt there is a Brocklebank around somewhere – probably in Australia as many British cars were exported new down under, and a surprising number have survived there. Just as this book was going to press, I heard from an enthusiast who had found a Brocklebank. It had been taken apart for restoration some 50 years ago, and the rebuild had not happened. Yes, you have guessed it, it was found in Australia.

In 1987 Nick Baldwin went to work with Supercar Classics and I was on my own. Wonderful editors such as Tony Dron and later Robert Coucher kept me on a slightly wavy straight and narrow. In 2000 I was unhappy at the way a new editorial team were treating my

submissions and I moved over to Haymarket's *Classic and Sports Car* magazine to help Mick Walsh write 'Lost and Found'. Soon I was working with Richard Heseltine and editor James Elliott and later the present editor Alastair Clements to whom I give many thanks. They were all very long suffering.

I am often asked, 'How on earth do you find all these cars?' The answer is quite simple; I do not find them, other people find them and my skill (if that is the right word) is hearing about the find as soon as possible and then asking the owner if I might write about it. My very sincere thanks go out to all owners who have put up with me badgering them for details of their find, the car's history and do you have photographs of it 'as found'? Photographs are to my mind very important. I hope readers of this book will get some idea of the excitement of finding a car in the barn (or other places). It does not have to be a Ferrari, the story behind a Model T Ford or Austin 7 can be just as interesting and sometimes amusing. Some are almost unbelievable such as the Ferrari that required Papal permission for it to be removed from its village resting place, or the MGB with only 1,000 miles on the clock that the owner thought was awful, but even so kept it for 35 years or possibly the lady who sent birthday cards to her car each year and they have survived with the car!

Michael E. Ware. September 2022.

# 1 | SOME STRANGE LOCATIONS

Old and supposedly abandoned cars can be found in the most unlikely of places as you will see as you read through this book. For this chapter I have picked out some which seem to be out of the ordinary.

Back in 2017, I was very surprised when I heard from the Wessex Archaeology Trust that they had unearthed a car on one of their digs. Army bases in Germany were being closed and the troops were returning to the UK. Larkhill on Salisbury Plain has been a garrison town since late Victorian times and many new houses were being built here for those troops. The ground had been cleared and as it is so near Stonehenge the archaeologists moved in. They found Bronze Age burial sites, traces of Iron Age and Roman life. The greatest surprise was miles of zig zag trenches which had been dug by soldiers in training before being sent to France in the First World War. Not only that, there were tunnels in the chalk which were of the type dug under enemy lines so that explosives could be set off under the German trenches. These tunnels had many messages and signatures on the walls and lots of personal items, rifles and live ammunition and ancient tins of food. Also excavated was a depression, which it was decided later had once been a practice artillery pit from training there in the 1950s. This too had been filled in with rubble, including the remains of a motor car, a very battered 1932 MG J2 (chassis number J2.192). The engine and gearbox had been removed, most of the body had disintegrated. Like the trenches and tunnels, it had been buried and forgotten.

Jeremy Hawke of the MG Car Club has seen the car and told me:

The remains of the 1932 MG J2 as dug up by the archaeologists.

The chassis side rails are quite good, the front axle is bent and the rear axle has 'no integrity'. Many of the solid bits are still there, as is the remains of the scuttle and the rear panel. The doors are just an imprint in the ground with hinges attached. Interestingly, the J2 engine was long gone and a Ford 10 unit substituted. This had a large hole in the crankcase caused by external forces rather than a 'blow up'. All things point to the car being buried at the end of the 1950s or early 1960s.

The tyres have a 1950s style tread. The MG Car Club records show this car as having been registered EN 5229 and sold by dealers J. Cockshoot & Co. of Manchester to Edward Riley. No other history is known. The rescued car was sold by

Witham Specialist Vehicles Ltd. and they donated their commission to The Army Benevolent Fund and the War Widows Association.

There are times when you find strange things at the bottom of the garden. Chris and Tracy Ward recently moved into a new home in St. Peter's Parish on the Channel Island of Guernsey. When Tracy's parents came to stay, her father was asked to help tidy up a very neglected but well-established rockery in an area of ground some way from the house. After the removal of some soil and large stones, his spade hit the top of a solid object which turned out to be an engine. First thoughts were that it was from a tractor. Further digging found a chassis with front axle, gearbox, bumpers, door glass and lots of very rusty bits. A plate on the gearbox says it's Daimler and the gearbox number (27509) is from around 1948. No chassis number has been found as yet. An English number plate has been found – GUK 880 – which is Wolverhampton from 1948. No Guernsey number has been found. Experts from the Guernsey Old Car Club and Kevin Bennett from the Daimler and Lanchester Owners' Club have come to the conclusion it is probably a 1948 Daimler DB18 and a piece of woodwork points to possibly a drop head coupe. So far there are no clues how or why this car came to be buried, but by the state of it, it was certainly a long time ago!

Continuing with those that required digging. The Volkswagen Transporter, Kombi van or microbus were often known as Sambas. At first the Volkswagen Transporter did not catch on in the USA, but by June 1960, the USA were Volkswagen's leading export market.

Unearthing the Daimler chassis from the rockery.

The half-buried Volkswagen Samba which was used as a storm shelter.

One such, a 1960 Samba Microbus, performed an unusual role in 1983 after the Oklahoma owner took it off the road, removed the engine and half buried it to provide a storm shelter from tornadoes. Twenty-five years later, a passing hunter saw the 'shelter', recognised what it was and told Volkswagen enthusiast Adam about it. Adam tried to buy it, but it was not for sale. Five years later Adam tried again. The owner had died but his brother agreed to sell it to him. They arranged for some dozen other Samba enthusiasts to help dig it out of the red soil bank into which it had been built. With the aid of a small mechanical digger, the cutting down of many trees and a lot of very hard spade work, they achieved its removal in around six hours. On the way home they took it to a car wash and the result proved it to be in much better condition than one might have expected.

In 2015 my Australian correspondent, Garrie Hisco, contacted me to say he had found the remains of a Dodson car, made in London. I had to find out more as I had never heard of it. It would appear that the Dodson (1910-14) was an almost exact copy of the Renault chassis, though *The Motor* reports: '… made with English threads and pitches'. It was manufactured by David Brown of Huddersfield but sold by Dodson Motors of Maddox Street, London, later moving to 34 Bond Street. Mr Dodson had formerly been the Managing Director of Renault England before moving to David Brown's. The Dodson car was made at the same time as the Valveless, another car manufactured by David Brown; later Valveless were reputed to have used the Dodson

The Samba being removed from its resting place and then to the car wash.

The Dodson was a good looking car when new, very Renault like at the front.

chassis. In 1912, Dodson, Valveless and SAVA, the latter a company for which David Brown had an agency, were on the same stand at the Motor Show.

The remains of the Dodson consisted of a chassis with dismantled engine, gearbox and the remains of two wheels, one of which has Dodson on the wheel nut. It is in a collection of cars and extremely difficult to see or to photograph. I enquired of the late Mike Worthington-Williams if he had ever heard of one and he told me he had

written about one in Australia in his 'Finds and Discoveries' column in *The Automobile* in July 1998. From comparing photographs, we were sure these are one and the same.

At the end of the 1960s, Jim Hepburn was at a show in Cooma, Victoria with his 1913 Fiat. A lady took great interest in the car, especially in the outside hand brake lever. She told him that when mowing in her back garden she struck an object

One wheel had Dodson on the wheel nut.

sticking up through the ground that looked just like that brake lever. Jim was invited to have a look, his visit ending with the mutilated remains of the Dodson being dug up. He sold it a few years later to the present owner who has done nothing with it. I was told:

> There is a chassis and the remains of an engine, it appears to be a four cylinder consisting of two blocks of two cylinders and a separate gearbox with what looks like a cone clutch. One of the blocks of two have been shattered. The brake and the gear lever are bent exactly as in the picture in Mike Worthington-Williams' article from 1998 which convinces me, amongst other things, this is the same car.

It is thought to be the only Dodson surviving, though the last time I wrote that about a car of this age a one family owner car turned up, also in Australia!

When Shadi Eddin was looking for a Ginetta G4 he never expected to end up looking in a shed on a Cornish cliff top! A keen Ginetta Owners' Club member, Shadi heard a rumour that a member in Cornwall had owned such a car for nearly

The chassis was in amazing condition for its age.

forty years and no-one had seen it in that time. He made contact with Michael Gay, a carpenter from Redruth, to find that he had bought the car in 1971, used it a little and then took it apart for restoration. Other things then took precedence and the car was still in pieces. However, Mr Gay had not thought of selling. It took nine months of persuasion and then he relented. Shadi went to see it and told me:

> His property [the shed] was precariously perched on top of a cliff face, the chassis was in amazing condition for its age, all the body panels were available, he also had the original engine block, radiator, gearbox, fuel tank, A40 back axle, wheels and suspension. It was all too good to be true. I made Mr Gay an offer.

He was very pleased to hear that Shadi was going to send the car to be restored by the Walklett family back at the Ginetta factory. When Shadi returned to Cornwall to collect the car he brought with him Tom Walklett, Ivor Walklett's son. The car is now being restored by the Walkletts and Shadi hopes to take part in some HSCC racing with it.

It is known that 15 URO was built in 1963 by Philip Emerton alongside another Ginetta being built up by journalist Chris Webb for *Practical Motorist* which has a consecutive chassis number and was registered 25 URO. After the build that

Gear lever bent in the same way as the illustration in Mike Worthington-Williams' article in 1998.

car was road tested for the magazine by Graham Hill who achieved 110mph, not bad for the 1,200cc engine. Shadi's car had three owners in the London area before moving to Cornwall in 1970 and was bought by Michael Gay the following year.

Built by Practical Motorist journalist Chris Webb.

In 2019 Marreyt Classics from Aalst in Belgium offered for sale a lovely 1960 Alfa Romeo Giulietta Spider Veloce. This recently restored car had been auctioned as a 'barn (or rather castle) find' in 2015. It had been found, along with five other 1960s Alfas, in the underground cellars of a castle. Kasteel Van Heers in the province of Limburg dates back to the thirteenth century. It fell on hard times and one of two brothers, Michael Demaistieres, lived there until 2007 doing his best to keep the rain out of part of it. They had been keen Alfa Romeo enthusiasts in their day. Michael had also built an Alfa Special and had raced it. The Flemish government had provided some money towards repairs to the castle roof, but then heard about the cars and took over ownership of the castle. The cars were auctioned to provide a little money towards the repairs. Sadly, no pictures were taken of the Marreyt Alfa in the cellars. This

The underground cellars of Kasteil van Heers.

car left the factory on 17 December 1960; its original colour was white. It has been fully restored by Italian Alfa specialists Carrozzeria Franco and Team Benetello.

It seems surprising to me that quite a number of abandoned cars have been found in underground garages. Was someone paying rent for all these years? Francisco Carrion had been a young Spanish lawyer living in London, but he is also a very keen old car enthusiast. He found a complete c1956 Bristol 404 that had been lurking in a long-closed Spanish garage for ten years but it has been off the road for over thirty and received very little use before that. It has 34,390 kilometres on the clock! Francisco told me that the Bristol was bought at the Paris Salon. The first owner was the grandson of the founder of a well-known Spanish

Lurking in a long closed Spanish garage.

bank, but he died only three years after taking delivery. The car was stored until the mid-1970s when it was put back on the road, but only used for a short time before again being stored. Later, the car was spotted in a shed which was in danger of collapsing. It was moved to the now closed service garage and has stood there ever since. Found under the seat was a picture of the car at the Paris Salon.

Francisco went on to tell me:

This car is not alone … in the same garage there are 14 abandoned cars including a Rover P4, BMW 700, Alfa Romeo 2600, Nathan-tuned Hillman Imp, 1930 DKW F2, Humber Hawk and a Cadillac which was used in the 1979 film *Cuba* starring Sean Connery. All the cars belong to an old man who has been renting the garage for decades. It had been a workshop since the 1920s and there are lots of old spare parts everywhere.

When a group of enthusiasts get together, they often reminisce about forgotten cars they have heard about in barns and stables. Usually, the lost Bugatti turns out to be an Austin 7 Special or that veteran car is a pre-war invalid carriage – that story was true and it was sold as a veteran to some unsuspecting enthusiast. For Adolfo Massari of LBI of Pennsylvania these stories are all worth following up. He told me, 'When mention of three cars sitting in an underground parking structure in Manhattan for the last 40 years was made, it piqued our interest.' Many phone calls later they were in contact with the owner. He told them the usual story, that he had bought them to restore but never did. He listed them as a 1937 Packard hearse, a 1937 Rolls-Royce with a fine body and a 1938 Delahaye Cabriolet. It turned out the cars were in a 'nondescript individual building in the middle of Long Island, New York'. The owner opened the metal doors of the underground parking lot: '… sitting before us, partly obscured by boxes, were three vehicles covered in dust and dirt that had been sitting there for quite some time [40 years]. We had stumbled onto something quite special'. Many photographs and video were taken before trying to move the cars. Extraction (so often overlooked by magazine reports) took two days as the

Left: 1937 Packard Hearse. Middle: 1937 Rolls-Royce. Right: 1938 Delahaye Cabriolet.

Extraction took two days to arrange.

vehicles were very tightly packed, had not moved for so long and were on flat tyres. At the same time, they wanted much of the dust and dirt to be left intact.

Once back in Philadelphia, work began on research, and still continues. The 1937 Packard was as described with coachwork by Silver Knightstown Body Company of Indiana. It had been a hearse/ambulance and finished its years as a cemetery vehicle in Brooklyn. The 1937 Rolls-Royce, still sporting its British registration at the rear (EGJ 44), was bought new by Sir Phillip Sassoon, a long-time Member of Parliament. As purchased, it had been fitted with a Barker open body. Mr Sassoon died in 1939 – one presumes the car was sold shortly after that. At some stage another body was fitted, a very stylish one built by the Paris firm of Franay, thought to have been similar to the coachwork which they displayed at the 1937 Paris Auto Show. At present no other history

The Rolls-Royce bought new by Sir Philip Sassoon.

is known other than the car spent some years in Texas before moving to the East Coast in around 1978. The Delahaye was not as described! It was not 1938 but a 1947 Delahaye 135M with coachwork by the Belgian firm Vesters and Neirink and had been displayed at the 1948 Brussels Auto Show. This firm, founded in 1923, only built seven

Rolls-Royce on the roof of a high rise building in Karachi.

Possibly a Markham Peasey Super Sabre body shell on a Scottish roof top.

bodies after the war before concentrating on trucks. It is thought the car spent part of its life on the island of St. Martin in the Caribbean. Later, it passed through the hands of early dealer Ed Jirst (Vintage Car Store) in New York who sold it to this last owner for $350!

Now here is a real mystery. Why, or even how, did a 1928 Rolls-Royce Barker bodied tourer, chassis (GWL 2), end up on the roof of a high rise building in Karachi? It is thought to be owned by the son of the famous Bollywood actor Sheik Mukhtar. When I saw the photographs I turned to my friend, Rolls-Royce expert John Fasal. John told me that he had first seen this car in Karachi in December 1983 when it was at ground level. It was in poor condition but still had its radiator. John went on to say, 'What on earth is it doing on the roof? When I saw it in 1983 there was enough of the car to use as patterns and the chassis was pretty complete, it would have made a worthwhile restoration.' John, who has seen almost all the Rolls-Royce cars in India, told me that the first owner was H.H. The Maharana of Udaipur and it later went to H.H. The Maharaja of Jodhpur.

You might be surprised at what you may find if you cast your eyes upwards. Whilst travelling on the road from Oban to Duror in Scotland, Francisco Carrion happened to look up as he was passing a garage workshops and was surprised to see a car on the roof. He asked the garage owner what it was and received the reply, 'I do not know the marque, but I think it was a kit car'. The only other information forthcoming was that it was an abandoned car in the 1990s, but 'we are not sure for how long it's been on the roof'. After careful scrutiny, we think it's a special built with a Markham Peasey Super Sabre body. The registration number is TYH 598 which is from Huddersfield, early 1961, which ties in nicely with the great special building period. These bodies were

built for the longer wheel base Austin 7 or the Ford 10, though this one might be on a Morris chassis.

There is a fascination with finding cars under water. Perhaps the one all enthusiasts want to find is the 25hp Renault owned by William Carter which was the only car being carried on the Titanic on the voyage on which it sank. Ernest Carter was travelling with his wife Lucille, two children and chauffeur. The family survived the disaster, but the Renault is still 13,000 feet below the surface of the Atlantic and as far as I know its presence has not been spotted by any of the submersibles that have surveyed the wreck.

Aircraft archaeologists have located many crashed aircraft on the seabed, some of which have been raised and restored. Railway historians seem to be well organised as the *Railway Magazine* of September 2007 has a long article entitled 'Lost at Sea' and listing 90 known ships that have been wrecked carrying locomotives. I have not seen any such listings for ships carrying cars. There are tales of ships carrying cars being lost in the winter on the Great Lakes in the United States, and I have only read about one such car being retrieved. There was of course the well reported story of the 1925 Bugatti Type 22 Brescia which was raised from Lake Maggore in 2009. The wreck was subsequently bought by Peter Mullin for his Mullin Automobile Museum in Oxnand in California. In 2014 the Poseidon Luzern diving club were practicing on Lake Lucerne and found a car in ten metres of water, in sight of the shoreline of a very isolated part of the lake. For members of this club

The Porsche 356 coupe emerging from Lake Lucerne.

this was not unusual, they had previously found more than 200 sunken boats on the lakebed as well as 40 cars, even aircraft. In this case underwater photographs showed this to be a c1954 Porsche 356 Coupe; interest was such that it was thought it should be raised. Using their rescue ship *Kon Tiki* divers retrieved the car. Its origins are a complete mystery. Before it was submerged the car had been stripped of its interior as well as engine and gearbox and licence plates. There are no roads in this area of the lake so it is assumed it was dropped from a ship of some sort. It is also presumed it was dumped as it was a stolen car or involved in some sort of insurance fraud. The car was recently spotted in a local driveway. There must be more to this story, but it has so far eluded me.

The car had been stripped of its interior and engine and gearbox.

The Porsche now cleaned up and stored in a local driveway. (A. Teufer)

Convair Mk 1 body shell in a Gloucestershire pond.

In March 2010 I wrote a piece about a Special that Martin Dayton had found adjacent to a foot path near the village of Staunton in Gloucestershire. What was unusual about the find was the car was part in and part out of a pond, and by the looks had been there a very long time. None of us could identify it so I appealed to the readers. Soon after publication I heard from Angus Dudley to say it was a special with a Convair Mk1 body on it. His father-in-law, Clive Wren, who formed Convair Developments of Leytonstone in 1956, had built this body and many others. Angus had, in fact, been to Staunton to see the car in the pond and remarked that it was an unusual colour, being blueberry blue. Another reader, Nigel Dobbie, also visited it and took some very good photos.

Later I heard from a collector of unusual and obscure cars from Greece, Alex Vazeos, who wanted to buy a Convair bodied special, and Angus Dudley told him that the one in the pond was the only one he knew of that was available. Ally Stuart and a team of helpers from Stuart Classics

of Ipswich have rescued the car from the pond. I was told that as well as the body and chassis: '… we have found the engine, gearbox, fuel tank, axles and various other parts'. The car had its registration plates with it, EKU 16, a Bradford number from late 1946. Bradford's records only showed the registration had been cancelled in December 1964. We assume this number was that of the donor car. With Convair only making this body in the late 1950s, it does seem unlikely that the special had come off the road in 1964. No history of this car has come forward. It so happened that my late brother-in-law was Chairman of the Staunton and Coarse Parish Council at the time, and he tried to find out locally if anyone could remember the incident of the car being put into the pond. No luck.

In 2015 I was driving away from Launceston after visiting the steam railway there. I took the A388 to Holsworthy which passes through Chapman's Well. Here was situated a roadside garage (the petrol pumps had already been removed) which looked to have been abandoned for some years. The forecourt was covered in mud and leaves. On the forecourt was a very derelict Triumph TR3, a Jaguar XJS, Triumph Stag and a Triumph TR6 behind. Through the moss-covered windows one could make out a Triumph TR5 under the ramp, with a Michelotti TR of some sort on the lift, also the rear end of a Porsche. A Ford RS Sierra Cosworth was in the corner. The contents of the garage workshop and the attached shop look as if they have never been touched since the day the owner locked up. A quite amazing sight for these days. *Classic and*

The body shell after being removed from the pond.

A very derelict Triumph TR3 on the forecourt of a disused roadside garage.

The interior of the garage just as it had been left in the last days of business.

*Sports Car* are very keen that readers do not trespass in their enthusiasm to get closer to abandoned vehicles so I did not go round the back to see what else might have been there.

Twenty-five or so years ago my friend Vivian Orchard, who has since passed away, took me to a secret location where there were two interesting cars stored. The oldest of the two was a 1912 2-cylinder Renault which had obviously been off the road for many, many years. It looked reasonably complete but very rusty, the wings are missing in my photographs. The coal scuttle bonnet with radiator behind looked complete, though the chassis was broken at the front. The pictures depict the absolutely typical derelict barn find. We were then taken to a large indoor riding school building where a number of items of farm machinery and old lumber were stored, as well as a small number of cars including a Morris Minor van. At the far end of the barn was a 1928 Rolls-Royce 20hp 6 light saloon with fabric body by Mulliner. This had obviously been standing a long time and was covered in a white dust. The car looked complete, but whether it was in running order was not known. We were sworn to secrecy at the time. I have kept an eye on this

1912 Renault had been off the road for many years.

1928 Rolls-Royce 20hp fabric saloon by Mulliner.

location ever since, and it has recently been sold to a developer. To the best of my knowledge, neither of these cars has come up for public sale. I wondered where they have gone.

A chance remark to John Fasal, the Rolls-Royce expert, at the Beaulieu Autojumble, provided the answer. Both were now in the possession of Tarka King from Dorset. I can now reveal the location was Norris Castle, a grade 1 listed building on the Isle of Wight, built in 1799, with 225 acres of land and a mile of sea frontage. The buildings were in a poor state of repair when I visited. The last owner died in 2014. It has since been bought to turn into a luxury hotel and wedding venue.

The Rolls-Royce registered YH 4229 was last driven on the road when it came to the Isle of Wight in 1964. It needed work so was just used on the estate for taking visitors down the road to the beach. By 1970 it was out of use and in leaky storage. It moved to the riding school in 1972. Tarka, who is a distant relation of the previous owners, kept an eye on it from afar. In 2015 he and his cousin Robert Frewen were able to acquire it. Removing it was made more difficult by a large bramble bush which had crept in behind and almost overwhelmed it. The absolutely bald tyres did actually hold air and the rusted spoked wheels did not collapse so moving it was not too difficult. When he collected it, he was asked if he wanted the Renault, a car he was unaware was on the premises. Unlike the time I saw it, chickens had been let loose around it and had laid many eggs in the vicinity. When trodden on, they gave out an appalling odour! Registered LK 4188, no-one has any idea of its history or how it ended up at Norris Castle.

The Rolls-Royce 20 and the 1912 Renault at the home of Tarka King.

1915 Chevrolet being used on the Mangapura Valley settlement.

The Rolls-Royce was given a quick overhaul so it could be used off the roads for Tarka's daughter's wedding. It is now receiving a body-off restoration. The Renault has, however, been offered for sale.

As part of a re-settlement scheme for First World War veterans, land in the remote Mangapura Valley of North Island, New Zealand was put aside for them to settle and farm. Only thirty took up the offer. The land was steep and laborious to clear, difficult to farm, access was never improved, and life was hard. By the end of the 1930s most families had left. One of the earliest to take up settlement was Edward Johnson, who arrived complete with his 1915 (1916 Model) Chevrolet 4-90 4-seat tourer. This he used on his farm but when he left, the roads were so bad he could not get it out. The full story of the settlement is told in the book *The Bridge to Nowhere* by Arthur P. Bates (Wanganui Newspapers, 1983). The government built a bridge into the valley in the late 1930s but by this time nearly everyone had left!

Len Crane was posted from the UK to New Zealand by Westland Helicopters. He recounted in a written recollection the story of his finding the car in 1973:

> A bush pig hunter told me there was the remains of an old car located in the remote Mangapurua Valley … I and two friends went into the valley on scramble bikes which was not easy as the land had reverted to dense native bush. We located the car still sitting in the same spot … the only way to get it out was by helicopter … we flew in, roped it up and put it on the winch. The pilot flew it out

and dropped it onto a flatbed truck which we had waiting at the nearest main road … when I returned to the UK a few years later [1977] I shipped the Chevrolet back in a crate.

Len has now decided that as the car has been in his care for 40 years and only minor work has been done on it, it should pass to an enthusiast to rebuild. Richard Skinner, a professional restorer, has now purchased the car. It is completely dismantled with no body aft of the scuttle but amazingly for an outdoor find, no-one has been in and stolen parts; there is even one complete headlamp and the key was still in the ignition.

For those of us who live in the United Kingdom and Europe, Alaska seems a long way away, remote and sometimes inhospitable. There is something fascinating about the Fiat Abarth with double bubble aluminium body by Zagato. When Fiat introduced the 600 in 1956, Abarth of Turin immediately made a 750 version. Fiat supplied Abarth with part finished cars and in return got a lot of publicity from the sporting success that Abarth cars obtained. A 1956 double bubble Fiat Abarth surfaced in of all places, Alaska. The owner raced this car at Tarracross raceway in Alaska as well as two Testarossa Ferraris! The Fiat was also used for road racing, but then was

The disassembled 1915 Chevrolet.

The 1956 Double Bubble Fiat Abarth found in Alaska.

converted for ice racing on Big Lake. It was fitted with a full race Buick V8 engine mounted further forward than the original. It had a Corsair transaxle and custom cut gears.

Sometime later it was sold and the new owner told me that he had been looking for this car for 40 years and as a young man he was fascinated by the man with the Testarossa Ferraris and the little Fiat. He had been told that originally the car had won its class in the Mille Miglia. When bought, the car was about to be dismantled as the engine was wanted for another car. As for the Mille Miglia story, who knows? Sales talk? I couldn't find reference to any such class win.

Amid all this talk of far off and exotic places, don't forget that there might be a surprise right on your doorstep. Here is one just three miles down the road from where I live in Hampshire. When Norman Reynolds retired from his family removal business, he started restoring old vehicles as a hobby. One day when he took his 1939 Morris ½ton truck for its MOT, a stranger came up to him saying if you are interested in restoring old cars you ought to meet my neighbour, he has four of them standing in his garden. By the

The undergrowth had to be cut down before the Austin Sevens became visible.

A shed with two Austins in it and a vine growing up the side.

time I heard about them, Norman and friends had done a day's gardening and cleared a number of trees and undergrowth from around these cars. Having heard of the state of these cars, I expected to find a run-down premises with overgrown garden. Not a bit of it; a very neat house with a Mercedes in the drive. A very long garden out the back in immaculate and beautiful order. Then a vegetable plot and a shed with two cars in, with a vine growing up the side, another shed and a greenhouse and two cars in the open covered in a variety of tarpaulins.

The owner, Dave Sheppard, had been a keen member of the Austin 10 Drivers Club and restored and rallied two such cars. In 1972 he tried to interest his sons in car restoration and bought three unroadworthy cars for the family to work on, and then another a little later. The sons soon lost interest and the four cars have sat in the garden since then. Dave has had serious back trouble so was unable to work on these

or his other cars himself. The two in the open are a 1935 four-door Austin 10 Sherborne, BTA 882, and a 1935 Austin 7 Ruby Saloon, AAA 454. Both are likely to be past saving but would yield spares. The others in the lean-to shed are a 1935 Austin 7 Pearl Cabriolet 'CME 667' and a 1937 Austin 10/4 2-seat tourer with dickey, EGC 953. I was told the cars had been on wooden blocks, but these must have rotted away as they were now standing on the earth. From a quick glance I imagine these latter two are restorable. There was also a host of spares including four Austin 10 engines, three engines for Austin 7s, spare axles, wheels and tyres, and a lot of electrical parts such as dynamos and starters. Dave Sheppard has now parted with the cars and spares to Norman but on condition that they were not moved until the runner beans were over as the neat rows of beans are between the cars and the only exit! Getting them out at the bottom of this very long garden was a problem as the gateway was only 5ft wide.

# 2 ACQUISITIVE COLLECTORS

One can imagine the excitement of an enthusiast who is present when a long-sealed door is about to be opened. The saplings growing up in front of it are removed, as are the piles of leaves and weeds. The doors creak open and there lies an entombed old car. Imagine the surprise and amazement if, behind the door, there is a collection of cars whether it be five, ten, fifty or one hundred. People who have collections of unrestored cars are, at times, a strange bunch. In this first story, the cars were not behind closed doors but behind a very strong barbed wire top fence. In 2014 I heard from Yvette VanDerBrink, Head of VanDerBrink Auctions of Minnesota who had recently sold a car collection owned by a most extraordinary man, Oliver Jordan.

By all accounts Oliver Jordan from Enid, Oklahoma was a tough, rough car collector. In 1945 he purchased an existing scrapyard (salvage yard). He bought and sold cars and parts until '… the City told Oliver to make changes to his business for zoning … no-one was going to tell him how he was going to run his business, so in 1953 he shut the doors – literally'. He continued to buy in cars and soon the property was covered in hundreds of collector vehicles from the late 'teens to the 1950s. He enclosed his land and collection with a high barbed wire fence and had a number of guard dogs. Many came to buy cars or parts but each time the answer was the same, 'No'. Yvette told us 'Mr Jordan was constantly trying to keep his privacy and guarding his land against expansion from the City of Enid'.

Oliver lived inside the fortress with his wife Ruby. His grandson Stuart Piontek came to help,

moved some of the cars around, took an inventory of them, and built a building to put some under cover. When Oliver died in 2004, they tried to sell the collection complete. There was great interest but no takers. Ruby passed away and the family sold this collection of over 250 cars and tons of spare parts in single lots at a no reserve auction.

The VanDerBrink listing of all the vehicles reads like an encyclopaedia of American cars of the period. There were no European cars at all. Here are just a few of the 250 cars that were on offer – a 1936 Cord 810 Sedan and a 1937 Cord 812 supercharged, a 1937 Lincoln all aluminium passenger sedan, 1929 Model A Ford breakdown truck (wrecker) which was Oliver's first tow truck, 1938 Chevrolet Master deluxe two-door sedan known as the 'honeymoon car', and 1937 Buick

1936 Cord 810 Sedan one of two Cords on sale.

Oliver lived inside the fortress with his wife Ruby.

Imagery Date:19956/2011    36°21'44.98" N   97°52'09.39" W  elev  1293 ft    eye alt   1837 ft

Over 250 cars were on offer.

fast back sedan. The oldest car on offer was a 1917 Maxwell, whilst one of the rarest was a 1924 Rollin. There was a rare 1940 Hudson Super 6 two-door sedan, a 1940 and a 1950 Kaiser, plus many trucks and some tractors. It must be said that many of the vehicles were in very poor condition and could only be described as parts cars.

Quite a different type of collection this time. Here the owner, Don Lacer from Junction City, Kansas was selling most of his collection in his lifetime. It numbers around fifty cars plus much memorabilia and a few trucks and even a side by side pedal vehicle. This collection was featured as an exclusive on www.barnfinds.com. They had the chance to visit and to photograph the cars and to talk to Don about his career and the collection:

'I am a Kansas native, born and bred in Junction City. We are Fort Riley's home town … My career eventually grew into a late model dealership. My father worked for the Union Pacific Railroad … whilst collecting cars along the way. During the 1950s and 1960s soldiers brought a variety of European cars to Fort Riley which included Jaguar, Delahaye, BMW, Riley, Mercedes-Benz, etc … my father would buy them. I can remember coming home from school one day and there were two Mercedes-Benz Gullwings in the driveway. My father would buy the cars, park them inside the warehouse and that is where they remained … At the time of his death he had 120 cars in his collection. Unfortunately, many of the cars had then to be sold.

Whilst the majority of the vehicles are American, there are a number of unusual (in the USA) European cars such as Citroen DS, Borgward Hansa, Rover 75 Cyclops, Austin Cambridge, Austin A35 Sunbeam Imp and a Riley RM. Don has added considerably to the collections as well.

Star of the show was the Manta Ray concept car, built in the 1950s by Glen Hire and Vernon Antoine of Whittier, California. Both were aircraft design engineers. It had a glass fibre fourteen-piece body shell mounted on a 1951 Studebaker chassis with Studebaker V8 engine, later to be substituted by one from a Cadillac. It was built as a styling

An unusual find in the USA, a Rover 75 cyclops.

The Manta Ray concept car alongside a Riley RM.

exercise and as such it ran but the emphasis had been on looks. In 1959 it was bought by Don's father and added to the collection. It is reputed he swapped it for a 1952 Morris, 1952 Volkswagen and a 1953 Packard. It has been virtually unseen ever since. Recently it has had work done on it in order that it can attend some shows.

Now for something quite different. Some years ago, I gave a talk to the Isle of Wight Austins. Afterwards a member, Alan Millbank, who has helped me in the past, gave me a packet of photographs saying '… these were taken in 1991 of a farmer's collection in a series of barns, I wonder if they are still there?' The name and address of the owner was also included. The photographs depicted a Model T Ford lorry, another Model T with a sort of toast rack body, and a third T with the remains of a very old, possibly horse-drawn, 'Eccles' caravan on the back. There was a blue and a green Austin 7, three six cylinder Austins, a Rolls-Royce saloon, an early 1920s ABC with horizontally opposed air-cooled motor, a Rytecraft Scootacar, plus at least six microcars. I wrote to the address, never expecting an answer, and received an almost immediate reply '… Come and visit, you will be most welcome. I have still got some of the cars but have parted with others'.

What a great day I had. Martin (not his real name) was a most interesting and hospitable 83-year-old, living in a rambling farm house surrounded by barns. During his very varied career he said, 'I have been fiddling with old cars for over fifty years, buying most for ten or twenty pounds each'. His collection of microcars came about because in the early 1960s he had the idea of making the ideal small car. He bought the microcars as a sort of 3D crib sheet, or possibly as examples of what not to do! He was later particularly struck by William Town's Minissima, but all he had as a reminder of that was a Corgi model of one. All but two of the microcars plus the Rytecraft Scootacar had been sold.

As we walked around, he showed me the two Austin 7s still there. A 1929 green one, UL 6373, that he had bought from a local farmer who had converted the rear end into a simple pick-up (with trailer) to collect cob nuts from his orchard. The other, another 1929 Chummy, was registered GC 145. Nearby the two Austin 6s '… smaller than the

7' quipped Martin. Both were convertibles. The 1934 example had been a taxi forty to fifty years ago when he bought it. The other, DPG 422, was the more modern looking 1935 model. Two microcars remained, a 1962 Peel 49cc P50, and the very rare German built Brutsch 49cc Mopetta. Both could claim to be one of the smallest cars ever built – they were strictly single seaters and with no room for even a shopping basket.

One that had me baffled was the Peel Yacht car. All that remained was a fibreglass platform for a

The fibreglass platform of the Peel Yacht car.

Austin Seven converted to a light pick-up for collecting cob nuts.

four wheeler of small proportions that I was told was designed to carry four people and would be placed on a yacht to give the yachtsmen transport when visiting port. I turned to George Gelling who had been the Chief Engineer at Peel Engineering. He told me that one Yacht car was, in fact, made. It had a 197cc Villiers engine hung behind the rear axle and driving forward by a complicated series of chains. He did not know what happened to it. Martin's example was definitely another moulding for a car that was never built. Hanging up in one barn was a mystery chassis; no-one had been able to identify it. It was either later Edwardian or early Vintage, narrow and long, and had come from the Sharpe collection long before they ever decided to sell up.

There was a barn loft with many bicycles, early invalid carriages and mopeds, engines, spare parts galore, and I am sure much more of interest if one had time to delve. Very collectable these days are pedal cars. There were four by Triang from the 1950s (kindly identified for me by Shaun McGee), a blue model Eighty, and another called the Racer, one variant of which was the Brooklands Racer. This particular one had obviously been part of a children's roundabout. A Veteran style Renault complete with its clumsy looking plastic, and now very rare, side lamps, another in the shape of a wartime tank, and a very 'crashed' Austin J40.

Still on the Isle of Wight, Barry Price has lived on the island for all of his life. He and his family run a garage in Newport. Barry is very interested in Isle of Wight history and has a huge collection of historic photographs. When it comes to Isle of

Wight built cars, only two makes are listed for the island, the Lifu steam car (1899-1902) of which one remains in the collection of the Ironbridge Gorge Museum Trust and the other make is Enfield (1969-76). Barry has an eclectic collection of classic cars including five built by Enfield. J.K. Goulandris, a Greek shipping magnate, formed Enfield Automotive in 1969 and employed John Ackroyd (later of Thrust fame) to build the cars on the Greek Island of Syros, with them being finished and distributed from Somerton on the Isle of Wight. John Ackroyd says 123 of the E8000 electrics were produced, of which the Electricity Council bought around half. Barry Price has the first prototype of the Enfield 8000. It is around 9in narrower and more rounded than the production model. This was bought from Somerton works as it was closing down. He also owns a running E8000 which was one of the cars used by the Electricity Council. There is an open electric in orange called

Prototype of the Enfield 8000.

Brooklands racer by Triang.

The Enfield Sphere, a prototype that never went into production.

Enfield Safari with body designed by John Ackroyd.

'The Enfield Sphere' which takes the form of a utility. It did not go into production and again was bought from Somerton works when it was closing down. The further two cars bear no relation to the electrics at all. One was the Enfield Safari built on Jeep running gear with a hand made two-door body designed by John Ackroyd. It was left hand drive.

Tucked away at the back of the collection and quite impossible to view closely, was a blue vehicle called the shooting car. Barry said it had an alloy chassis, a Porsche two-litre engine and Land Rover gearbox. He said the roof could be unclipped leaving a pair of seats at the front and a single seat behind on which would sit the person doing the shooting, or there was plenty of room in which to stand. Enfield also made a one-off four wheel drive V8 called the Chicago which is with another enthusiast on the Island.

Electric cars are very much in the news these days, but Guy Ligier is not normally associated with such vehicles. Guy Ligier was a successful French racing driver and later owner of an F1 team. He was also a good businessman. He went into sports car building with the Ligier JS, the initials standing for his great late friend Jo Schlesser. In 1980 he changed direction and produced the JSR, a squarish two-seater micro car powered by a 50cc Motobecane engine with automatic transmission. It quickly became the best-selling microcar in France.

John Cave, Chairman of the Battery Vehicle Club, heard about thirteen Ligier JSRs that were being offered for sale near Cambridge. He went to see them. They had been standing for many years in a very leaky barn. In the end he decided not to purchase because he already had too many commitments. However, he worked out the story behind them. In 1985 a company was formed called 'City Wheels'. Their coloured brochure says, 'The City Wheels Transport system is designed for moving around city centres, large factories, exhibition sites, leisure parks, airports– in fact anywhere that demands low cost, short distance transportation'. John was told that to launch the scheme some thirteen Ligiers were bought from France and converted by a firm in the Midlands

A line of Ligier JSRs, part of the fleet of 'City Wheels'.

C376 SBL was featured in 'City Wheels' brochure.

to be battery electric powered and to use a swipe card for access and for starting. Ligier did make an electric version and it seems more probable that these were built as electrics. It would appear that City Wheels did not receive the expected finance they needed and failed. Some twenty years later the white and red cars were lying very neglected in a farmer's barn. C376 SBL, which is featured in the City Wheels brochure, is one of these cars. Coventry was one city interested in the scheme and have a City Wheels Electric Car in the collection of their Transport Museum.

Whilst John Cave was in the Cambridgeshire barn where the City Wheels vehicle resided, he photographed four other vehicles. Sadly, the person showing John the Ligiers had no idea of the history of any of them. There was a white Enfield 8000 electric and a Bond 875 made between 1965 and 1970. For a three-wheeler it was unusual in having the engine in the rear, an 875 version of the Hillman Imp engine down rated for use in the Commer Imp van. From the pictures, it looks as if it had been bombed by bird droppings. John Surtees is said to have driven one of these at Brands Hatch and reached over 100mph. The third car took a bit of puzzling out, a three-wheeler with virtually no bodywork. It had wheel steering to a girder fork with single wheel. I think it's a version of the Raleigh Safety Seven, built by bicycle

Bond 875 with Hillman Imp engine.

Believed to be the chassis of a Raleigh Safety Seven.

makers Raleigh of Nottingham between 1933 and 1936. The fourth item is a four-wheeled chassis and I have no idea what it is from, probably dating from the 1930s.

Jim is a thrifty Scotsman, now aged 70. He had spent all of his working life as a constructional engineer based in the Yorkshire Dales, whilst working abroad as well as the United Kingdom. He loves cars but has never had the right sort of money to buy them complete, so over the years he has collected eighteen unrestored and unloved classic and vintage project cars, and at least five motorcycles. My photographer friend David Miller and I visited him at his home in an eighteenth-century cottage. Leading from a living room was a place that at one time had been a workshop. Now it was filled with the motorcycles (British and Japanese) and household and workshop leftovers. On one side, a 1948 Alvis TA14 saloon which was hardly recognisable because of the stuff on top of it. Also a 1928 Dodge Standard Six saloon which had come from Uruguay in 1989, unusually as a runner. In fact, he had driven it around the village green before storing it. Just outside in a lean-to was a 1927 Dodge tourer which came as a failed restoration project from Australia in 1989. It is really two cars being made into one; this one is undergoing restoration. An interesting aside, when Jim buys an incomplete

car, he makes a note of the items and parts that are missing and spends a long time on eBay and the like all over the world and buys the missing bits. On the Alvis, for example, the engine had dropped a valve, so he bought spares for the engine from Red Triangle twenty-five to thirty years ago. Jim told me, 'They are still sitting on the shelf.'

We then journeyed some fifteen miles away to his hillside store, previously a workshop or storage shed. From the outside you can just see what looks like a classic car suspended from the roof. Inside is the family caravan, the rest of the space is chock full of some fourteen cars, some stacked two high at the back where 'shelving' had been created

The Jensen CV8 which was used as a stepping stone to get to see the cars at the back.

The Dodge Standard Six which had come from Uruguay.

around scaffolding poles. Each of the cars on the top shelf are engineless so were not too heavy to raise up there with a block and tackle. Even with a wide angle lens the collection was very difficult to photograph. David, who has always wanted a Jensen CV8, was horrified to find that the only way to photograph the cars at the back was to follow Jim and stand on his CV8, a car he bought some years ago on eBay for £1,000. The Chrysler engine was missing some of the ancillaries. He has now obtained the missing bits, but he has now also acquired a V12 Jaguar engine and automatic gearbox as a possible replacement. Jim is no purist, he just wants to get the cars restored and out there in use. I asked Jim why he had no less than four Reliant Scimitars. He replied, 'There was a period when you could pick up a rough Scimitar for £300. Having a separate chassis makes the Scimitar a good candidate for building specials, so I picked up three for that purpose. The fourth was my main use car from 1986 to 1997, fitted with a Rover V8 engine and five speed box.' One Scimitar chassis was to be shortened to be fitted with a rough condition Cobra Replica body shell he had been given. The fibreglass work required 'was going to

be a challenge'. Some years ago, Jim acquired a set of fibreglass panels for a Jaguar XK150 from someone retiring from the classic car world. He says, 'These panels are not an Aristocrat body but I think are a one-off set commissioned by a businessman many years ago.' An engineless Scimitar sat next to part of the fibreglass shell on the top shelf. In two different places were to be found a complete and unused set of fibreglass panels from a 1960 Edwards Brothers (EB) body shell,

The Dodge tourer came from Australia as a failed restoration project.

originally designed for the Ford Ten chassis in the 1960s. Jim intends to mount this onto a Triumph Herald chassis he bought just for this purpose.

There is a very rusty looking (only surface rust) c1960 Austin Healey frogeye Sprite with original steel bonnet which was bought completely dismantled from Liverpool some ten years ago. 'One floor panel cut out for replacement by the previous owner but replacement not carried out.' A Riley RMA had disappeared under other cars. Jim had bought this in the early 1990s. It had been dry stored since the late 1960s when the owner had stripped it for restoration but never proceeded with it. 'A very good basis for restoration,' says Jim. There is a long story attached to WRW 210, a 1958 Convertible Hillman, similar to one Jim had as a student. From 1962 it had been owned by a family called Hillman (no relation). Husband George died soon after and Mollie, his wife, kept the car on the road and in use from then until she died in 2003. Jim thinks it was kept running as a memorial

Fibreglass panel for a Jaguar XK150 (top left). Engineless Scimitar (below right).

to her late husband. When sold in 2004 it still had an MOT certificate and Jim bought it as he considered it 'a lovely and heart-warming story'. He also has a 1969 Hillman New Minx, the last to bear the name, which he bought from the West Midlands.

The rusty looking c1960 Austin Healey Sprite.

The 1946 Rover 10 and 1946 Austin, both saloons, were purchased in 1979 for £40 each from a coal merchant in Dumbarton, Jim's place of birth. Both were 'fairly derelict'. He has since been able to buy a 10hp and 12hp engine for the one missing from the Rover and the remains of a rotten identical Austin, which will produce mechanical spares.

The very heavy rains in July 2019, which devastated property in the Yorkshire valleys, caused a mud slide to fill the back yard of Jim's property on which he was planning more storage. He intends to find space to restore four cars at a time. In this way he hopes that if he gets stuck on work on one car, he can move on to the next, and so on. Jim has a thing about having good quality leather for the cars he intends to rebuild. To obtain this he has acquired many old sofas from which he strips the leather. The resulting pile of leather is currently stored on the back of the 1928 Dodge. The wood from the sofas is cut up small and provides fuel for the family's wood burning stove. The surplus foam from the sofas is stored in quantity on the roof beams of the car store! He has far more foam than car seats! Jim has restored one car from the collection, a 1951 AC Buckland tourer which he purchased in 2008 in poor condition. He said, 'The AC wet liner engine was in bits so I opted for a Rover SD1 2,300cc to get the car mobile. The Rover engine is

working well, coupled to an LT77 gearbox.' Sadly, this car lives outside as there is no room elsewhere to keep it. I wish Jim well with his future restorations and hope he achieves some of his ambitions for the cars. He says he is not intending to acquire more. I would like to thank Tony from York who has only recently met Jim, and as a reader of 'Lost and Found' convinced Jim that I should be allowed to write about his collection.

In 2005 I was invited to North Walsham to meet Mrs Maureen Johnstone who was selling two cars from her late husband's collection. One was an Aston Martin DB6 that had been on the manufacturer's stand at the 1967 Motor Show, and the other was a donor Aston Martin car. Both cars had been standing out at the back of the bungalow for over ten years since her husband's death. The Show car's first owner is recorded as S.M. Sommerfield who bought it off the Show stand. The second owner in 1974 was Basil Mountford, a senior member of the Bentley Drivers Club and partner in the Bentley restoration business Hoffman and Mountford. He converted the car into a light weight with Perspex windows and uprated Vantage engine. His wife had raced it at a Bentley Drivers Club meeting at Silverstone in 1974 where she finished fourth. Mr. Johnstone had bought the car in 1986. Among the problems was some frontal damage to the

AC Buckland with an engine from a Rover SD1.

The Aston Martin DB6 (left) which had been a show car in 1967. 1948 Healey Duncan (right).

nearside which had been repaired with inches of filler. Alongside the Aston Martin was a 1948 Healey Duncan that was not for sale and was to be placed into the large garage alongside. I was not invited to see inside the garage, but I knew there were some more Healeys. I did, however, keep in touch with Mrs Johnstone, sending her a Christmas card each year. In April 2012, she rang me to say that she had made up her mind to sell the rest of her late husband's cars and Bonhams were coming to take the cars away later that week. I hastily returned to North Walsham. Malcolm (Mac) Johnstone, Maureen's husband, had bought these cars to work on in his retirement but he sadly died in 1996 before he retired.

The garage beside the bungalow looked as if it was for one car, but over the years Mac had extended it three times, both in length and width, and it now contained six cars, some of which were in pieces.

After the removal of a part-restored Volkswagen Beetle, the property of one of Mrs Johnstone's daughters, the 1948 Healey Duncan was first out. JUC 1 was by now in poor condition, the entire framework of this pillar-less windowed saloon appeared to have rotted. Mac had bought it in 1982; though it had arrived on a trailer, it was then in running order. The previous owner had been J.E. Mattocks of Melton Mowbray who had it from 1965 to 1982. The next car out was a very desirable 1952 three-litre Alvis Healey registered FF 8100. Mac had bought this in 1995 from Mr J.B. Mills of West Clandon, near Guildford. This had been in

1952 Alvis Healey which had last run in 1985.

the same family since 1963 and they had last run it in 1985. It had 40,000 miles on the clock. This model, officially known as the three-litre Sports Convertible, has all enveloping bodywork designed by Gerry Coker of Panelcraft. It is thought twenty-eight were made, though three retained the Riley engine and transmission. One of the most difficult cars to move because of locked on brakes was a 1950 Silverstone Healey GCY 610, which Mac had bought from Harold Coats of Chelmsford in 1986. It came in pieces and Mac had done some work on this; there were four newly restored wings for this car stored in the loft.

Possibly the rarest Healey was a 1948 Drone. JPW 227 looked rather like a home-made special. It was a device by Donald Healey and Duncan coachbuilders to produce a car which could be priced at under £1,000. Hugh Gaitskill had just brought in a crippling sixty-six per cent purchase tax on any car over £1,000. The frontal design was influenced by Cord and to get it down to a price,

1950 Healey Silverstone which was very difficult to move.

even the passenger seat and spare wheel were extras! A few buyers of the Drone immediately took the body off and had a coach built body to their design fitted. The Johnstones Drone came to them from an owner in Norway who had owned it for a couple of years. He swapped it with them for an MGA and a spare Healey chassis. This was in 1990. Before it went to Norway it passed through the hands of Stewart Skilbeck and was sold to Norway by broker Richard Pattinson. It is thought that fourteen Drones were made altogether, of which at least three had their bodies changed. Bonhams believe this is the sole survivor in original form. One Drone body survived until at least 1998, registered DYE 961 (then changed to RSU 604). Someone had picked up a discarded Drone body and had built it onto a 1937 Triumph Vitesse chassis. Peter Lomas from Cheshire was the last owner recorded by the Pre-1940 Triumph Owners Club. They wonder where it is now.

Also in this stash was a 1934 Singer 9 Sports four-seater in a very stripped-down condition. It was sold new by Turners Ltd of Croydon who were Singer agents. The first owner was Frederick Chase DFC, known to have been a fighter pilot in the Second World War. He was the son of the vicar of North Walsham. Relatives have said he sold it in 1950 in order to buy a Rover 75. Malcolm Johnstone bought it in 1978. It is thought he used, or had every intention of using, the car as he is recorded as buying spares for it and he had a Singer Owners' Club membership until 1985. At some time, the DVLA had issued the car with a new number, TSV 371. The unrestored Healeys and the stripped-down Singer were sold by Bonhams

1948 Healey Drone with minimal bodywork by Duncan coach builders.

The almost totally dismantled 1934 Singer 9 four-seater.

in June 2012. It is thought likely that a Bill Nichols of Cheslyn Hay in Staffordshire bought the Singer and was responsible for a partial rebuild. It then passed through the hands of two dealers. I have been talking to Alan Crosby from Coventry who later purchased the car. He told me, 'The car was just about a running project and looked acceptable from a distance. On closer inspection it was found that not a lot of the car was original or even correct and was in a poor state …' The restoration of the car is now complete.

Still on the subject of Healeys, in 2015 Paul Delderfield was on a walking holiday in Wales when he spotted an online advertisement for a 'Healey Saloon project'. After a telephone call, a rather clandestine meeting was arranged in a supermarket with a man with the keys. Paul told me, 'When the barns were opened not one but six cars were laid up in the 1970s.' The cars were a Jowett Jupiter with body by Farr of Blackburn, a Riley 2.5 RM, a Talbot 90 drophead, two Healey Tickfords, a Healey Westland and a yellow closed Healey with strange looking bodywork. Paul went on to say, 'I only wanted spare Healey parts but the opportunity to buy a number of Healeys at once was a chance in a lifetime.' Paul bought from the daughter of the deceased owner, the Healey Westland coupe, the Healey Tickford saloon, as well as the yellow saloon. Research has shown that this latter car is Healey chassis number twelve and the third oldest surviving. The first owner in 1946 was J.S. Douglas of Burnley. At first, we thought that the body was constructed by Bambers Garage of Southport as their plaque was on the dashboard, but further research found a number of other makes of cars with known coachbuilders had the same plaque, so it is now assumed this was the supplier's plate. The rest of its history is unknown until sometime in the mid-1960s it was bought by Douglas Day and put away in his barn. There is a rumour it was used in a sci-fi film in the 1950s. Surely someone recognises it with those huge side windows and half oval doors? The 1952 Jowett Jupiter is one of four such cars bodied by J.E. Farr & Son Ltd of 34 King Street, Blackburn. It was built for Mr F. Hamilton Payne from Stalybridge. By 1966 it was in poor condition in Colwyn Bay and was likely to be scrapped. It was saved by Mr A. Turner and was then bought from him by Douglas Day and put away in the barn.

The third oldest Healey to survive, but who built the body?

As a freelance motoring writer, I meet all sorts of interesting people. When working on a restoration story for *The Automobile,* I was taken to a lovely farmhouse and surrounding farm buildings. On opening the doors of a large storage building (almost too posh to be a barn) I was expecting to see modern gleaming farm machinery, of the sort often seen on BBC's *Countryfile* programme. Instead, there were several rows of classic cars covered in the dust of ages and most not used since the 1980s. The father of the family, now in his eighties, and two sons used to own a garage before turning to farming. I was shown around by one of the sons who said to me, 'Because we had space, family and other cars just got parked up rather than being sold.' I can mention just a few. Possibly the most interesting was a 1967 Jaguar E Type S1 2+2. Father had bought it in the 1970s with the idea that it should be his wife's car. She scraped it down one side and never drove it again. It was repaired for

1952 Jowett Jupiter with body by Farr of Blackburn.

1967 Jaguar E Type S1 stored for nearly forty years.

used since 1984. In the corner next to it, a 'hillbilly' pile of bits that I was told was a stripped Triumph TR6. I also saw a Triumph TR3 used regularly by Father in his early working years. His son told me he had never seen it running! Many cars were difficult to reach but along the back row was a Singer Vogue, probably an MOT failure from the garage days, a Triumph TR5 bought as a restoration project, and a Triumph GT6. A white Triumph TR4, another project – 'Dad bought it and repaired it and had it resprayed; it has been in the shed ever since.' A real surprise was a Bentley S3 which was purchased from Canvey Island in 1984. A previous owner had replaced the Bentley radiator with one from a Rolls-Royce. It did some wedding hire work and has not been driven since the early 1990s. There were many other cars not mentioned. None were for sale.

older brother to drive in the 1980s, then given to younger brother as a 21st birthday present. Used for a couple of years and stored since.

A red Triumph TR4A was one of Father's cars used for his work in the 1960s. It was given to a brother when he passed his driving test, and not

Ian Hellings from Illinois is a most unusual collector. He moved from Australia to the USA where he started collecting microcars and invalid

A Triumph TR4A not used since 1984 and next door to a 'Hillbilly' that was once a TR6.

carriages, both powered and unpowered examples, as well as other cars. Most of his microcars are restored and in running condition. However, the first car I saw on my visit was an old friend I had written about in 'Lost and Found' in October 2003. The Curlew Coupe had first been registered in May 1950. This diminutive wood and aluminium car was built by the Crowborough Engineering Company of Newton Aycliffe. It was never fully developed as the money ran out and the only one made was then stored by one of its backers, Kit Calvert, until his death in 1985. It was later sold by Tennants Auctioneers. It went to a microcar enthusiast who, because of a move to France, passed the car to Ian Hellings. An unrestored 1955 Iso Isetta was awaiting attention. This is an Iso factory-built car before the rights were bought by BMW, who turned it into one of the most successful bubble cars ever. The William Towns designed Mini Engined Elswick Envoy was able to take a driver seated in a wheelchair, but

The William Towns designed Elswick.

never really caught on. In another large shed, in partial darkness due to a lights failure, were large cars all awaiting rebuilding. A 1952 Australian built Hillman Minx, a 1951 Rover Cyclops (again an Australian built car) with a 1952 Rover alongside. Tucked behind a Humber Super Snipe and Humber Imperial was a 1953 Packard. There was also a partly disassembled Austin Healey Sprite and a very complete looking 1942 Packard 120. A Riley RMD drophead coupe was very desirable, nearby a beige Austin Princess R and a Borgward Isabella. Most unusual were two American Metz, one from 1915 and one 1917, both of which combined friction drive with chain drive. Their slogan 'A speed for every need'.

Kathy and Robert Porep are collectors of quite a different type. They believe in getting things done. They live in farming country around Woodstock, Illinois. Theirs is a collection of contrasts, a barn full of lovely restored and running classics, including a Nash Healey, a Kaiser Darrin, no less than four 1961 Pontiacs (the favourite car), two 2-seat

Not a Rolls-Royce but a disguised Bentley.

The 1950 Curlew Coupe originally built in Newton Aycliffe, near Darlington.

A 1952 Hillman Minx built in Australia.

1922 Maxwell bought from a local farmer.

Thunderbirds, four Chevrolet Corvettes, and many others. Next door is another barn with the unrestored cars where I spent the most time! Just inside the door was a 1922 Maxwell which they had bought in 2010 from a farmer just five miles away. Though unrestored, it had a very sound body. It was running but the cone clutch was stuck. The Poreps have a real liking for Cords. In this barn there were three, the first, a 1937 supercharged version, is now just a body shell. It had been fitted with an Oldsmobile engine driving the rear wheels, not

the first such conversion I had heard of. The second was another awaiting a restoration, the third a Phaeton built in 1936. Elsewhere there was a fourth Cord whose restoration was well under way; this was another 1937 supercharged example. A huge 1936 Ford panel van dwarfed the next door pick-up which was a conversion on a 1925 Auburn. I had written about this car when I saw it in Rockford in 2002. It had been owned for twenty years by Don Nelson, a Model T Ford expert. Originally this pick-up wore coupe bodywork by the Fabric Body Company. We think the body was converted in the late 1930s. In the corner, an orange coloured car had me fooled. It was a 1954 Hudson Metropolitan. When Hudson and Nash merged, a number of 'badge engineered' models were produced; this was Hudson's version of the Nash Metropolitan.

As well as cars, there were tractors in the barn, along with unrestored petrol (gas) pumps, enamel signs and a dismantled Smith DSA Miniplane – ('Darned small Airplane') – a single-seat, single-engined sport aircraft designed in the USA in the 1950s and marketed for homebuilding. In the nearby immaculate workshops was their latest restoration, a 1936 Cord, making five in total.

On the right Hudson's version of the Nash Metropolitan.

A 1925 Auburn which had been converted to a pick-up.

Original lettering for 'Jacoby Farms' milk.

Some collectors go a stage further and open their collections to the public, often calling them museums. There are few collections of unrestored vehicles. I recommend you to the Beller Museum in Romeoville, Illinois, a collection of around fifty Model A and B Fords (1928 to 1934), with a few other makes as well. Not all are on show at any one time. This collection has been put together by Jordon Beller who claims to have had 27 jobs in his life, the last being that of an eye surgeon. Jordon likes to find Fords which are mainly complete,

original and in 'oily rag' condition. He likes to leave them unrestored. I can only mention just a few.

The 1928 Route car has a country built body for use by a door to door salesman. The 1928 Model A standard open model has a lovely patina of age but is also a daily driver. Alongside, a 1929 Model A open cab pick-up was used for milk deliveries by Jacoby Dairy Farms of Pittsfield, Massachusetts, and still has their name on the door. The next car was originally a Model A Ford Sports Coupe but was very cleverly converted

Model A Ford route car designed for door to door salesmen.

A Plymouth Roadster under a mound of rubbish.

during the last war to resemble a factory pick-up in order to gain a supply of petrol coupons. The very motheaten looking 1932 Model B Standard Tudor was known to Jordon when he was a child. He tried to buy it many times as it lay derelict in a back yard. After it had been fifty years in the open, he was able to get it. There is a display of period and post-war speed equipment for the Model A and Model B and a very large and comprehensive library. In the adjacent building is a huge collection of spares, most neatly stacked and catalogued. The museum is open by appointment: www.bellermuseum.com

Sometimes abandoned cars get overgrown to such an extent that you have no idea that they are there. In an entry on the website for 'The Old Motor' they gave details of a plot of land which included a very dilapidated and abandoned house with grounds that was in the process of being cleared. David Mount, a contractor based in Asheville, North Carolina, was given the job. As they were about to start on the abandoned building, his 13-year-old daughter stopped him saying there were the remains of a car in the cellar under mounds of rubbish and rafters. After unearthing and removal, this car turned out to be a very rare Plymouth Roadster. The extensive grounds were covered in a very invasive plant called Kudzu

which spreads rapidly and climbs up and over bushes and trees. Under this carpet of weed were found nine other cars. How they came to be there or for how long or who had owned them is a complete mystery. The first cars to come out were an underslung Model T Ford Speedster with either a Whippet or Overland radiator, and a very rakish Ford V8 engined Speedster on a Model A Ford chassis.

In the States they have weekend morning meetings of classic cars called 'Cars and Coffee'. Kevin Richards of Culpeper, Virginia, a previous contributor to 'Lost and Found', took his MGA to such a meeting. Here he met up with Mike, an old friend of his father's, who told him about an MGA, a

Underslung Model A Ford Speedster.

Packard and a Bentley that had been sitting locally on a vacant plot of land for some forty years. The lot was near Kevin's office, and he gave it the once over. All he could see was a vast thicket of bamboo but no cars.

A year and a half later he passed the plot again and saw that it was for sale. There was a little diagram of the site on the sale board which showed that there were two garages at the back of the site. Kevin takes up the story; 'Mike ventured through the dense bamboo thicket and lo and behold, a tin shed garage containing an MGA. A separate cinder block garage with collapsing roof housed the Packard and Bentley.' Mike approached the realtor (estate agent) and gained permission to visit the site officially. He determined that the MGA was last on the road in 1972, the Packard had taken the brunt of the collapsed roof and had water damage and was likely only to be good for parts. The Bentley was no such thing. It was a 1939 Rolls-Royce Wraith with a body by Rippon of Huddersfield.

It turned out that another buyer had got there first, but after two months he did not collect them. Kevin and Mike made a bid and were able to purchase the MGA and the Rolls-Royce.

Neighbours told them that all three cars were driven in there in the 1970s and just left but no-one could be found who remembered an owner. The MG had been sold new locally and it still has the decal of a local dealer in Arlington. The Rolls-Royce still retained its British licence plates of BVH 505. It was ordered new by Clarissa Thresh of Shipley and it is thought she left it in her

MGA last on the road in 1972.

will to her driver. In 1965 it was in the hands of a hire firm in Bournemouth which went broke. The records of the Rolls-Royce Enthusiasts' Club show that it was in the USA in 1974, owned by someone called Knowles. There is a rumour that on arrival from Britain it was owned by an Army General from Fort Benning in Georgia.

The Bentley turned out to be a Rolls-Royce.

The 1939 Rolls-Royce Wraith still had its UK number plates.

Lancelot Hill of Bowral, New South Wales (his tie is under the sweater).

I wish I could have met Lancelot Hill of Bowral in the Southern Highlands of New South Wales, Australia, who died leaving a most interesting collection of stored classics. According to his firm's website, he followed his father into the antiques business in a building that used to be Cobb and Co's coach staging station. 'His shop was not a jumble of randomly collected treasures … everything has an associated context – a series of delightful theatrical vignettes.'

Lance's friend, Rory Johnston, contacted me to say that he had just extracted a wonderful 1936 Jaguar SS100 2.5 litre, chassis number 18024, from the barn behind the antiques shop that has some unique features that appear to be factory fitted. He told me that in his earlier years Lance had loved motor racing and competed a lot, as did his sister in a Lotus 7 and a Swallow Doretti. He thinks the SS100 was bought from a doctor in the New South Wales seaside town of Wollongong, south of Sydney, in the 1950s. He raced it regularly in local events for around six or seven years and then the car got stored as his business took more of his time. Rory went on to describe Lance as '… always well dressed and he always wore a tie, proper old school. His car knowledge was huge and once a

1936 Jaguar SS100 which Lancelot had regularly raced.

year he would travel to the UK to buy stock for his antiques business and look at cars and go to race meetings. He loved the UK and all its traditions.'

Rory's firm 'The Classic Throttle Shop', situated right by the Sydney Harbour Bridge, went on to sell this time-warp collection, which also consisted of a long term stored 1955 Aston Martin DB2/4, Jaguar XK140 FHC and Jaguar Mk IV, along with a 1952 Jaguar XK120 Roadster in need of a full restoration, and is listed in the wonderful Jaguar book by John Elmgreen and Terry McGrath 'XK in Australia' as one of the fastest XKs, and has a certificate to prove it, recording 129.31mph over the flying quarter mile. Also a superb original 1972 Ferrari Dino with factory Borrani wire wheels and only 37,000 miles from new. Not for sale is a race prepared MGTC (UK registration RKU 335) which Lance drove with Lloyd King.

The original Turner raced regularly by Wayne Sutherland.

MGTC originally registered RKU 335 in the UK.

Under the bonnet, a mess made by squirrels.

Howard Hayes of Virginia was an enthusiast for British sports cars and he raced some at Sports Car Club of America meetings. After his death it emerged that he had kept most of his cars in three sheds along with a varied collection of spares and some body shells.

Russell Filby of the Turner Register has been telling me about no less than three Turners that were in this collection, two of which had been raced at some time. Chassis 30/149 was not known to the Turner Register and was thought not to have survived. Russell told me, 'The orange car was covered in thick dust and under the bonnet had become a nest for squirrels but following its excavation and a clean-up, the car appears remarkably complete and in good condition for recommissioning.' The paperwork tells us that its

first owner was James Pinson the Third of South Carolina (1972), then Dennis James (1972 to 1973) and then Wayne Sutherland (from 1975), both also from South Carolina, and finally to Howard Hayes in 1978. It is known that Wayne Sutherland had raced the car at many tracks during his ownership. Russell says, 'To remove the car the driveshaft had to be disconnected as the rear axle was locked up solid.'

At this location was an engineless black Turner with no documentation. It has obviously been raced. It is an early 803 model with sloping rear bodywork. Russell did have on the records of the Turner Sports Car Register that Howard Hayes had owned another Turner (chassis 30.251). At first

Kevin Richards, who was in charge of releasing these cars from their barns, could not find this car, which could have been his road car at one time. Russell brings me up to date:

> It turns out that this car was stored in another location which when opened up

The black Turner with no documentation.

1959 Turner, a very original car.

revealed the Turner for the first time since the 1980s. This car would have been built in 1959 and supplied to Tri City Sports Cars of Ohio, who were the US Agency. No ownership was known to the Register prior to 1987 when Hayes made contact with the Club, but the title shows the prior owner to have been George Erwin Dausman of Oakton, Virginia, from December 1968 until July 1978 when ownership passed to Howard Hayes. It is incredibly original and retains its original matching number BMC 948cc engine.

Kevin Richards, who had first heard about the Turners and other cars in this collection, has been telling me about this amazing collection of British sports cars that he bought in 2019. He said:

> Three years ago we had been told of a gentleman who had passed away who had a collection of odd fibreglass cars and the family were trying to make heads or tails of the collection and how best to sell it ... the majority of the cars were in West Virginia, about an hour and a half from where I live ... we found everything from Gilberns to Turners, Arkley to Elvas, and even a Lotus 7. We made a bid and left'. Kevin heard nothing for three years but then he got a phone call '... that not only had the offer been accepted but we had to get all of the cars off the site before April 2019 because the buildings were to be demolished.'

Kevin had three months in which to arrange the move and further storage.

The Gilbern originally UK registered 584 GBC.

The Notchback Elva had a British racing history.

A list of the contents shows, amongst others, the three Turners and a Gilbern (formerly 584 GBC). A past owner of this car had been contacted; he went on his honeymoon in it. Four Elva Courier including a 'notchback' which had been raced in the UK by a member of the Cemian Motor Club at a 750 Motor Club 6 Hour Relay race. One of the Elvas had been burned out at some time. At least four MGBs, an engineless Lotus 7, which is thought to be the second Lotus 7 imported into the USA, three Sprites or Midgets, a TVR and an Arkley MG Midget. There are a number of glass fibre and other body shells and many, many spare parts.

Do you remember the tremendous stir caused some time back by the finding of a large collection of cars in a vast Portuguese shed? This story bounced around the internet for months. I never did hear what happened to them.

In the USA there was another story doing the rounds, of a smaller collection this time, but if true, they are mouth-watering. They include a Shelby Mustang GT5000, three Lamborghini Countach, Cadillac Eldorado, Buick GSX, and a Porsche 911 Speedster from 1989, reputed to have only forty-one miles on the clock. Eagle-eyed readers might find more. Is there a Lamborghini Espada there? One site said, 'The owner's father started collecting cars in the early 1980s and eventually most stopped being driven and were parked here.' Unless it's a film set, it would appear that the cars exist somewhere, but as to the full story …

Engineless Lotus Seven, one of the oldest in the USA.

What is the story behind this collection?

# 3 | THE YEARS OF INVENTION TO 1918

For me, one of the most interesting periods in the history of the motor car are those formative years from 1886 to, say, 1916. During this period hundreds of individuals and small manufacturers were making the 'horseless carriage' as early cars were often called. A good name really as some of the early cars were horse-drawn adapted to have a motor installed, whilst others followed common bicycle practice, making a frame or, if you prefer, chassis, from tubing and putting a motor into that. Panhard-Levassor in France in 1891 were the first to put together what became for many years the accepted layout for cars. They had a vertically mounted engine at the front of the driver, a friction clutch and form of gearbox, at first with chain drive to the back axle, later to give way to the shaft drive to a differential.

Finding Veteran and Edwardian cars (to 1918) in an abandoned state is getting very much rarer so this chapter has a variety of finds from all over the world. Finding very early examples is exceptional, as we will see.

The 1890s saw a number of manufacturers turn to making an automobile. Some, like the French firm of Maillard, did not at first prove successful enough to go into production. Thomas Nicolas Maillard was the founder and owner of a company making cooking stoves. In 1895 he built a car, possibly even two. It would appear that the company built the entire car, with the exception of the axles and wheels which came from the Petit factory in Bar de Duc and which also supplied such parts to Panhard-Levassor. The engine is believed to have been built in-house. It is an underfloor horizontal engine lubricated on the lost oil principle. The

1895 Maillard prototype.

final drive is by chain to the wheels, whilst variable gears are selected by belt drive. Still bearing its horse-drawn ancestry, the look and size of the wheels and the carriage lamps are examples. The car was discovered in a former Maillard cooking stove factory and was bought from the family by a collector. He was so proud of the car that he kept it in his living room! In the late 1980s he sold it to the last owner who stored it without trying to get it mobile. From photographs it looks very original and complete just as one would love to find an old car. The firm did make it into production and they appeared at the 1900 Paris Salon but had stopped manufacturing cars by 1903.

This next one is a very early car from France. One evening, Clemens Heddier from Coesfield, near Dortmund in Germany, was looking through some internet sites. On an unknown French site, he found advertised a 1901 Voiturette Bertrand. Though he collects pre-Great War cars, he has always wanted a London to Brighton eligible car. He replied and was told that a number of people were after it, he should come at once! He decided to buy the car without prior inspection. The next afternoon he set off on the 1,300km drive to Aurillac in France to collect the small car. The Voiturette Bertrand was a two or four seat car made in Paris for two years from the end of 1900 until 1902. The make's first appearance in public was at the Salon de l'automobile at the Grand Palais in Paris. The Autocar reported that on the Bertrand stand '… were two nice looking machines – a tonneau and the other a four seater …' We also learned that it had a single cylinder De Dion Bouton mounted at the front which was connected to the back axle by a very long drive belt.

Early history of the car is not known.

Its early history is unknown and it may have been one family owned from new. It is estimated that it must have been off the road since around 1929. At some stage a winch had been mounted on a framework on top of the car being driven by a belt from the De Dion engine. The last owner started a restoration twenty or so years ago. He overhauled the engine and most of the mechanical parts. Fifteen years ago, it was then put back into store. The owner's son, who was not interested in old cars, was the one who put it up for sale. There is thought to be only one other in the world. Clemens Heddier does not want to start the restoration until he has done more research.

Darryl Grey from Adelaide in Australia was looking for a new project. He had just completed the restoration of a 1926 Bullnose Morris. He saw an advertisement for an Edwardian Renault without

An Edwardian Renault without a body.

body. The car was 500 miles away but Darryl was sent a set of photographs that convinced him he should go and visit with the trailer. It was much as he had expected except that some of the parts had been badly affected by a fire. The new chassis went to Tozer, Kemsley and Fisher in London and from there was shipped to Brisbane, Queensland. No record of early owners exists until 1930, when it was with a farmer in Victoria, the uncle of the recent seller. The farmer had plans to open a veteran and vintage machinery museum, but this never happened. The collection passed to his family on his death in 1990 and after nearly 70 years of storage, the incomplete Renault was bought by Darryl in 2011.

He learned from Jack Kemsley of the Renault Freres Club in Great Britain that this was a 1912 car, model CB which, if it had been bodied in Europe, would most probably have had a Coupe de Ville body. Darryl decided on something a little simpler. With the help of Renault enthusiasts all over the world he has now completed the restoration. He told me:

Whether the fire damage was deliberate or accidental is not known, but the fire was very hot and had melted all of the bronze bushes in the burnt items which included the torque strut and its spring loaded damper housing, the wire wheels, the cross shaft, the gear and hand brake levers, and much more … the steering column had sagged under its own weight in the heat and the bronze bushes in the steering box had melted and solidified as a puddle inside the bottom of the box.

After eight years of very careful restoration the Renault has just been completed and it looks a very fine car.

A cyclecar has been described as a small ultra-lightweight vehicle, bridging the gap between the motorcycle combination and the motor car proper. Quite a few appeared before the First World War but the short lived phenomena was mainly post-war. Some are described in this book's later chapters. 'I first saw a Bedelia at an historic motoring meeting at Dijon in the mid-1960s. It was love at first sight and I resolved to try and find one. It took over forty years!' This is how John Fitzpatrick from Melbourne described his first sighting of one of these extraordinary cycle cars. Bedelia were one of the first into the cycle car market before the First World War, commencing manufacture in Paris in 1910. The late historian Mike Worthington-Williams described them as resembling 'a long wooden coffin on wheels … [the engine] driving the rear wheels through enormously long belts. The driver steered from the rear seat by a series of wires and bobbins to a crude centre pivot front axle.'

A few years ago, Nick Harley knew John Fitzpatrick was looking for such a device and found a 1914 example for sale in a French automobile magazine. John takes up the story:

> It was owned by a brocanteur [second hand dealer] in Nimes. He had found it in a shed that he had been asked to clear. That is as much of the history as I know. It had obviously been stored for a long time and contained some interesting detritus, such as cigar butts and a rats nest made basically out of chewed up comic books

The car has had some modifications, probably done in its earlier years. It had a fixed front axle

A 1914 Bedelia found in a shed clearance.

The Renault after eight years of careful restoration.

John Fitzpatrick with the Bedelia. 'It is wonderful to drive.'

with sliding pillars and coil springs at the extremities. It has a BSA engine of around 600cc.John has restored it mechanically, leaving the body much as he found it. He told me, 'It's wonderful to drive. Light as a feather. Cruises at 60kph and steers beautifully.' Sadly, having got his 'dream car' he has had to sell it due to a move back to France and 'old age and decrepitude on my part'.

I have not been very successful in hearing about finds of early German-made cars. However, this Wanderer is unique. Wanderer is probably the least well known of the makes that went on to form Auto Union in 1932. Wanderer was an old established firm making typewriters, later bicycles, and it was early into motorcycles. The first production car came in 1911, however they had made an experimental car back in 1904, a two cylinder motorcycle engine four wheel car. It was named the *Wanderermobil*. Niilo Santii from Finland was restoring a veteran Reo when he saw a picture in the *Mobilisti* magazine of the remains of an interesting looking veteran. The

The remains of the 1904 Wanderer as bought by Niilo Santii.

magazine was not sure what it was and suggested a Reo. Always looking for spares, Niilo went to have a look. The elderly owner, Pentti Kaista, said that his father had bought this car that he called a Wanderer in around 1910. In 1926 he bought a Model T Ford. He then converted the little Wanderer into a garden tractor, shortened the chassis and took off the wooden body. Pentti then showed Niilo all that remained of the body; the bonnet lost in undergrowth behind a shed. Niilo bought the remains and has done much research and is convinced he has the factory prototype number one with the air cooled engine from a second prototype they built. He told us, 'The first attempt was chain driven with one cylinder engine, but only the chassis was finished. They used the same chassis for the second car, which had a motorcycle engine with two cylinders. It was driven by a propeller shaft and was air cooled.' In his researches he traced someone who had read all available factory papers on the motorcycles and in them was reference to Wanderer selling one of the prototype cars in 1907 to a member of the public. Niilo has restored the car, lengthened the chassis using the original springs found on a shelf in Pentii Kaista's shed. The original wheels were missing but one hub and a few rusty spokes survived from the prototype. By looking at illustrations Niilo could work out they were exactly the same as the motorcycles. The reproduction of the original body was built from contemporary illustrations. He found traces of green paint on the chassis and the yellow was the colour Pentii remembered it being painted when his father had it.

Whilst the name N.A.G. (*Nationale Automobil-Gesellschaft*) may not be well known to some

NAG taken apart in 1918.

British readers, by 1914 this firm was one of the largest car producers in Germany. Gerd-Henning Schoenewolf from Germany contacted me about a 1914 8/24 N.A.G. tourer that he has purchased. What is so unusual about this find is that it would appear that the car was taken apart in around 1918 and never put together again. Gerd-Henning told us '… all the parts, especially the mechanical parts, show no signs of wear. Following the war, the car was left in the city of Namur in Belgium and whoever found it, took it apart and stored the parts in a bakery. There it remained until the mid-1960s when the person I bought it from collected all the parts from all over the building, from the cellar to the roof rafters. Part of the body had disappeared'. This man did nothing with it at all and recently sold it to Gerd-Henning who has put together all the parts to see what else is missing. Of the major components only the mid part of the body and the front wheels are missing. He believes it to be the only remaining example of this model in the world.

A type of car that was unique to the USA in the early years of motoring was the high wheeler. It is the nearest thing to a horseless carriage you could get. It was popular for a short time because of its high wheels which made it very useful in the outback where the roads tended to be rutted and muddy. These cars were usually very simple. A few of these pioneering cars have survived, often having been kept by early owners for a long time, possibly out of nostalgia but often just because they were used in a farming area, barns and outhouses were plentiful so they were just pushed to the back of the barn. The Schacht Manufacturing Company

The restored Wanderer.

The mid part of the body of the N.A.G. was missing.

of Cincinnati was one such. They made cars from 1904 until 1913, but unusually continued to make trucks until 1938. Gustav Schacht had been making horse-drawn buggies for some years before launching his first car. When that appeared, it showed its buggy and high wheeler ancestry but from the casual glance only the radiator sticking up at the front and the steering column and wheel

give an indication it was self-propelled. An early 1904 example has surfaced and was being offered for sale by Shawn Miller of Significant Cars of Indianapolis. It appears to be in very original condition albeit time-worn. Shawn told me, 'When I found it, it was not in a barn but rather stored in a very nice manufacturing company's warehouse. The owner had inherited the car from his partner in the venture, who had, in turn, inherited it from a family member in the 1980s ... obviously it was stored in a barn for most of its life given its somewhat weathered state.' Shawn has withdrawn this car from sale and he now feels it is so unusual (possibly only four survive) that he wants to keep it and add it to his personal private collection of over forty cars.

It is not often one has the chance to study a car which is genuinely unique and which has survived for 109 years without having been repaired or restored. In 2015, whilst visiting the wonderful collection of cars belonging to Bob Lederer outside of Chicago, Illinois, my eye was caught by a neglected looking veteran in a nearby store

1904 Schacht from Cincinnati.

awaiting its turn to have some new wings made for it in Bob's body shop. This turned out to be a unique car, a 1905 Wisconsin – they only made one and this was it. It was made by the Wisconsin Machinery and Manufacturing Company in

1905 Wisconsin with its unusual engine.

Canal Street, Milwaukee, Wisconsin. The car is owned by Tedd Zamjahn who kindly let me have a copy of an interview with Otto W. Brown in 1962, a motor engineer originally from Leipzig who helped with the building of this car. It must be remembered this interview was conducted some 57 years after the car was built and it does leave us with some historical loose ends. It is suggested that this car was a test bed for a new engine which was planned for production for use in automobiles. It's a large two cylinder engine with a peculiar looking combined block and crankcase – the restoration engineers I spoke to were keen to take it apart to see how it worked! Otto Brown claimed that he designed the engine and that the bodywork was built locally. It was always his intention to put at least one seat behind the front two. The resulting rear end is rather like a flat bed. According to Otto, 'It was never used as a truck around the factory. It was primarily used around town.' He does record

The only Wisconsin ever made.

one full day journey away from the works. The local 'Register of Automobiles and other similar motor vehicles' show that it was registered on 12 July 1905. Otto Brown says 'The car ran at between 15 and 20mph. It was used for two to three years, then stored. When the Company moved … in July 1913 they took the car with them, where it was stored in a shed. It was sold in about 1920 for twenty or twenty-five dollars and towed away.' We now know it was bought by Francis Nolan who kept it for 42 years during which time water leaked onto a front wing and rusting much of it away. He sold it in 1962 for $850 to Don Mericle. His widow sold it in 2011 to Tedd Zamjahn who is having the bodywork repaired before starting on the mechanical side. Whilst Otto Brown says this was the only engine they built for automobiles the company went on to produce different types of engines for marine use. 'At the peak, fifty to seventy engines per day were being built.'

The Model T Ford was the world's most successful car of its time (1908 to 1927). Besides being built in Detroit and other factories in the USA, it had twelve overseas establishments of which Old Trafford in Manchester was the largest. This car was known affectionately by many as the 'Tin Lizzie'. Immediately before that model came the Model R (1907) and Model S (1908), both very similar and both had many of the characteristics of the 'T'. Both are much rarer! Only 2,500 of the Model R, for example, were made in total. Ron Zimmer has been telling me about the Model R that he bought a little while ago from a Chevrolet/Cadillac dealer in New York City. The name is O. Ploetner, which can be seen in faded gold leaf on the side of the car; it had been used in early years for advertising purposes. The Company had started out selling Fords from the earliest years of production; later they switched to Dodge and the Ford R was '… buried right away at the start of World War Two so that it would not have to go

Model R Ford not used on the road for over seventy years.

for the scrap drive'. It had been there ever since. The car had been advertised on eBay. 'When there were no bids I made an offer and found it to be mine.' The car is in wonderful original condition and it is so rare to find a car which we know has not been on the road for seventy-five years or more.

There were, of course, Fords before R and the S, though not many came to Britain. At one time I had written an article in which I had mentioned the 6,336cc Model K which I had been told was difficult to sell. Mark Dixon, Assistant Editor of *Octane* magazine, contacted me about an enamel sign that had been offered on eBay. The vendor had thought the sign was c1930 but mention of both 15hp and 60hp on one sign suggested that it was, in fact, advertising the Model N and Model K which dated the sign as 1907. As the prices on it were in English money it must have been very rare. It was purchased by Charles Stapleton, a very keen early Ford collector. When he went to collect the sign, he was told by the vendor '… that the sign had been dug up in the back garden of a garage established by his grandfather on the London Road in St. Albans in 1905. He sold cars and motorcycles and rode a bike in the TT. The garage closed in 1996'.

An early British enamel sign for Model N and Model K Fords.

The late David Skinner from Chandlers Ford in Hampshire had spent most of his adult life tinkering with Model T Fords. In 2005 he purchased a 1911 British assembled Model T Ford which had been taken to pieces by a previous owner who had also burnt the body work because it was infested with wood worm. The first owner, C.L. Bembridge, worked for a firm

This 1911 Model T Ford was converted to a pick-up.

David Skinner bought the dismantled Model T Ford at auction.

of agricultural merchants in Lincolnshire. It was registered CT 775. He kept the car taxed until 1930, later converting the tourer body into a form of pick-up for use around the farm. He, or maybe his family, kept the car until 1960 when they sold it to Dudley Christie who put it away in store. I do not know who took it to pieces or who burnt the body. Dudley sold it at a Model T Ford Register auction as he knew he would never get round to its restoration. David, then retired, bought it and took on the pile of pieces and completed the rebuild in the form of a Model T Ford Torpedo tourer. I saw it a few days after it had passed its first ever MOT after eighty-one years off the road, and a few months before its 100th birthday.

Sometimes when you discover a long unused car you may find yourself in the dilemma of not being sure whether it should be conserved, possibly taken to an oily rag stage or restored.

The restored 1911 Model T Ford, photographed when 100 years old.

This was certainly the case with this 1913 Model T Ford.

Guy Zaninovich from Detroit told me about it:

This original 1913 Model T Ford tourer has just been removed from an old Californian nondescript two car garage where it has been stored since 1960. The person I purchased it from bought it in 1960 with the idea of restoring it, and fifty years later it remained untouched and in the same spot. The car has not been driven since he parked it up in 1960. When I got it, I drained the oil, hooked up a gas tank, got some spark to the coils, cleaned the carburettor, unstuck a valve, and it fired on the third pull of the handle.

The previous owner had bought it from the original owner and they both lived in Auburn, California. A Model T Ford expert to whom we showed the pictures said, 'It looks like an extremely original and correct car. If it came my way, I would definitely grab it with both hands and gloat at length!' It is interesting to note that there is hardly any

1913 Model T Ford – restore or keep as is?

wear on the three pedals so it's likely to have had an easy life. I am not quite sure why a strap has been affixed around the radiator. To restore or not to restore …?

Finding hidden Model T Fords in the USA might not be too difficult. To find one that has been stored for over eighty years must be very unusual. This Model T Ford from 1914 was taken off the road and barn stored in 1933. It still has a 1933 licence plate on the rear. It has now

1914 Model T Ford stored since 1933.

come up for sale due to a change of plan. Says the seller:

> The car is in exceptional condition because it has not been messed with since 1933. The only accessories that I am aware of include the Prestolite acetylene generator tank on the left running board that had replaced the carbide generator as well as the late Model T Ford magneto driven horn with switch

mounted on the steering wheel and speedometer. The tan canvas seat and interior side panel and door covers … probably installed by the dealer that sold the car new.

The seller, who has another Model T Ford, said, 'I decided then to never try to make the car run and drive again, or even clean it up at all.' Now he has put it up for sale he claims he will 'not allow anyone to pick this car up other than in a safe covered trailer, truck or van'. This is one of the longest 'off the road' cars that I have described in thirty-eight years of writing about such things.

Jack Cashman was born in 1918 and worked on a Missouri farm before joining the Navy. He then worked in a chemical plant and in the 1950s he started collecting old cars. His son told me, 'We always had four to six old cars around at any one time, a lot would not stay long as he would trade them and get something else he was interested in.' Jack had grown up with Model T and Model A Fords. In 1950 he was in the local barber's shop and mentioned he was interested in a brass radiator Model T Ford. In the next chair was the owner of the local cinema. He told Jack he had one that was stored in

1916 was the last year for the Model T Ford's brass radiator.

an old lady's garage; he hadn't seen it for years. 'Pay the storage bill and it's yours.' That bill was $15. He bought the Ford, which was made in 1916, and used it for parades and special events, and then put it into store. His son said, 'It's been sitting quite a while as [Jack] got older he didn't have the energy to mess with it much, but he never lost interest in it; it was always his favourite.' Jack died in 2006 and his son has just sold the Model T to Richard Skinner who runs Tudor Wheels in Cadnam, Hampshire. Richard is the son of the late David Skinner mentioned previously and whose name crops up in other chapters of this book. Richard is delighted with his purchase. It came covered in years of dust. He told me that 1916 was the last year of the brass radiator. The car is very complete and original. The engine is free and the folding hood was absolutely correct. For many years the seats have been covered in plastic and are very sound underneath. As it was moved from the container the tread came off the two front tyres. Richard could not understand why there were piles of mud with holes in them affixed to the inside and underside of the car. He was very relieved when told they were not from termites but previously the homes of mud wasps.

'Mud with holes', previously the home of mud wasps.

Ransom Eli Olds had two major makes of car named after him. Firstly, he was involved with Oldsmobile but when the curved dash model needed replacing, he fell out with his fellow directors. He left in 1904 to form a car bearing his initials, the 'Reo'. This was a successful venture as Reo cars in those early years were always near the top of the best sellers list. In 1910 they built a 35hp four-cylinder with shaft drive and in left hand drive form. One such is now a magnificent 'oily rag' car. No owners are known before Jim Keith bought it

1910 35hp Rio with probably its first owner.

early in the Second World War. He had found it in a barn on the northern outskirts of Charlottesville, Virginia. He was a Navy pilot who was later to be called back in 1950 for the Korean War, and sold the car to Bill Pettit of Louisa, Virginia. The present owner, Greg Cone, a vintage aircraft engineer, told me 'The Pettits had accumulated a sizeable collection of automobiles and owned the Museum of Motoring Memories in Natural Bridge, Virginia, from 1958 until 1967. The Reo was not on display but kept at home. That's where I first saw it, but it was beyond my means … I eventually succumbed to ownership in 1990.' It turns out the car had a mechanical problem and it had not been run by any of these owners. Greg was able to trace the problem which involved the magneto and it now runs well. He told me, 'It is my intention to conserve the car's condition and preserve it as a reference piece.' However, he has a real problem; the original tyre size was not available when I wrote this piece in 2015 and Greg desperately required some Michelin 860 x 85 high pressure beaded edge tyres.

Greg Cone 'eventually succumbed to ownership in 1990'.

Another very original car. A Russian immigrant living in Sebastopol, California, was running a successful vineyard in the early 1900s. In 1911, he purchased a new Model 33 Buick five-seat passenger touring car. Many years later the Horseless Carriage Club of America were made aware of the car but the by now elderly owners would not sell. After their deaths, leaving no heirs, the car stayed in store. HCCA member Douglas Rich heard that the abandoned vineyard was coming up for sale and the machinery was being broken up. He was able to purchase the car at just over its scrap value. Having looked at it closely, he felt that it was beyond his restoration capabilities and sold it to fellow member Judd Houser. At that time, it is thought that the car was last run in the early 1950s. The engine was found to be in good condition, but the drive train needed repair. Some items such as the hood and hood bows and the windscreen had been lost, though the support base for the windscreen and its brackets were in place. In 2009 the car was re-assembled and in 'as found' condition took 'Best Original Car' at the

Utah Concours d'Elegance at Salt Lake City. Since then, it has hardly been used and was offered for sale by Laferrie Classic Cars of Smithfield, Rhode Island in 2019. Tom Laferrie describes the appearance as 'desert tan', a pigmented patina resulting from storage in a benign climate. He goes on to say, 'Remarkably, the black leather upholstery, whilst

The upholstery, whilst brittle, is almost all intact.

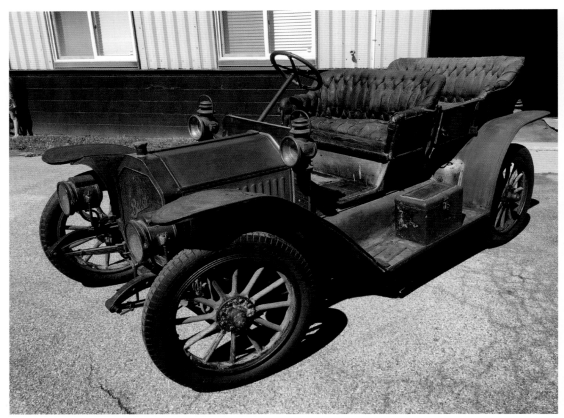

1911 Model 33 Buick bought new by a vineyard owner.

brittle, is virtually intact. A 1915 Californian registration medallion remains on the dashboard'.

When John Willys bought Overland in 1907, the Indiana Company was bankrupt. So much so that the first 465 cars he made were constructed in a circus tent. In 1909 the company moved to the factory previously occupied by Pope Toledo in Ohio. He was successful and by 1910 production was the third largest in the USA behind Ford and Buick, and the following year they became second! Jim Manz, a well-known collector from the Illinois area, is married to Gail, whose father had been an Overland dealer in Illinois in the 1950s. My friend David Kerr, from Chicago, takes up the story:

> In the 1950s he got a call from a man in Texas who said that his family owned a 1913 Overland tourer that they had owned from new. He thought that Gail's father should buy it for old time's sake. He was interested but insisted that the man bring the car from Texas to Chicago for him to see. The owner then jumped into the Overland and drove it from Texas to Illinois which must have been some undertaking and a slow drive but suggested he had supreme confidence in the car. After delivering the car and receiving $500 he took the train back to Texas.

Gail's brother ended up with the car which he took apart but then lost interest. Gail and Jim took over the car and it's been sitting in store ever since. They sold it in 2015 and it is at long last to be restored.

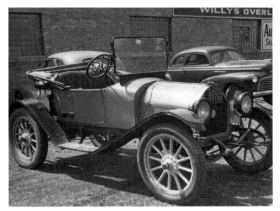

1913 Overland tourer which has been owned by one family from new until the 1950s.

The Overland photographed in 2015 before restoration started.

There is a tendency to forget that Scotland had quite a thriving motor industry, over fifty makers at one time. One of the most productive was Argyll who were as famous for the size and opulence of their factory as they were of their well-built motor cars. Founded in 1899 they were making fifteen cars a week in 1904. In 2014 Garrie Hisco from Adelaide had been to collect a vintage car for one of his clients. After loading it, a group of them retired to a café. He told me:

> A gentleman sitting next to me in the coffee shop asked me if I was interested in other cars as he had some vintage Dodge parts and a vintage Citroen Torpedo. He said he was too old to restore them and if I wanted them, I could have them. After Christmas and the New Year I went with him to a remote farm in the Adelaide Hills, near Murray Bridge, where he showed me the barn which had been sealed up for the last forty years. It took us a long time to break in.

At first, Garrie was excited by the c1923 Citroen 5CV torpedo, also known as the 'Cloverleaf' or 'La Lemone'. This was missing the body but otherwise seemed in good order and mainly complete. The Dodge parts were from a 1920s Dodge but mixed up with them were a lot of parts for a much older car; amongst the parts was a complete radiator with the Argyll badge on the front. It is surmised that these came from a 1905 car. When laid out, it was found that the chassis, engine and body were missing but much remained, such as the radiator,

Parts for a 1905 Argyle.

bonnet, bulkhead with windscreen fittings, gear-box with all linkages and steering parts, and much more. He could not find out much history behind these cars; the owner had said that many years ago he had been asked to clean out a shed by a widowed lady who was moving house after her husband died and that is where they had come from.

In 2015 an antique dealer from Japan brought a 1906 five-litre Daimler with five-seat tourer body to restorer Richard Peskett. The owner had no idea of its background history and just wanted it re-fet-tling to MOT standard. It is thought it had been unused for some time. Registered AC 752 Richard was sure it must have had its coachwork replaced at some time, possibly in the 1950s. To his trained eye, the coachwork and the wings did not look right, though the chassis, engine and running gear was very original indeed. It turns out that the first owner was Cornelia, Countess of Craven whose husband owned a number of early Daimlers. Richard had access to a photograph album belong-ing to William Billingham who had been chauf-feur to the Craven family. A photo in the album showed a new Daimler fitted with a lovely landau-lette body by Rothschild of Paris, with the registra-tion number AC 752.

Richard's diligent research has now proved that in 1911 the coachwork was changed to that of a ten-seat estate bus and the Cravens used this until 1932 after which it was put in store. The next owner left it in the open throughout most of the war, leading to the deterioration of the bodywork. Eventually it passed to that great enthusiast from Newbury, the late Francis Hutton Stott. It next turned up at the sale of unrestored cars from the A.W.F. Smith col-lection at Cross in Hand in 1968. Here it was on offer as a running chassis. For technical reasons it was withdrawn from the sale and John Mitchell, well known for making cars for films, built the present body. The next owner, a very keen Veteran Car Club member, Nick Ridley, used it with great gusto for a couple of years before selling it to

1906 five-litre Daimler when it belonged to Cornelia, Countess of Craven.

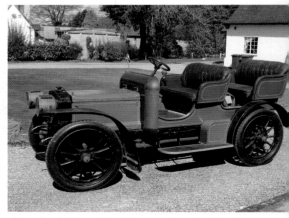

The re-bodied Daimler when in Richard Peskett's workshop in 2015.

Dennis Lucey in Southern Ireland. Lucey owned the Killarney Motor Museum and also supplied a number of cars to a Mr Sullivan who was building up a collection in Honolulu, Hawaii. The Daimler went to Honolulu. In May 1991 his collection was sold by Sotheby's, but before that at least a couple of Daimlers had been bought by a collector in Japan. It was reported to me that Mr Lucey was no mechanic so did not use his cars very much, nor was it used when in the Sullivan collection. Evidence on the car seems to suggest it has not been driven in anger since Nick Ridley – some 45 to 55 years ago! I was present when this five-litre was started up for the first time for years at Richard Peskett's workshops. What a lovely sound, what a lovely car! A very practical and quick car suitable for many Veteran Car Club events. It is now being fully restored by its new owner, Brian King of County Kildare.

There is something fascinating about the large horsepower Napiers of the Edwardian period. Perhaps Selwyn Francis Edge's publicity machine is still at work! In 2013 Chester McKaige moved to Tasmania 'as it is becoming increasingly difficult to enjoy vintage motoring when dealing with Melbourne's increasing traffic congestion'. He took with him his collection of eight veteran and vintage motor cars, including his 1904 40hp Napier and the 1925 three-litre Bentley that was his late father's first car.

The Napier left the factory in April 1907. There is no record of the type of coachwork fitted, possibly a landaulet is the view taken by Chester. It is thought to have ended its life on a large farming property in North East Victoria. Certainly two owners later it was in that area. Writing in Bill Boddy's *Vintage and Thoroughbred Car* in 1954, P.J. Cocks recounts car hunting in Victoria where he liberated a three-litre Rochet Schneider. He went on to say:

> As I approached the house my gaze fell on a horrible sight. There was the Napier, or what was left of it! The rear section of the chassis had been cut off and the tracks of a tank had been put in place. The Napier was obviously serving as a tractor. When I found the owner he explained that when he acquired the farm just before the war, both the Napier and the Rochet Schneider were in a shed.

The Napier at one time had been a tractor.

Later, the Napier went to Arthur Lang who 'used to go around country properties collecting the sad remains of cars, tractors and anything else he could find'. On Arthur's death much of the collection passed onto a mutual friend, George Rushden who himself was a hoarder rather than a restorer. The next owner was Ron Elsbury, who bought the Napier at auction. He had a new radiator made for it and was largely responsible for putting it back on its wheels. Due to other commitments, Ron sold the car a few years ago to Chester who has finished much of the work started but never finished, working from the rear of the car to the front. His next undertaking will be the engine and gearbox.

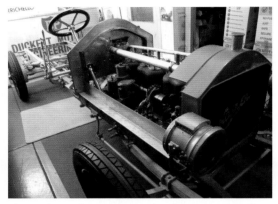

The Napier under restoration by Chester McKaige in Tasmania.

Emerging into the sunlight recently for the first time in forty-five years is a very rare and unusual car, a 1909 Little Briton. Star were a successful cycle-making firm which began building Benz-type cars in 1899. The Star Cycle Company Limited of Wolverhampton, which had offered from 1905 smaller models, less expensive but soundly built than its parent Star Company, was re-named as the Briton Motor Company Limited in 1909. The twin cylinder model that had been marketed by the Cycle Company as the 'Stuart' became the 10hp Briton. The Briton company was in liquidation in 1922 and was bought by C.A. Weight who made a few more cars, probably from leftovers, ceased production in 1928. He then took on an agency for Caterpillar tractors.

The Briton car that has recently re-appeared is the oldest known, being made in 1909. It is a twin cylinder of 1,915cc. It is Veteran Car Club dated. It is registered IT 442 which is an Irish number

from County Leitrim. The history is very vague. It is known to have been in preservation in Ireland as it was rallied there until the early 1960s. By 1968 it was in the hands of C.G. Weight of Tractor Spares Limited of Willenhall. It was his father who had bought out the Briton Motor Company in 1922. In the early 1970s it was acquired by a group named 'The Wessex Machinery Museum Limited'. I have a catalogue of a steam and car show in Southsea in 1975. The entry for the Briton reads 'acquired … from the successors of the British Motor Company'. Surely a misprint for Briton Motor Company?

The contents of Wessex Machinery Museum Limited were auctioned on 8 May 1976, but the Briton was not included. It surfaced from storage in Hampshire and was purchased by Richard Skinner of Tudor Wheels. After he had put it back into fully working order, the car was sold to Martin Obbard from Powys.

Recently Martin was given a tip-off by Andrew Tanner of the Veteran Car Club that the remains of a four-cylinder Briton, just the chassis, axles, gearbox and engine, and many boxes of bits, was being auctioned by Richard Edmonds. He put in an online bid and bought the lot. When he collected the items, he found there was also a box of paperwork which helps sort some of the history. J.H. Dudley-Ellis and his cousin unearthed the remains of the car 'amongst coppice and undergrowth … at Alciston, near Polegate in Sussex, at the very end of a track near an old wartime Air Ministry hut'. It is thought the missing body had been some form of truck. It later came into the hands of specialist dealer, the late Cecil Bendall,

The Little Briton in store in Hampshire.

As restored by Richard Skinner.

The remains of a Briton found in Sussex.

who later sold it to a Robin Ellis. The Veteran Car Club were approached by next owner, Neil Evans of Martock in Somerset, and the Club gave the unrestored chassis and other pieces a provisional date of 1910. It looks as if Mr Evans then did quite a lot of work on the chassis and wheels, possibly into the 1990s. As all then went quiet one can only assume that perhaps Mr Evans died and only recently has the part restored car been offered for sale. The Veteran Car Club lists six Briton or Little Briton cars, of which only two are the four-cylinder version. Martin's is the oldest, the other is in the Black Country Museum.

Writing in 2011 I suggested that I had never written about a car that has spent nearly 100 years in one family ownership. The car in question is a 1913 Singer Sports Roadster now owned by Jock and Liz Robertson. It was purchased new by Robert Robinson who owned the Chowilla Station on the banks of the Murray River near Renmark in South Australia. Richard Fewster, who lives in Renmark, has been telling us about it. Richard runs Ruston's Roses, which houses the National Rose Collection of Australia. He is a car enthusiast and has a small motor museum on his site in which the Singer now stands on a loan basis. The car came directly to Australia from the makers and is fitted with its original British body. It

The part-restored bits of Briton, now owned by Martin Obbard.

is not known why a Singer was chosen. It was in regular use for over twenty years before being superseded by more modern vehicles and put into store. For some time it was in the open down by the Station's rubbish tip where it survived two Murray River floods. It was Jock's late uncle who had the car saved from its riverside fate and had it tucked away in a shed. Jock and his family, who are very conservation minded and run the station to that end, are determined that the Singer should be

1913 Singer Sports as bought by Robert Robinson in around 1920.

'Saved from a riverside fate and tucked away in a shed.'

restored. It was missing its engine, though this has now been found; it had been powering a pump at one of the Station's reservoirs. Over the years some parts have been lost, such as a bonnet, hub caps, spare wheel, dashboard and gauges.

We asked Richard Fewster how it is that cars like this exist on farms in Australia. He told us:

> It was quite common for people living on Station properties not to trade in their old cars when a new purchase was made. I have been to many outback properties where three or four generations of old cars and motorbikes still reside in various forms and conditions. Many sedans were cut down into utility vehicles to perform other duties on the property. I suspect whilst the Singer's engine was removed to power a pump, the overall strength and small size of the car reduced its appeal for being converted into a utility.

The British firm Talbot, founded in 1903, was financed by the 20th Earl of Shrewsbury. After a very successful day at the Fromes Hill Climb in Herefordshire in 1907, where they won the gold medal, the Talbot cars were subtitled 'invincible'. 'Barn find' may be an over-used word these days but a genuine barn find 1914 15-25 Invincible Talbot with a body by J. Rothschild et Fils turned up in 2016 in an Irish sale held by Auctioneers Fonsie Mealy of Castlecomer in County Kilkenny. This car, CR 1351, was first registered in Southampton to Brigadier General Brady. I do not know when it went to Ireland but a copy of the logbook shows that it was continuously taxed in Ireland from 1927 until 1937. The auctioneers say it had been unused for forty years. There was a farm yard clearance sale of vintage tractors, parts and scrap at the property some nine years ago at which the car was offered for sale, but the reserve was not reached so it went back to the barn. The deceased owner's son later offered it for sale. In the same auction was a 1939 Vauxhall 25 saloon which, from its very rusty condition, had been off the road for many years as well.

Now for something quite different. Some readers may be lucky enough to own a car once used by their grandfather; few, I suspect, own a production model *built* by their grandfather. Such is the case with the 1914 Wilton light car that Roy Halsall of East Knowle, near Shaftesbury, completed

1914 Invincible Talbot being pulled out of a farm barn.

restoring in 2014. His grandfather, a cycle racer, cycle maker and cycle dealer, built a number of cars under the name of Wilton; named after Wilton Road in Victoria, London, where they were at first built. Wilton Cycle and Motor Company manufactured cars from 1914 until the early 1920s.

Roy had been hoping that someone, somewhere, might have one. Mike Worthington-Williams heard that one had emerged in Victoria, Australia. Car Number 4, built in 1914 and registered LK 9391, had been taken when nearly new to Australia by a wealthy sheep farmer. This car had been used by the works for publicity purposes, along with a competition appearance (with the other car in the accompanying picture) to win a silver award in the 1914 Land's End Trial. Its history is a little vague; we only know of the last few owners after the war. One of these had mended (not very well) accident damage that had occurred in the past, which included a change of back axle. By 1960 it was in Ballarat. Alan Mills of Castlemaine,

who was looking for a pre-Second World War car, heard about it and spent twenty years trying to buy it. He succeeded in 2007. It was soon afterwards that Roy heard about it and asked if he would sell. Alan was pretty sure he wanted to keep it, but in the end felt that sending it back to the UK to be rebuilt by the maker's grandson was the right thing to do. When Roy opened the container he found a very worn out car, partly dismantled but

A worn out and partly dismantled car.

Two 1914 Wilton light cars being used for the firm's publicity purposes.

It took seven years to restore.

with nearly all the parts present in accompanying boxes. It took Roy nearly seven years to complete the rebuild.

At times it is very difficult to accurately identify the pile of pieces that you found in a long disused garage. In the case of pre-1918 cars, the Veteran Car Club has a Dating Advisory Panel on which sits some of the best experts in the country. They will, for a fee, try and identify your find and tell you its date of manufacture. Sometimes they have to admit they are beaten but you can rely on them to continue trying to find an answer. In the case of this car, I am not sure if it was taken to the Panel or not, but I do know major research into its history has been conducted by Ariejan Bos and Laurens Klein.

For those of us who love the unrestored old car the greatest sale of this century must have been the Christies auction of the Sharpe family collection on 30 June and 1 July 2005. The three Sharpe brothers had been collecting cars since the 1960s when such finds were much easier to acquire. The 216 cars, plus motorcycles, bicycles and automobilia that were in good or reasonable condition had, for years, been on display at the Ramsgate Motor Museum. Approximately three quarters of

the collection, mainly unrestored, had been kept in a variety of locations and buildings near to their Gables Service Station in Rayleigh, Essex.

I attended the sale and was intrigued by a double page spread in the catalogue describing a car that had not been identified, titled as 'c1902 Aster engined car +/- 18hp tilt seat tonneau'. It was very scruffy and missing its bonnet. No-one who saw it could identify it. It sold for £23,500. The catalogue stated that the car had been bought by a lady and her

The car on offer at the Sharpe sale.

Radiator, bonnet and water pump were missing.

brother in 1903 and used around East London. Later it developed a radiator leak and the radiator was sent away for repair never to return. In 1914, the car was taken to pieces and stored in the cellar. The brother joined the Army and sadly was killed. In around 1960 one of the eagle-eyed dealers who looked out for cars for the Sharpe Brothers heard about the car and rescued it from the cellar and loosely re-assembled it, finding little missing other than the radiator, bonnet and chain drive water pump.

The buyer at Sharpe Brothers, who wishes to remain anonymous, has sensitively re-commissioned the car and had it running. It is driven by two vertical water cooled Aster engines set across the chassis. Further research has revealed that, except for the body, this car is almost identical to one of the three Gladiator cars entered in the 687-mile Paris to Berlin road race of 1901. The Gladiator cycle manufacturers from France had strong English connections and is listed as having started making cars in 1896. By 1903 about eighty

The Gladiator competing in the 1901 Paris to Berlin race.

per cent of the factory output was sold in England. It is reported in the *Motor-Car Journal* of 1901 that one of the racers had come to England and had been re-bodied with a tonneau body. It was not uncommon for racing cars to be rebuilt for future road use. Has the mystery been solved?

# 4 | BETWEEN THE WARS

Many of the servicemen returning from the First World War had experienced motor transport when abroad. They may have been trained to drive or maintain vehicles. When returning to civilian life, they could be tempted to spend their gratuities on owning private transport for themselves. The motor industry quickly got back onto its feet and offered a wide selection of vehicles from the cheap to grander cars for the more wealthy. For the 1920 Motor Show there were over 170 different makers on display. Cyclecars, which had appeared for a few years before the war, now became more commonplace as the motor industry tempted the would-be motorist away from either the motorcycle or the motorcycle and sidecar to something usually with four wheels, though often very flimsy.

The 747cc Austin 7 of 1923 (see Chapter 5) was the death knell of the cyclecar.

Before the Great War, Hendon was developed into Britain's leading airfield by Claude Grahame-White. Here he built an aircraft factory for the manufacture of biplanes. Once the war was over, and war contracts ceased, he decided to diversify and built the Grahame-White cyclecar. A number of photographs survive of twenty or so of these cyclecars lined up outside the factory, claiming to be a week's production. No-one knows how many were built in total, probably only a few hundred were sold. Bob Jones, who has made a study of this make, only knows of two that survive; one he owns and one now owned by David Williams, a cyclecar and historic BMW enthusiast. David's car was found and literally dug out by David Hodgson

Graham-White Company claimed this was a week's production.

many years ago from under a large bramble bush in Essex. Bob told me, 'It came with the remains of a body, but without bonnet, engine or gearbox … He obtained an engine [Precision 350cc] and back axle from David Baldock in Kent that had been used to drive a saw bench at some time. He was still short of a gearbox so later on I let my gearbox be copied.' At some time during this rebuild some paraffin was spilled onto the rear part of the existing body which revealed the original registration number MC 6442 which until then had not been known. Later the car passed to Steve Clare, a decorative art glazier, who got it into running order. David Williams improved the running and now takes it to appropriate cyclecar events, including the well-known 'Festival of Slowth'.

It is not often that a long stored vintage Bentley re-appears, especially one as early as 1923. This car was delivered new to Australia on 2 June 1923 and purchased by Massey Burnside of Melbourne. Nothing more is known of its history until the Bentley Drivers' Club have it recorded as being owned by D.J. Dow of Melbourne. It then passed to Peter D'Abbs who, in 1954, sold it to the present owner. He used it for a few months and then took the body off and fitted it to a 4½-litre Bentley chassis which he then used for daily transport. Later, when the 4½-litre was to be sold, the body was removed and placed back on the 3-litre chassis.

This chassis has now been in store for just under sixty years! The owner is now long retired but was described to us by Leon Mitchell as 'a respected restorer of fine vintage cars and motorcycles'. Leon, who is acting for the now elderly owner, went on to tell us:

> The current custodian began restoration of the car when he retired … it has a strong focus on originality and the work was carried out with passion and the desire to give the car the restoration it deserved. To some extent the restoration could be deemed 'old school', eschewing recent trends to use re-manufactured parts in place of genuine Bentley items.

The car is complete in every detail, though still only part assembled. Its chassis number is 276 and it has the correct engine number 285. The body is the original by Vanden Plas. It has the correct beaded edge wheels and tyres and no front wheel brakes. The 3-litre Bentley was announced in *The Autocar* in 1919 but the first cars were not delivered until September 1921. In that year 21 were sold, with 204 following in 1922. When this car was offered for sale in 2013 by private treaty it created tremendous interest and has gone to a new owner in the UK.

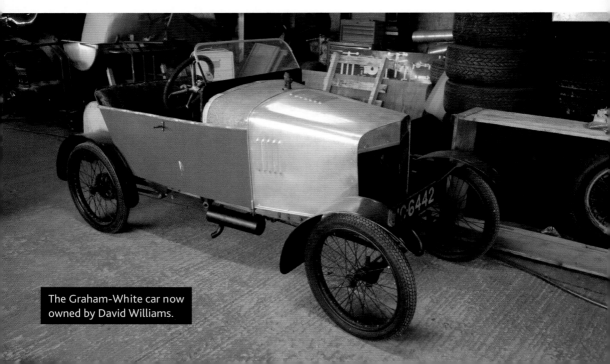

The Graham-White car now owned by David Williams.

1923 vintage Bentley when under restoration by the now deceased owner.

When offered for sale the Bentley created tremendous interest and was sold to a UK owner.

Like the Bentley, it is not often you discover a Bugatti lying unused. Quite by chance I can relate background stories to four Bugattis in recent years. During his summer vacation, Mario Laguna went to view a private collection of some forty cars situated on the Spanish Mediterranean coast. Having admired the collection his eye was caught by a shape under a sheet in the corner. When uncovered, a dismantled 1928 Bugatti Type 44, less body, was revealed.

The Bugatti Trust have told me that it was purchased new from the Bugatti agent in Barcelona. It would appear that the car was first registered in Palma de Mallorca (Majorca). Its registration PM 4283 is still with the car. The Bugatti Trust

The Bugatti when fitted with a four-seat cabriolet body.

lost track of it around forty years ago when it was owned by F. Henri Berlin from Madrid. They have a couple of pictures of it then with a four-seat cabriolet body.

The present owner bought the body-less chassis over twenty-five years ago from a hotel owner on Mallorca. It is reputed that at some stage the original body was removed and substituted by a coupe one built locally, but the hotel owner did not like this and scrapped it. The index card held by the Bugatti Trust gives the body as a two-door coupe, which has been crossed out in pencil and 'no more' written in. Mario told me, 'The present owner helped me to arrange out of doors all the parts of the car. We found at least ten greased and paper-wrapped factory bearings, the gas tank, factory nuts and bolts, cables, steering wheel, and much more. Sadly, the dashboard and instruments are missing.' The present owner is unsure what to do with it. Some fifteen years ago he entrusted specialist Enrique Godo in Barcelona to sand blast and paint the chassis. The engine is in original condition, as found, and is fired up on occasions. He rather likes it as a show chassis but feels he ought to commission a special body with sporty characteristics.

Various parts of the Bugatti.

The background to this next story came from Christopher Gardner of Switzerland around Christmas 2013. It concerns a doctor who had a dream of providing a unique and up market health spa and convention centre in a northern Italian village. He hoped that the added attraction of a collection of vintage cars would make this centre something different. The centre was built in a glass fronted building with the cars inside and virtually no way of getting them out again! The centre never opened. The cars existed only as a rumour of a 'Tomb of Important Cars'. From 1971, the cars were locked away in a climate-controlled environment. Always one for a challenge, Alessandro Bruni (aka 'The Truffle Hound') decided to track this rumour down. He found the cars and traced the now 90-year-old owner. It took a donation to the sisters' convent down the street to be able to view the cars and, soon after, Bruni was able to obtain a 1928 Bugatti Type 44 (straight 8, 3-litre) with Spider coachwork by De Costier Freres of Boulogne in a very art deco style.

Alessandro trailered the Bugatti across the Alps braving snow and ice just days before Christmas. He told us:

It is a dream come true to find a Bugatti never seen before and encased in a glass room for over four decades. The condition is remarkable, totally original and pristine, with hair-line cracks in the paint and an American Indian mascot – the previous owner was known as 'Chief' or 'Capo'. It has not been driven since 1971. I made a stop en route to fill the dickey seat with good Italian

1928 Bugatti Type 44 after removal from the original health spa building.

'I felt like St. Nicholas delivering this Bugatti in the festive season.'

wine and cakes so we could have a Merry Christmas with three good litres of red wine and the finest three litres of Bugatti I have ever seen. I felt like Saint Nicholas delivering the Bugatti in this festive season. I was greeted at the home of the new custodian, a Swiss Bugatti collector, at 3 am with cookies and hot chocolate. The Bugatti will be made running again without any other restoration or the disturbing of its superb original condition.

In 2012 Brightwells Auctioneers of Leominster were involved in the exhumation of a very interesting 1931 Bugatti Type 51. Brightwells' James Dennison has been telling me how they found the car in an overgrown garage in Worcestershire. 'The car had been lying there unused for years and trees had grown in front of the doors, so we had to cut these down and move half a dozen rotting 1980s cars out of the way before we could gain access.' Various JCB type vehicles had to be brought in to do this. The owner was Alan Riley, who had died earlier that year after a long illness. James described him as follows; 'Alan was a well-known and slightly eccentric character who spent most of his life as a mechanical engineer and test driver in the experimental department at Austin BMC in Longbridge.' He had numerous Bugattis and other exotic cars '… all of which he bought and ran on a shoestring as the pay at Austins was not great'. After the Bugatti was put in the garage, Alan still had access to it through a small back door. James said, 'It gradually became covered in

The Bugatti covered in rubbish as Alan was a hoarder.

Possibly the car Count Stanilas Czaykowski won the 1931 Casablanca Grand Prix in.

rubbish as Alan was a hoarder who could not bear to throw things away.'

Alan had acquired this green Bugatti in 1987 when he swapped it for a 1931 Alfa Romeo 8C 2600 and a Maserati 250F! Alan always believed that the car was the actual one driven by Count Stanilas Czaykowski to win the 1931 Casablanca Grand Prix. Czaykowski was Polish by birth and lived in Paris and always drove Bugattis. In 1931 he purchased one of the first Type 51 Bugattis that were sold to a private owner. Later he was killed at Monza when driving a Bugatti Type 54. James Dennison went on to tell me, 'We have had the car inspected by a Bugatti expert and it is almost certainly a very skilfully executed reproduction, although it may contain substantial parts of the original chassis of the Czaykowski car. Further research is underway.' Whatever the outcome, it is a desirable Bugatti.

Willem Leonhardt was a wealthy Dutchman who, on a business trip to Nova Scotia, met Norvel

Parsons, and later, in New York, his actress daughter, Mona Parsons. They married and settled down in Holland. Leonhardt, who had owned many luxury makes of car and had taken part in a Monte Carlo Rally, in 1938 bought a one-year-old Bugatti Type 57 Ventoux which was painted chocolate brown. When war came, they hid the car. Willem and Mona and friends formed a resistance group to rescue shot down British airmen. Later, this group was infiltrated, and Willem went underground. Mona remained but was imprisoned to act as bait to get Willem to return. She was placed in a number of prison camps and with a friend, finally escaped when her camp was bombed. After much walking they crossed the Allied lines where she was at first treated as a spy, but luckily she had stumbled across the North Nova Scotia Highlanders who believed her story (see www.monaparsons. ca). After the war the car was disinterred and later sold; the new owner by coincidence taking it to Canada and then it went to Australia via Texas. In 1967 it was bought by Rob Rowe who was instrumental in getting historic racing up and running in Australia. Rob was too busy to do anything to the car and it remained stored until 2010 when it was mechanically restored. When Rob bought the car, it was completely covered in grey paint; he had it painted red. In this form it was recently sold by Motorclassica in Melbourne. It has now joined Clive Palmer's collection at the Palmer Coolum Resort in Queensland.

The Model T Ford Register of Great Britain produced a book in 2014, *The English Model T Ford:*

The 1938 Bugatti Ventoux when owned by Rob Rowe in recent years.

*Beyond the Factory,* which has 240 pages devoted to non-factory coachwork and additions you could purchase to improve your Model T Ford. In the USA, of course, the business was much bigger. One of the firms so doing was the American Top and Body Company of Delphi, Indiana who marketed theirs under the name of 'Faultless'. In 2016 Mark Hyman Limited of St Louis was advertising a 1921 Model T Ford raceabout for sale which is almost a running catalogue of Faultless parts. He says, 'It still wears its Faultless alloy side steps, cycle fenders, radiator grille cowling, cut down speedster body with tapered tail, special hood, roof and windscreen frame - all original items from the period.' It is almost complete but unrestored and very original.

A period in its history is interesting as told to me by Shawn Dougan of Hymans:

It belonged to a guy in California who owned a race track, and this car was used as a pace car or safety car. If you look through the rust on the hood it says 'Highland Mill' on one side and 'California' on the other. On both sides of the rear body 'Safety Car' is written, again under the rust.

In November 2013 a container arrived from the USA in which was a 1935 Ford V8 three window coupe. David Acon from Eastleigh had fallen in love with its shape when he saw it advertised. On opening the container, he was delighted with his superbly original purchase. Assembled new in Canada this was an intended Colonial model. It was shipped to Dagenham as a kit and built up here in right hand drive form and with the special 'economic' model 60 2,226cc engine to better fit the British tax system. This was an engine with faults and many cars were returned to the factory for a replacement Model 62 engine, which this car has. The first owner was a doctor from Maidenhead who used it until his death in 1940, after which it was laid up. His widow re-commissioned it in 1950 but hardly used it, putting it back in store. Two schoolboy friends were allowed to get it running in 1962, but they left it with an engine full of water which then froze in that winter's 'big freeze' and caused damage. The car was auctioned in 1978 and purchased by an American who eventually took it back to the USA but did nothing with it as no-one could mend the damage to the engine. There it lay until David Acon rescued it.

What is amazing is that it has done only 19,652 miles in its entire life and has been basically well stored. I saw it recently and whilst the paintwork is dulled in places and the interior slightly moth eaten, everything is there and works. David sent the car to the Flathead Emporium run by V8 specialist Jim Turnbull in Holton Heath. He has repaired and rebuilt the engine with great attention to period detail. It is now ready for 'oily rag' events where, I am sure, it will cause a stir.

Jim Turnbull spends most of his time these days rebuilding Ford V8 flat head engines for customers. One of his clients sent him the engine from his Bren Gun Carrier which was duly rebuilt and collected. Six weeks later he rang up to ask if he was interested in buying some 'military stuff'. His friend had overheard a conversation in a village

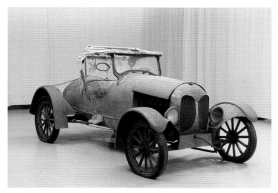

Model T Ford Speedster for 1921 with many Faultless accessories.

1935 Ford V8 three-window coupe as purchased by David Acon.

The engine of the Ford V8 as rebuilt by Jim Turnbull.

pub about a shed full of wartime military equipment. It turned out that 'somewhere near Bristol' was a fifteen acre plot of ground that had been a scrapyard. When it came up for sale the local farmer bought it to add to his farm and to get rid of the scrapyard. On the land was a shed that had been used to store ex-MOD equipment which was locked up, I think, in the late 1960s and left. Included in this stash were a number of brand new Ford V8 bare block assemblies (i.e. no internals) still wrapped in their original wrappings in crates still with original markings – Jim was able to buy eight of them. It's not just cars that get left and forgotten!

Keith Egerton from Shropshire, now in his eighties, used to run a local garage. In 1960, a customer brought in a 1933 Ford Model B saloon for some work, but then refused to pay for it. Until recently he still had the Ford stowed away in a shed in his garden. The registration number RD 4139

Ford V8 bare block assemblies new/old stock as bought by Jim Turnbull.

1933 Ford V8 Model B Saloon 'covered in quite deep surface rust'.

'The interior trim was mostly gone.'

Restoration took five years.

was not on the DVLA records, so Keith contacted Andy Maclean who is the Vehicle Authenticator for the Model A Ford Club of Great Britain. Andy also edits the *V8 Telegraph*, the magazine for all Early V8 enthusiasts. When the paperwork on the car arrived with Andy, he was delighted to find that there was a buff logbook, the last tax disc for 1961 and insurance certificate, which means there would be little trouble in recovering the number.

Keith wanted to sell and Andy knew of a member looking for such a car, Edwin Phelps from Somerset. Andy and Edwin went up to see the car. The car was covered in quite deep surface rust, but Keith had rubbed it back in a couple of places to show the blue paint underneath. Andy said, 'The covering of the sliding head roof had disintegrated, although the framework was there; the driver's side rear passenger door had fallen off and was on the floor at the back. The interior trim was mostly gone, although the driver's seat was intact.' Further investigating showed that it was a numbers matching car. A deal was done, and the car went down to Somerset. Enter Jim Turnbull

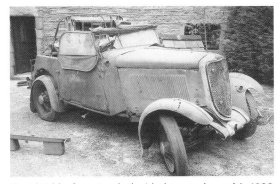

David Tebbs from Leeds decided to purchase this 1933 Wittingham & Mitchell Model Y Ford.

again from the V8 Emporium, who heard about the car and persuaded Edwin to sell it to him. I saw it when visiting Jim at Holton Heath to talk about his business in re-building Ford V8 engines. He has already had the engine running and hopes he can keep the car mainly in 'oily rag' condition.

Phil and Margaret Denson have owned and restored a number of Model Y Fords, one of which was used regularly in County Kerry where they have a holiday home. Knowing that an open tourer model of the Y Ford called the 'Kerry' had been marketed by W. Harold Perry (body by Whittingham and Mitchell) they decided that ought to be the car for use in Ireland. Once they started looking, they found it to be a very rare model, with only three of the type known to Registrar Sam Roberts. One of these owned by David Tebbs in Leeds was in a poor condition but could be for sale. At first Phil thought the work would be beyond him but several months after first viewing they decided to purchase it. This was in 2008. Restoration took five years and it has now made its first trip to Ireland.

It was registered OD 6420, a Devon number, in 1933. Nothing is known of its history until 1960 when it was owned and run by Mr Batch in Norwich. Phil told us, 'Apparently his parents had bought it off the local milkman for twenty pounds in 1961 for him to run but when he could not get it through the MOT in 1964 it was sold for scrap.' At some time it passed to Belcher Engineering in Diss and to David Tebbs in Leeds in 1989. It has been off the road for nearly fifty years. An interesting aside is from a W. Harold Perry brochure which Phil has obtained. He told us, 'This has been altered by a sticker, with the Kerry name on it having been placed over the name "Terrier". Perry had

Model Y Ford converted to a high sided pick-up.

The Fordson badge on the Model Y Ford.

originally called the model Terrier but Leyland objected as they had a truck of that name, so Perry was forced to change it – note Kerry is also a type of terrier dog.'

Karl Grevatt was looking for a pre-war light commercial for publicising Charlecote Mill where he is the miller. He saw advertised on eBay a 'barn find' Ford, which he bought sight unseen. It turns out he has a version of the Model Y Ford van (based on the car chassis) that had been converted by an unknown coachbuilder to a pick-up, but in this case with high wooden sides, probably for carrying light but bulky loads such as hay. These high sided vehicles were sometimes referred to as 'sheep or pig cratches'. It has bench seats running down each side so might have also been used as a shooting brake. There is an extra forward facing lamp on the cab top. Not knowing what he had bought, he took it to a vintage Ford Rally at the British Motor Museum. It created great interest and would appear to be the only example of this

conversion known to exist! The vehicle is badged as a Fordson, a name used only on commercial vehicles; the light commercials were the last to receive this name.

RG 9012 was a Reading registration for 1936. It is known that it was found in the back of a box van in 2005 on a farm in Wiltshire, its last tax record seems to have been early 1980s. Karl told me, 'The amount of very dried cow dung stuck to the underside has suggested a life of being used off the road … condition when found could best be described as 'tired and worn' but substantially complete and very original … there is only a little woodworm that causes concern, makes a change from rust!' The Ford is nearing the end of a sympathetic restoration and may soon be seen around the Stratford-Upon-Avon area delivering flour from the water driven mill.

In 2020, early on in the Coronavirus pandemic, I saw on television that Karl Gravatt and Charlecote Mill were run off their feet with orders for their flour.

I cannot resist including this American Ford because of its size and rarity. In 1940, Ford of America made eight chassis which were delivered to coachbuilders Sebierts (about whom I can find no details). The eight chassis were fitted with luxury limousine bodies. They were 21ft 9in long with two doors on the driver's side (front and rear), whilst there were four doors on the nearside. There were two fold down steps on the driver's side to allow access to a luggage compartment on the roof. These eight were designated for the armed forces. Six went abroad and all trace of these has

1940 Ford (of America) made eight of these long chassis cars which were bodied by Sebierts.

been lost. The other two were retained in the USA, one going to an Air Force base in Maryland, again all trace lost, whilst the only survivor was used on a base in Texas. After the war it was sold to the Whipple Stage Company in Prescott, Arizona, whose name can still be seen painted on the luggage compartment on the roof. This company used it as a shuttle between Glendale and Phoenix. In the late 1960s it had been sold to Len Gasper in Arizona and then to Phil Hansen in Chicago. The present owner bought it in 1977 and I think it had not been used on the road since then which, if true, is rather a pity.

Now away from Dagenham and Dearborn, we go to Abingdon. Terry Andrews has been a member of the MG Car Club for some thirty years, owning a number of Triple-M cars. He did not know that he was looking for yet another car to restore when a friend rang him out of the blue. He had found an unusual-looking MG under a tarpaulin in a garden in Hampshire. From the photographs on emails which followed, Terry could identify the car as a 1934 MG Magna L1 type Continental Coupe, a very rare version of the Magna of which MG only made one hundred. His friend quickly decided the car was too far gone for his restoration skills and it was offered to Terry. The car needed to be moved urgently and was bought unseen, just on the pictures. A few weeks later he went down to his friend's workshop to see the car first-hand. What Terry quickly realised was that, though this car was in poor condition and would need a complete restoration, it was very original and complete, with such detail as the original little wire baskets over the rear wheel arches, original 'dolls eye' switch for the interior light and the carpet door pockets. The only instrument missing was the clock. It had all the right numbers and was almost complete down to the last detail. He thinks it came off the road because of a clutch problem. It had probably only had about ten years of road use and the mileage reading of 61,000 is believed to be genuine. He tried very hard to wrap up the car for the very wet journey home so that it did not fall apart, but even so some of the woodwork disintegrated.

Whilst the car was drying out in his garage, Terry started on the research. He found that this blue car was first registered AWL 723 in October 1934 and was sold by agents Laytons in Oxford to a Mr Huskinson. However, the car had been made ten months before in January. Even though MG only made 100 of these, I think pretty coupes, they were very difficult to sell because of their high price compared with the standard model hence Wilson McComb christened them 'Kimber's Folly'. Nothing more is known of the car until the replacement buff logbook in 1947 shows it now painted red and living in Teynham in Kent. Then there were a number of changes in quick succession in Kent and Sussex until being classed as 'untaxed' by the Southampton Licencing Office in 1951. It was bought by the family of the previous owner to be repaired and used, but it never was. Subsequent inspection showed that the engine had been completely overhauled but never run. It had been garage stored until about eight years ago when it was placed in the open under the tarpaulin, but one of the doors was not shut properly and the damp got inside. It was only

MG only made 100 of these L1 continental coupes.

The engine had been rebuilt but never run before being left under a tarpaulin.

being sold because the family were about to go into sheltered housing. There may be ten of this model left in the world (most of which would appear to be 'under restoration') and Terry has formed a self-help group for people who are restoring them.

The prototype production Jensen of 1935 has been in a part dismantled state in Canada for near sixty years. After I had made contact with the new owner, restorer Rob Staruch, I wrote up a short history of the car distilled from research in the library at the National Motor Museum in four different books, various magazines and then the internet. Much of the information was repeated in these various references. I sent this history to Rob, who kindly rang me up to say that after extensive investigations on the car itself, much of what had been written was incorrect! Also, almost all sources illustrate the car outside the home of racing driver Ron Horton. Rob Staruch is convinced this is not his car but prototype Number Two which was built but destroyed in an accident!

Alan and Richard Jensen's first car was a homemade Austin 7 Special, followed by a Jensen designed body on a standard 10; this resulted in an introduction to the New Avon Body Company. Later they had a short skirmish with Patrick Motors before joining coach-building company W.J. Smith and Sons, which shortly changed its name to Jensen Motors. They made bodies for a number of different makes including a series on Ford V8s.

Desirous of producing their own car, they commissioned Rubery Owen to build a chassis. The engine was a Standard Ford V8, possibly fitted with twin carburettors, though only a single is fitted now. The Jensen designed body was that of a sleek open four seat tourer with an ash frame panelled in aluminium. Access to the rear seats is by a door on the nearside which opened forwards allowing the scuttle with twin aero screens to open upwards to aid ingress. The car had a long sleek appearance and a slightly V-shaped sloping radiator grille. It was registered EA 7000 with West Bromwich. It became known in the factory as the 'White Lady', and the name has stuck.

It is thought the car was sold in 1936 and used until 1939 and then again after the war until 1957. It was then sold to a Bristol dealer who had it on his lot for some three months. John Huva, a supervisor for the Spacecraft Division of Telesat based

The 'White Lady' after being found by Rob Staruch.

in Ottawa, purchased it. He used it until the end of the year when he sent it over to Ottawa where he drove it until 1968, after which he laid it up. By 1975 he had completed the building of a garage large enough to allow him to work on the car. He removed many of the exterior parts but then the work stopped; it remained in pieces until the end of 2016 when Rob Staruch bought the car and was able to rescue most of the bits. He described the garage as being like 'entering a tomb'. First he had to remove a false wall behind which the car was situated and there it was, covered in twenty years of debris. He has had the car running and he told me he was not sure whether to restore or just complete the re-assembly. Subsequently it has been sold to a UK enthusiast.

I do like it when cars which have been out of use for years are found to be very original and, in this case, still with its original upholstery, which had been covered since new. In 1896 Ernst Zurcher and Hermann Luthi made Switzerland's first motorcycle engine. They moved over the border to Pontarlier in France where in a new factory they made Zedel engines and complete motorcycles. In 1906 they made their first car and continued in car making until the outbreak of war. Production restarted in 1919. In 1923 Jerome Donnet, a manufacturer of seaplanes, bought the business and under his control the cars were renamed Donnet-Zedel, and continued until 1934.

In 2017 Ivan Dutton was on a rally in France driving his Model A Ford. He called in to see his friend John Champ of Eygaliers who had a knack of finding old cars in France. Ivan spotted a rather grand looking early vintage saloon, a 1924

Toned with printer's blue to enhance reproduction, this print shows the White Lady, S1 parked outside Ron Horton's home in Barnt Green, south of Birmingham, around 1936. Copies of the photograph were pasted into promotional brochures made up to illustrate the Jensen 3½ Litre range. Opposite: with her wings re-painted maroon, S1 attends a car rally in England in the 1950s.

Ron Staruch is convinced this illustration was of prototype number two but is very similar to the number one which he found.

Donnet-Zedel. He was told that it was probably last on the road in 1962 and since then had been in a sort of museum collection. Ivan offered to swap his Model A for it, and much to his surprise, the deal was agreed.

'Oily Rag' is a name we give these days to very original cars that have survived unmolested even if they are shabby. I have recently seen this car and it is amazingly original. The odometer shows 39,000 kilometres, and this may well be a true reading. It has its original paint, which has peeled a bit around the windows and on scuttle and bonnet, all original lights and fittings. The interior was remarkable, all the trim seats and door trim had since new been covered over with cloth. On the doors, this cloth was on fasteners for easy removal. The original cloth underneath was quite unworn. It is thought that the car spent some time in the South of France and the owner did not want the original upholstery to fade in the harsh sunlight.

Ivan took the 2,100cc engine apart, had everything checked and cleaned, the only item needing renewal being a worn gear on the oil pump drive. To get the oil sludge out of the gearbox and back axle, both had to be heated with a blow lamp, but everything inside was perfect. The brakes have iron shoes and steel drums and did not need replacing. The wooden wheels were perfect. The

The very original 1924 Donnet-Zedel now owned by Ivan Dutton.

Protective cloth over the original back door covering.

The interior of the Triumph when in the poly tunnel.

car needed re-wiring. I was taken for a ride and the car rode beautifully and the brakes were extremely good. This will be a sure-fire draw on any rally field.

During the First World War, Triumph motorcycles were widely used by the British and other armies. In 1921 Triumph were persuaded to expand into the car market and produced their first car in 1923. From 1928, Triumph produced some 15,000 of their Super 7 model which was not much more expensive than the Austin 7 but with the great advantage that it had hydraulic brakes. They made many different body styles and according to the Pre-1940 Triumph Register, only three of the boat tail version are known to exist.

The first owner of the 1928 Triumph Super 7 boat tail GM 28 was James Anderson who was given it as a 17th birthday present. His father, Alexander Anderson, was the founder of the very successful Motherwell firm, Anderson Boyes, who held many patents for the manufacture of coal cutting machinery. James, in due course, became Managing Director. He used the car until 1937 when he got married. There is then a gap in its history until 1955.

The only thing known about this period is that Alexander Anderson's grandson found the car in a sorry state in a local dealership and bought it back, only to have the number transferred to another car. In around 1965 the dilapidated car was sold to Tom Forrest, reputedly for 50/-. The last tax disc with the car dates from 1955.

The present owner, Arthur Harvey, a near neighbour of Tom Forrest, takes up the story:

My first sight of the car was in 1969 shortly after we arrived in Scotland, when Tom was embarking on a mechanical restoration of the engine and chassis. The remainder of the restoration ran out of steam in about 1972. It was then parked unfinished under cover in a polytunnel … at some time the floor level of the polytunnel was changed and the car was found crossways on at the back of the polytunnel on a floor ten inches lower

1928 Triumph Super Seven had been stored in a poly tunnel.

than the main structure and buried under a considerable amount of garden and garage debris. It had to be lifted and turned sideways onto the higher floor, all completed with only one inch clearance!

Tom's original restoration work was good, but the body was in a very poor state, although very little appears to be missing. Incidentally, the magneto which had stood untouched for forty odd years in the Scottish climate, started the engine first time without any work being done on it – definitely a feather in the cap for the often maligned Joseph Lucas!

It is said that the Trojan was the only car ever to be advertised in the *Church Times*; certainly a lot of vicars seem to have owned them. To many the Trojan make might bring back memories of an out of date looking car on very thin wheels with solid tyres (later to have conventional tyres). For those not quite so old, red vans for Brooke Bond Tea. In between these

1931 Trojan RE Saloon known as the 'Guildford'.

The rear engine was mounted in a removable box.

the Company experimented with a number of more traditional looking cars and the Trojan Museum Trust has just been able to acquire a 1931 Trojan RE saloon (rear engined) known as the Guildford.

Talking to David Hamblin, who runs the Trust, I found out:

> The RE was designed by Leslie Hounsfield and was meant to have a variety of innovative design features. One was the reason for the rear engine … [it was] mounted in a box at the back of the car, which also housed the gear box, drive chain and in the original design, the radiator, the idea being you could drive your car to the nearest Trojan garage, they would then unclip the back box complete with back axle and the complete braking system. They would then replace this with a 'courtesy engine', you could then drive away to return later to collect your fully serviced engine.

The rear radiator was not successful and it was replaced at the front requiring some 25ft of hose to connect to the engine; this never worked well.

The registration OY 1527 is a Croydon number; this was where the factory was located. Its continuation logbook shows Chris Bird of Harrow (a long term Trojan fan) had it from 1959 until 1962 and was probably the last owner to run it regularly. After various owners in Cornwall, it passed to a Mr Tucker of Launceston in the 1960s and later to his son. A few years ago, he offered it at auction and the Trojan Museum Trust tried to buy it but it was withdrawn. Recently Paul Tucker was persuaded to sell. The Trust believes only around 100 REs were made and they think five survive.

Not all big saloon cars of the late vintage and pvt period are ponderous carriages. The George Roesch designed Talbot 75 was quite quick for its size and remarkably silent. Doug Reid from Oxfordshire certainly hopes that his 1931 Talbot Saloon will come up to these standards when he has rebuilt it. This six light saloon with sliding head has an exceptionally large opening roof. Doug told me, 'It was erected on 10 August 1931 at Clement Talbot's works in Barby Road, Kensington, West London. It was registered YY 86 on 28 October 1932 and delivered to Talbot dealers Pass and Joyce in Hanover Square, Mayfair, on 30 December 1932.' It would appear the car spent much of its life in North London.

The first owner is not known but in 1938 it was owned by Leonard Adams and tax discs indicate it was on the road during the war. An insurance document found under the seat shows he still owned it in 1947. Later owners include Ian McGinty (no date), Christopher Ortner 1976, and restaurateur Roman Unterhofer in 1983. The latter had acquired the car with a friend in 1976 in payment of a debt and he bought out the friend in 1983. He did nothing to the car other than keep it in a dry garage where it stayed until released by Doug in 2012. It is thought the last time the car ran on the roads was 1957. Doug Reid told me, 'I think the car's milometer, showing just under 70,000 miles, is almost certainly correct and that the car has been exceptionally well maintained during its working life; something which has become apparent as the car's mechanicals have been dismantled.'

The firm of A.J. Stevens and Company were highly respected motorcycle manufacturers. In the late 1920s, they entered the commercial vehicle field. In 1930 a small Coventry Climax engined car was first shown to the public at the Motor Show. Around 1,200 cars were made before the car side went into liquidation. In 2013 a garage was being cleared in Sidcup after the death of the owner, Mrs Lawton. In it was found an AJS saloon car. It had been owned from new and had been the pride and joy of her military policeman husband, Robin Lawton. In a role reversal, Mrs Lawton had always done the servicing on the car, so after he died forty years beforehand, she did not want to part with it, but in turn did not use it. Registered in Surrey in 1931 PL 6563 the car has now passed to a family friend, Dean Tredget 'who has worked in the motor trade and is determined to get it renovated and back on the road'.

Ken Lee, Registrar of the AJS Car Club, has been telling me that seven other metal bodied AJS saloons are known to the Club. The 9hp production was taken over by Willys-Overland-Crossley who made around 300 more before they too went into liquidation in 1933. PL 6563 seems to be all original except that it has a Jowett rear axle. It is assumed that had been fitted when no replacement parts were available. When Willys-Overland-Crossley failed, the spares were bought by R.H. Collier Limited who then scrapped them all in 1939.

After his death in 1976 the 1932 Singer owned by Frank Field-Buss was kept by the family in and around Sittingbourne. In 2013 Martyn Wray, Secretary of the Singer Owners' Club, was able to purchase it and has been looking into its history, hampered by the lack of a logbook. At first it was thought to be a Singer Porlock but he soon realised it was something rarer than that, a Singer Special

Removing the 1931 Talbot Saloon was a bit of a problem.

1931 AJS metal bodied saloon.

1932 Singer Special Sports, a model made for one year only.

A rare unusual Mickey Mouse badge.

Sports, made only for one year and records imply that possibly less than 100 were made in total. The car has the Singer Junior chassis with the new 9hp engine. Very few have survived. This would appear to be a very original car which came off the road in 1963 having done 52,491 miles.

Registered in East Sussex PN 8872 on 31 March 1932, the car was supplied by Rock, Thorpe and Watson of Tonbridge, though the family say that Frank Field-Buss went to Singers and collected the car personally. Martyn told me:

A meticulous owner, he kept every tax disc, including some from the early 1940s, hence the wartime white flashes on the wings, up until 1963 when he stopped driving. He also recorded all his work on the car – oil changes, brake linings, new tyres, etc, on a short piece of floorboard! … It transpired he was the only person ever to drive the car … all the instruments are in good condition and working apart from the clock that is mounted to the right of the steering wheel and may or may not have been a standard fitting but is definitely period. The fish tail exhaust with Singer on it is exceptionally rare.

When acquired, the Singer had an unusual badge on the radiator. It was a Mickey Mouse emblem. Unlike a mascot, this one has very little depth to it so one assumes it fits onto the radiator itself. It is silver and blue and looks like an old style Mickey Mouse from the 1930s. However, it is very similar in style and pose to a sketch by freelance artist Ray Johnson from the early 1960s.

Douglas F.H. Fitzmaurice from St. John's Wood founded a company called Airstream Limited. He designed streamlined cars in 1930s. One company which took up the design was Singer who first showed the Singer Airstream at the 1934 Motor Show. At first they said they were going to produce 750 at £300 each. Its slogan was 'The car of tomorrow – today'.

It was the first British production car with a streamlined body in the form of a full width four door pillar-less saloon on an 11hp chassis with independent suspension and fluid drive, the most striking feature being the 'waterfall' bonnet, very

Singer press release photo when the model was first announced.

Seating 'hammock like upholstery fixed between two pillar steel frames'.

The only other Singer Airstream is in the Caister Castle Collection.

much in the style of the first Chrysler Airflow. The seating was unusual, having hammock like upholstery fixed between tubular steel frames. Like the Chrysler, the Singer was ahead of its time in looks and the public did not take to it. I have seen figures of only 100 or maybe 300 cars made. It is well recorded that band leader Jack Payne bought a number for members of his band. It is believed that just two survive, one in the Caister Castle Collection in East Anglia, and one in New Zealand – the latter was offered for sale in 2019. This car was imported in 1935 by Tench brothers of Christchurch for a lady owner. Jen Hall, the daughter of the late Trevor Chambers of Sefton, North Canterbury, near Christchurch, New Zealand, who is selling it on behalf of the family, told me:

[Later it went to] a man in Rangiora who had lost both his legs. He found the pillar-less doors allowed him easy access to get in and

out and the fact that it was clutch-less meant that he could drive it easily. Dad purchased it for £10 in 1965 from our local garage proprietor John Younger, as it was going away for scrap.

She believes that her father never drove it but did trailer it to some local car shows for a number of years but would take it out of its shed and happily show it off to any enthusiasts who came visiting. It was hoped that a British enthusiast might feel inclined to buy this car and bring it back to the UK but that has not happened.

KMK 736 is a 1939 Singer 9 roadster with the name of 'Betsy'. This is the model which came out just before the last war and was back in production again in 1946. Pre-war examples are, therefore, rare. No history is known of 'Betsy' until 1957 when it was in the Hungerford area. In January 1960 it was bought by Mrs Cynthia Face, the landlady of the John of Gaunt pub in Hungerford. Caroline Franklin remembers, 'It was not starting at the time … so we pushed it from the pub to our house, holding up the traffic. Fortunately, it was not far.' The family had lots of adventures in the Singer on holiday and driving locally around Wiltshire and Berkshire. She said, 'Driving in the winter was a bit chilly – we used to put clothes pegs under the bonnet so it was lifted enough to let hot air through onto the windscreen.' The car was laid up in 1967 with head gasket problems; the last tax disc is on the car, and apart from a move to Ramsbury, it has slumbered since. It has, however, been carefully dry stored. Caroline Franklin asked Cameron Brownlee to sell the car for her and it

The 1934 Singer Airstream coupe recently offered for sale in New Zealand.

1933 Singer Roadster 'Betsy' was laid up in 1967.

has recently found a new owner in York, who was actually looking for an old Morgan at the time but was very taken by the background story to the Singer. It could well be the oldest surviving example of this model.

The Standard Motor Company was founded by Reginald Maudslay in 1903 and the name came about in a heated discussion with Alexander Craig, the Chief Engineer. 'I don't want any of these new ideas Mr Craig, I want my cars to be composed purely of those components whose principles have been tried and tested and accepted as reliable standards. In fact, I will name my car the Standard car'.

Through the good offices of the Standard Motor Club, I have been put in touch with Carl Burge who runs the intriguingly named firm 'Remember When UK'. This specialises in buying, restoring and selling K6 red telephone boxes and other street jewellery. A friend of his suggested he might like to meet his mother, who was in the process of selling up her mother's Edwardian house. A visit was arranged to this house which had been vacant for some years. The interior was very period with '… Edwardian sideboards, chairs and charming period wallpaper … Bakelite light switches, braided cord light fittings and brass curtain poles everywhere'. As they were leaving, Carl was asked 'Would you be interested in an old car?' There, in a dilapidated garage and in a very dusty condition, was a 1936 Standard Flying 12. The car had been in the family since the 1940s and was last taxed in 1955 after which it was put away in the garage. The first owner had purchased it new from the Standard dealer in a town only a mile

1937 Opel Six 'thought to have been stored for some forty years'.

away and the speedometer showed it had covered only 34,000 miles. Carl, who had previously been in the motor trade, made an offer for the car which was accepted and is keen to get on with the car's restoration.

The pre-war Opel is a make that is not so well known in the UK, possibly because General Motors 'who took over Opel' already had Vauxhall in this country. A 1937 2-litre Opel 6 cabriolet has, however, been found in Belgium which has spent much more time off the road than on it! Sadly, it comes with no history. Daniel Vanderpoorten, who had recently acquired it, believes it has not been driven for around fifty years. He was told a number of stories about it, none of which can be proved. He did say that it was common practice to hide a car away at the beginning of the war, first of all from the Belgian authorities who would confiscate them, and then from the Germans. One way of ensuring that the car could not be moved was to hide it away and place the wheels in a very secure place. It is clear this car was put back into use after the war and only came off the road when the owner died. It is thought to have been stored for some forty years in an underground garage in Antwerp until bought by the last owner, who did nothing with it. Whilst the car needs a complete restoration, the engine is free and the rest of the car very sound. The upholstery is in excellent order. Daniel told me, 'This is a very rare car as many were used during the war by the Germans, some on the Russian front, and then by the occupying forces who just drove them into the ground'.

Ray Dietrich and Tom Hibbard when working for Brewsters in the USA were itching to go out

'Would you be interested in an old car?' – 1936 Standard Flying Twelve.

on their own in the coachbuilding world. In 1920 they formed Carrossiers Le Baron, more often known just as Le Baron. In 1927 the company was taken over by Briggs and moved to Detroit. Shawn Miller of Significant Cars in Indianapolis has found a 1934 Lincoln Convertible Coupe by Le Baron. It is thought only four of this model survive. Early history is not known but in the 1950s it was purchased in Rochester, New York by Dr Helmut Prahl for use when he was at college. Early in his career he moved around, finally putting the car out to grass. Shortly after, a rudimentary shed was built around three sides of the

'Still with all the dust and racoon nests in it.'

car. Over the next thirty years vandalism and the weather took their toll. In 1992 the family moved to Door County, Wisconsin and took the Lincoln with them where the car was put into a very nice dry garage. Dr Prahl had every intention of restoring the car, but it never happened. Shawn Miller bought the car from his widow. He told me:

> Two days after I had retrieved it I took it to the Classic Car Club of America Indiana Grand Classic event still with all the dust and racoon nests in it. This was the first (and possibly last) time that such a barn find had been presented at this event, which is, of course, a judged event.

When researching for the book *The Fate of the Sleeping Beauties* (in the UK published by Veloce), one of the three authors, Kay Hottendorff, fell in love with the Cord that featured in Michael Dovaz's extraordinary collection of unrestored cars. He found that nearly thirty years later this car was still 'sleeping' in a collection in the south of France but on enquiry, it was not for sale. Kay was determined to find one he could afford. Only 2,900 Cord 810/812 were made, 668 of these were supercharged and only 428 supercharged sedans,

1934 Lincoln Continental Coupe by Le Baron.

1937 Cord Custom Beverley stored for sixty years.

the latter being the only model Kay thought he might be able to afford.

He searched the world for news of an unrestored example. He attended auctions where Cords were for sale, but the bidding just went too high. After one such abortive visit, he despaired and put an item on the web forum of the American Auburn, Cord, Duesenberg Club which read, 'There must be another unrestored Cord waiting for me somewhere else in the world'. A week later he was offered a car, a 1937 812 Cord Custom Beverley' (supercharged). He told us, 'It had been stored for sixty years untouched and dry in a garage in Southern California. It was in very original condition and even had its 1952 licence plates.' Kay has been able to purchase it and bring it to Germany. He has since traced the first owner who sold it in 1949 for $50. It was the second owner who used it for three years before laying it up in 1952 and not using it

again. 'Perhaps one day I will start a very careful technical restoration, keeping the exterior and the interior almost unchanged.' For more details of the Cord that inspired this story see Kay's web page at www.TheFateofTheSleepingBeauties.com.

The Delage D8 120 was the last eight cylinder car produced by Delage. It was the fruit of a convergence between Delahaye and Delage. The engine was basically a Delahaye six cylinder engine with two extra cylinders added. The car was sold in chassis form and loved by the extravagant French coachbuilders. Toby Ross of Ross Classics in France has rescued what was once a lovely D8 Delage fitted with a Chapron 'Mouette' copy body. Chapron from Paris loved to build on the long chassis which devoted half its wheelbase to the engine. The first owner was the celebrated aircraft designer and manufacturer, Louis Breguet, whose planes were some of the first in France and continued in aeroplane manufacturing until after the Second World War. Louis Breguet had the rear of the car modified to give a larger boot. We do not know who did this alteration. In the 1930s he was working on the Gyroplane, a form of helicopter. In the course of business, he met Igor Sikorsky who later went on to build the first stable, single rotor helicopter to go into full production. They became good friends and the Delage was sold to Sikorsky in the USA. There is a rumour that later he left the car as a sculpture in front of his house for over thirty years. Toby Ross told me, 'The presumably already rotting car was left behind a factory, again open to the elements, which finished nature's work, and this is where we found it. We shipped it

The dashboard of the Cord looks very complete.

Louis Breguet had the rear of the car modified to give a larger boot.

Delage D8 120: 'the already rotting car was left behind the factory'.

back to England where it is in storage while look-ing for a new custodian.' It is the sort of car that, if fully restored, would easily grace the lawns of any present day top class concours.

Andrew and Frances McDougall from Melbourne, Australia have rescued a 1940 Alvis SP25 saloon with body by Charlesworth which had been stored since 1980. This is known to be the sixth last SP25 built by Alvis and must be one of the very last private cars built by the firm before changing completely to war work. It was registered in Coventry EVC 565 and sold to Brooklands of Bond Street, London. The first owner of the car is unknown. It may have been requisitioned by the government as in July 1940 the government took over the stocks of all new or unregistered cars. Car production had continued on a lesser scale until July 1940, nearly all of which had gone for export. This was the time of the so-called 'phoney war'.

In 1950 it was bought by Alvis enthusiast Michael May, who used it for towing his racing

One of the very last Alvis cars built before the factory went over to war work was a 1940 Alvis SP 25.

Alvis. He changed the engine from the original 3.5 litre to a 4.3 litre which had come from an Alvis drophead being prepared for the cancelled 1940 Monte Carlo Rally. He also fitted hydraulic brakes. In 1963 it was bought by Dr Iain Mathewson, a doctor from Aberdeenshire, and was described at the time as having a body that was 'tired and loose'. He was posted to Borneo but used the Alvis for all his home leaves, often touring complete with caravan. In 1975 he migrated to Australia taking the Alvis with him to Mackay in Queensland. He took it off the road in 1980. Andrew and Frances are Alvis enthusiasts and have two other Alvis but wanted a saloon. It was a 4,958km journey from Melbourne to Mackay to collect it. The rebuild of the wooden framed coachwork is a new experience for Andrew.

Mario Laguna has a long memory. Back in 1985 he read in a classic magazine about a Fiat 2800 with coachwork by Touring of Milan. The car was described as 'built on Mussolini's orders for his fellow Fascist General Franco'. Ever since reading that piece, Mario has been looking for that car.

Eventually he found it in Spain. More recently the owner has allowed him to look through the car's papers. It is car number 000436 and was sent by the factory to Touring in September 1940 and the Superleggera body was completed in April 1941. The car was then sent to Fiat's agents in Madrid, presumably for General Franco's use. By 1942 the car had moved to Portugal where it was owned by Fiat's Senior Director in Portugal, Mr Boldari. By 1976 it was owned by Mr Deupes de Perpessac who worked in the French Embassy in Estoril. By 1980 it was owned by Miguel de Lacerda of Durham. It was

he who wrote to the then historian of the Fiat Club, the late Michael Sedgwick, who thought that only six cars of this type were built and that this was a 'one off'. He also thought that the car was designed in the style of the Alfa Romeo Freccia d'Oro. The current owner has had the car a few years and on obtaining it, stripped it down to find out its true condition. Mario told me, 'The car retains all its original panels, there is no rust and no evidence of crash damage. The six cylinder engine has been overhauled and is in perfect running order'.

It is interesting that a coach-built car such as this should be constructed in wartime. Nick Georgano writes in his *Beaulieu Encyclopaedia of the Automobile* (Stationery Office, 2000), 'Passenger

'The car retains all its original panels.'

Built for Franco, the Fiat 2800 with coachwork by Touring of Milan.

car production continued in Italy further into World War Two than in any other country, the United States included.' In the section on Touring Coach-building he wrote, 'Anderloni [of Touring] realised the importance of the latest developments in airframe construction ... that led him to develop and patent the 'Superleggera' principle, which used an outer skin of aluminium panels resting on, but not rigidly fixed to, a cage-like steel structure.'

In 1927 Daimler launched a new series of cars called the Daimler Double-Six. Its 7,126cc V12 engine was basically two 25/85 blocks set at sixty degrees on a common crankcase. Later they made a smaller capacity version, the Double-Six 30, which still had a V12 engine but with capacity reduced to 3,744cc. Most of both models were fitted with large formal coachwork and it is thought only 800 were made. They are now very rare.

Robin Hanauer was doing his nightly trawl through eBay and in one of the more obscure corners found such a car advertised. It had an accurate description of its condition and said it was minus engine, gearbox and radiator. Few people seemed to be interested in the auction and so Robin bought it and collected it from the north of England.

No history is known, other than a demolition contractor had been asked to level an old house and outbuildings. In an open-fronted outbuilding was the Daimler. It looked very forlorn, but interesting enough for the contractor to have it moved to a nearby property and saved. It was described as a 1928 Daimler Double-Six with Hooper formal coachwork and that it had been built for a director of Walls ice-cream. It is now thought to be a

The Daimler viewed with great difficulty at the back of a barn.

year or so later than described, there is no entry in Hooper records at the Science Museum for such a car and chassis number, and surely only the top coat of vanilla paintwork has any connection with ice-cream! Robin believes that, apart from poor storage, the car has been vandalised and much of the aluminium stolen. It is, however, sound both in chassis and body, even the dashboard is complete, albeit with all the instruments smashed. One of this model's distinguishing features, and very expensive to replicate, are the piano style wire wheels. Robin has six of these but only one is relatively complete. I viewed it (with difficulty) at the back of his barn hemmed in by two Morris Minors, an XK120, Mk I Land Rover and an Austin 7. Restoration will be delayed, partly because of cost, and partly because an engine and gearbox are required.

Daimler Hire Limited exhibited a most unusual vehicle on their stand at the 1936 Olympia Show. It was a twenty foot long Daimler Double-Six limousine which had been specifically designed to transport a disabled or invalid owner in comfort. The body had been built by Lancefield coachbuilders of London, W10. From the exterior it just looked like a large limousine, as *The Autocar* wrote 'From the exterior merely a conventional four door six light limousine of unusual size, but anyone attempting to enter the rear compartment from the offside would discover that the "door", although provided with hinges and handle, is a dummy and does not open'.

Inside and behind the division on the driver's side is fitted a full length bed which in turn can swivel and be accessed from the outside through the nearside door. In this way the occupant could be removed still lying down. Beside the bed is a very comfortable looking armchair, whilst another

1928 Daimler Double-Six sold without engine, gearbox and radiator.

Daimler Double-Six limousine – the rear door is a dummy.

A fold down wash basin is fitted alongside the microphone for speaking to the chauffeur.

is fitted into the division and can be folded away. A wash basin is fitted to the near side, hidden under a hinged panel. There is a heater with controls on the bulkhead and a telephone communication with the driver. There are silk blinds on all the windows in the rear. There is a compartment in which can still be found a porcelain bed pan, porcelain male urinals and other similar medical accessories.

Luggage can be carried on a hinged platform which drops down at the rear. Cases can also be carried on the roof with a special rack which folds down when not in use. Access to the roof is via hinged steps built into the car's centre pillar which can be seen when the front door is opened. Only nine of these Daimler Double-Six chassis were built, two of which went into royal service.

This car is in very original, though unrestored condition and was obtained by Derek Malloy in Northern Ireland in 2009. The previous lady owner

in turn had inherited it from her late father's estate. In a letter to *The Driving Member*, the magazine of the Daimler and Lanchester Owners' Club, he asked for help with discovering its history. Virtually no history came with it. It was originally registered in London DLY 258. The first and subsequent owners are not known. There is strong hearsay evidence that the car was intended for use by King George V who in his later years was in very poor health, but he died (January 1936) before he could take delivery of it. This sounds a very likely story. Presumably it was never delivered to the Royal Mews and so is not recorded in Royal motoring history. It is thought to have gone to Ireland in the late 1940s where it was registered MZ 8074. The idea then was to convert it to a hearse but this never happened. As built, it would have had a 50hp engine fitted, but at some time this has been changed for the straight 8, four and a half litre engine.

The full length bed which can turn and swivel.

Various medical equipment still stored in a special compartment.

# 5 THE TWO GREATS - AUSTIN AND MORRIS

Austin was founded in 1906 with Morris in 1913. Between the Wars and afterwards these two were the big rivals in the British family car market. In the small car sector, the Austin 7 probably was the most successful, though Morris was the first to get a mass-produced car down to £100. They were also great rivals in motor sport and class record breaking at places like Brooklands.

Post-Second World War there was much talk of a merger of the two companies which finally came about in March 1952 when they became the British Motor Corporation (BMC). Whilst it was described as a merger it soon became quite obvious that Austin was in charge. Later this was to become the British Leyland Motor Corporation. From the 1950s the company's biggest rival was probably Volkswagen, a design that members of the British Motor Industry declined to take over when offered to them after the war.

Dave Waller of the Austin 7 Owners Club kindly put me in touch with Dave Simpson who is the owner of a 1927 Austin 7 Chummy which has been off the road for seventy years. He bought MK 7188 in pieces in 1980 from an owner in Dulwich, South East London. When he saw it, it had been completely dismantled. He told me:

> The chassis was leaning against a wall with the body resting on the floor. Piled into the body was everything else, including the dismantled engine, gearbox, bonnet, doors, hood and side screens, windscreen, radiator, wheels and wings. A wooden Sunlight soap box containing the instruments, magneto,

carburettor, armoured wiring loom and all the other small bits topped the pile. Unfortunately, the seats and some trim had been discarded as they had been attacked by mice and woodworm.

It would appear that the previous owner had bought the car in 1945 and had taken it to pieces soon afterwards. Recent inspection has showed damage to the crown wheel and pinion, which may have been the reason for it being taken off the road. Most of the tax discs back to 1929 were still with the car. It was repainted black in 1939 with wing edges painted white as the car was used throughout the war as the buff logbook reads 'Joint Recruiting Office, War Office'.

Dave Simpson intended to work on the car soon after buying it '… but life and other vintage projects got in the way'. He reassembled the car recently to see what he had got or, more importantly, what was missing. He has now taken it apart again and has started a recommissioning operation. He told me, 'It has never been my intention to

The car was loosely reassembled to see what was missing.

restore the car but I want to try and keep it pretty much as it was when last used. Wartime paint, although done using the Valspar and dirty brush method, will be kept'.

Whenever enthusiasts discuss restoration, the subject arises as to whether a car should be restored, or, if it's very original, should be conserved. The fabric covered body of the late 1920s was not only a fashion style, it was also a cheaper way to build bodies. It did have its problems, the British weather being one of them. A 1928 Austin 7 fabric bodied saloon with right hand drive was exported new to Valencia in Spain and went into daily use with a local doctor. Little more is known of its history except it was in Alicante in 1948 where it stayed until the early 1960s. It was still running in the mid-1960s when it became sidelined by a faulty back axle. It was put into a dry barn where it stood for forty years. It was discovered by a Spanish enthusiast who recognised the importance of the vehicle.

In 2017 it was bought by Julian Parker whose company are coachbuilders and historic vehicle conservators. Julian has strong views in relation to originality, restoration and conservation. He was

'Cleaned and treated every item.'

Conservation or restoration? - 1928 Austin Seven fabric saloon.

Conserved warts and all.

determined to do a full conservation on the car. He took it completely to pieces; I mean every nut and bolt. He cleaned and treated every item and put it back exactly as it had been – over 1,000 hours of work. When Julian showed me photographs of the car as bought and as conserved, it was very difficult to know which was which, except for the dust and flat tyres on it as it arrived. He hopes this will be a standard by which other conserved cars can be judged. It was planned for it to have its first outing at the 750 Motor Club's Austin 7 Rally at the National Motor Museum, Beaulieu in 2020, but this was cancelled because of the Covid virus restrictions.

David Wall, the restorer from Wroxham, first heard of this 1928 Austin 7 in the 1970s but was not allowed to see it, let alone buy it! He told me:

The 1929 Austin Seven outside the shed in which it had been stored.

Thought to have been off the road since 1951, a 1929 Austin Seven.

'Its structural condition is better than it looks.'

Every time I passed by that garage it crossed my mind. It turned out that a friend of mine knew the owner and put in a tentative enquiry. A few weeks later the doors to its shed were opened and after a few weeks' negotiation, it was mine. It came with its stable-mate, a 1934 Austin 7 (AXM 47) saloon still wearing wartime 'blackout' white on the running boards.

The owner of the cars is deceased and no paperwork came with either car, so history is at present unknown. VF is a Norfolk number, whilst AXM is London. David believes that the early saloon might well have been taken off the road in the 1950s, certainly it would have failed the MOT 'ten year test' when it came in 1960. The owner had every intention of restoring it in his retirement, but then other things took his interest.

At a Hobbs Parker auction in 2019, three lots were entered by the same farming family from near Ashford in Kent. A Series One Land Rover, an unrestored 1930s Lagonda saloon and a completely unrestored 1929 fabric bodied Austin 7 saloon. Ken Kimber bought the Austin 7 and has just started on 'a sympathetic rejuvenation'. No paperwork came with it, so he is unsure of any history. He thinks it was registered YC 5791, a Somerset number. He told me, 'The car has never been fitted with two rear lights and the presence of a 1951 tax disc suggests that this may be when it was last on the road.' He has asked the family if they remember why it came off the road but they did not know. The engine was seized which might have been the reason. According to the factory records at the British Motor Museum it was despatched from the factory on 26 March 1929. He said, 'Its structural condition is actually better than it looks.'

The number JA 2392 was issued to a 1932 Austin 7 by Stockport County Borough. Nothing is known of its history until 1969 when it was bought by Peter Crush from Cheshire for £130. He was at that time on leave from the Hong Kong Police where he was an inspector. He admits to knowing nothing about Austin 7s but was happy to have the car sent to Hong Kong for him to use there, where it was registered AP9057. When he was due to return home in 1971, he sold the car by auction and it was bought by Gerald Stockton,

an American who took the car back to the States when he returned home at the end of 1973. Here it was registered as an historic vehicle with the registration 'Chitti'. It is thought he was the person who painted it bright yellow. From California it was sold to Norton Viny living in Cleveland. It later passed to a Mr Harrah who used it for a while and then laid it up. In 2017 Patricia Harrah advertised the car on Craigslist. The ad was seen by David Harrison from Stratford-Upon-Avon, who was able to purchase it and have it repatriated to the land of its birth. Inspection of the car showed that it had been fitted with some very non-standard parts, typical of the special building era of the 1950s and 1960s. These included a Nippy cylinder head and manifolds, Morris Minor hydraulic brakes, 16in wheels and a hardy Spicer prop shaft. The engine was a later replacement. It is thought these modifications were made to the car by an owner before Peter Crush. David went on to tell me, 'The paintwork is indescribable, over 4mm thick in places and with serious rodents' nests in the back – half a black bin liner's worth. There had been a significant lightening of the rear floor where

The 1970 Hong Kong licence disc.

The Hong Kong Austin Seven now back in the UK.

rodents' uric acid had eaten away sizeable chunks under the seat.' The car has now been restored, David choosing to take it back to its 'warmed up' format of 1969.

Quite a lot of Austin 7s went abroad during their lifetime. I have been in contact with Peter Huser from Switzerland, who is selling a 1931 Austin 7 Saloon on behalf of his brother who has owned it for thirty years. Peter told me, 'I saw the car advertised for sale in Surrey in the summer of 1990 when I was on holiday in England. I told my brother Tom about it. He was a professional restorer of antique furniture and he thought the car would make a great advertising vehicle for his business.' He bought it in its unrestored and part dismantled state. His idea was to convert it into a

'Paintwork is indescribable.'

MV 8528, a 1931 Austin Seven Saloon in store in Switzerland.

reproduction of a 7cwt Austin 7 RN van. He had all the skills to do the woodwork necessary and felt that suitably lettered out it would convey the period feel for his furniture restoration business. However, as so often happens with successful specialists, the business takes up more and more time, and so the Austin just sat in a barn exactly as bought. Tom has just retired and is now too old to attempt a restoration, hence the sale.

The history of MV 8528 (a Middlesex number) is unknown until 1957 when it was owned in Watford by Arthur Marret, then a Mr Evett of Rickmansworth, moving to Betchworth, Surrey a year later, owned by George Williams. It then had four more Surrey owners before David Spencer-Phillips of Bures Manor, Reigate, was given it in 1965 by his late stepfather as an 18th birthday present. I have recently been talking to David, who says he had many happy trips in the car including one to France where he took a picture of the car at the Arc de Triomphe. He actually got out of the car and took the picture; there was little traffic in those days. The next owner did nothing with it and according to the logbook he never had it on the road. The car was sold to well-known Austin 7 engineer Mac Bonar, who lived locally to Bures Manor, who sold it to Peter Huser. We are not sure who took it apart with the intention of restoring it.

One of the first chassis to be bodied by William Lyons' Swallow Sidecar and Coachbuilding Company of Blackpool was the Austin 7; this model first appeared in 1927. This was an open two seater with rounded tail and an optional hardtop – the latter now very rare. Records seem to indicate

that under forty of this model survive to this day. Peter Martin, living in Broseley, Shropshire, is the Southern Correspondent of the Scottish Austin 7 Club and one day when visiting his local baker's and wearing the club cap he was stopped by a lady who got into conversation with him saying, 'We have got an old Austin 7 in our garage.' Peter enquired if she knew which model it was, to which she replied, 'It has Swallow written on the front.'

The car was local to him and the next weekend Peter went to look at it in a barn on a smallholding. It was in a sorry state. The 1930 car still belonged to the lady's 80-year-old but spritely, father. Whilst in the RAF he had used this car in the 1950s travelling back to camp in Wiltshire. Later, he ran a motor business and the Austin 7 came off the road in the 1960s. When it came time to retire, the garage business was sold and the Austin 7 moved to a barn where later the roof collapsed on it. It stayed in this wet and unprotected environment for two years before being put into the dry on the smallholding. The car appeared to be mostly all there, but at some time it had been fitted with cycle wings.

The Austin Seven Swallow was in a bad state.

At the time of Peter's first visit, the family were still hoping that they could arrange to have the car restored. However, they realised this was not going to happen, so it was entered in a Brightwells Auction in 2012 where it fetched £8,400, just a little above the auctioneer's estimate.

Of the many versions made of the Austin 7, perhaps the ones used by the military are some of the rarest. Some were made for general military use and had a body by Mulliner, whilst a few were designed specifically as radio communication cars. It is thought that three of these latter survive, including one in fully restored condition, to be

Austin Seven radio communication cars, bodies by Mulliner.

seen in the Royal Signals Museum at Blandford Camp. Ashley Hollebone is both a military vehicle and an Austin 7 enthusiast, having restored various versions of both genres. He has always wanted a military Austin 7 and followed up a lead which took him to a shed at a caravan park in Lincolnshire. He told me:

When I heard about this one, I went to look at it but had to work out what I was looking at as it was buried underneath a heap of parts and other items and looked far from appealing. I knew what it was a [military signals car] and decided it was worth the effort that would be needed to restore it. Although it looked in a bad state, I seemed to have more or less everything for it, including all the bodywork.

Registered MV 5046 from new, nothing is known about its military career or when it left Army service, though most had been superseded by 1939. It was probably sold into civilian use at one of the many military sales of ex-WD equipment and vehicles. At this time, it would appear to have been converted into a van. The last owner found it in a ditch well over forty years ago and it has been moved from shed to shed over the years. Ashley suggested that a van conversion would have been relatively simple due to the square design of the original military coachwork.

It is well known that the Austin 7 was built under licence in other countries – in Japan as the Datsun, in the USA as the American Austin (which became the Bantam), in France as the Rosengart, and in Germany as the Dixi, the latter being made

'It looked far from appealing.'

It had been converted to a van for commercial use.

Adolf Hitler viewing a WOC version of the Austin 7 Nippy at the 1935 German Motor Show.

by BMW in the old Dixi factory. In 1931 BMW tried to get out of their contract with Austin, which they succeeded in doing in February 1932. At this point the contract was taken up by a consortium of manufacturers operating under the name of Willys Overland Crossley (WOC). They had a manufacturing plant at Berlin Adlershof. The cars came to Germany in pieces and were assembled at Adlershof. Whilst they made a relatively few Austin 7 saloons, they found the sporty Austin 7 Nippy and Speedy sold much better. There is a photograph of Adolf Hitler at the 1935 German Motor Show inspecting a Nippy built by WOC. An apprehensive Lord Austin looks on. Hitler is reputed to have said, 'Once I also had such a car.' If true, it is more likely to have been a BMW Dixi.

Another car that Ashley Hollebone owns is a left hand drive 1935 Nippy made by WOC. He bought it some time ago from an enthusiast in Oxfordshire who is believed to have imported it. It looks to have had a hard life, just look at those reinforced hinges on the door! It is similar to the British built Nippy, but Ashley told me, 'Interesting features include a scuttle mounted fuel tank, export fan, the steering

box and also being left hand drive means that the pedal assembly is quite different from the normal Austin 7.'

Moving on from the Austin 7 we turn to the Austin 10. Miss Sarah Isabel Mogey was a graduate from Queens University in Belfast and took up a career in teaching. In 1933 she bought a brand-new Austin 10/4 saloon which was given the name

Ashley Hollebone's Willys Overland Crossley-built Nippy – just look at those two non-original hinges.

The 1933 Austin Ten 'Neddie' owned by Sarah Mogey.

Miss Mogey sent a birthday card to her car each year.

'Neddie'. She taught in Belfast and then moved to Bangor where she spent many years teaching at Glenlola Collegiate Girls School. She used the car virtually every day until she retired. Thereafter it was put away in her garage under a large sheet of polythene. She purchased a Mini and continued driving until her nineties.

I wish I had known Miss Mogey, who loved her Austin so much that she would send it a birthday card each year and some of these cards survive. I enjoyed the story that she was a diminutive figure and often sat on her pupils' exercise books to enable her to see over the steering wheel. An ex-pupil, Diana Gadd, also mentioned the books but also that one day the pile of books fell over as she was driving. She also told me Miss Mogey once offered a girl a lift home at lunch time, the girl thanked her but refused adding that she was in a hurry! Then there was the time when it had been snowing and 'Neddie' was driven to school as usual. However, Miss Mogey told the Principal that she would have to go back home as 'Neddie' was not very good in the snow. Having driven 'Neddie' back home, she then walked through the thick snow back to school to continue her teaching. Jillian Caruth remembers that in 1964 the 6th form leavers thought it would be a good idea to hoist 'Neddie' up the school flag pole! I am so glad they did not attempt this.

There is a letter on file with Sarah Mogey's will which hoped that any new owner would 'use their best endeavours to restore the car to its previous condition'. That on restoration of the car 'you will fit a plate, preferably on the dash board with the words '"Neddie" previously owned by Miss

The owner was so short she had to sit on the school exercise books to see over the steering wheel.

The new owner intends to look after the Austin Ten 'sympathetically'.

Isobel Mogey BA, Glenlola School". 'Neddie' has now been acquired by Al Rohdich from North Coast Auction Rooms, Ballybogey near Portrush who told me that he intends to look after her sympathetically.

I heard that Don Abbitt from Surrey had recently rescued an Austin Jubilee model, registered DGO 297. I looked long and hard for it in my Austin reference works. I discovered that this was a model brought out in 1935 by Salmon and Sons of Newport Pagnell under their 'Tickford' name. In Dennis Maynard's book on Salmon's, he says, 'Introduced in 1935 this model was a coupe cabriolet with four lights. It was available in both two and four door form. The two doors were more often simply referred to as a coupe rather than a coupe cabriolet'. He goes on to say that at the 1935 Motor Show, Salmon's exhibited this body on five different manufacturer's chassis. Their advertisements, of course, referred to their special hoods. 'The perfect "open-closed" car at last – instantly adaptable to any and every occasion. As handsome and beautifully finished as any coach built saloon: yet opening so readily, so simply at the turn of a handle that a child could operate it.'

Don Abbitt told me:

> I purchased the [1936] car from the second owner's son, who is in his eighties. The car was taken off the road in 1968 and when his father died some twenty-five to thirty years ago, he put it in his back garden with a cover over it. When we collected the car from Hayle on the Cornish coast, the weather was awful, rain and wind, so we did not have much chance to ask about other history.

Don only knows of one other on an Austin chassis which he hopes to see soon. Don says, 'I have started the restoration and am very pleased with what I have purchased'. I am sure it will be rebuilt to the high standard of his Austin 18hp Woodie. The Jubilee model was expensive, costing £325, much more than the £210 for the 12hp Austin Ascot, for example.

'They put it in the back garden with a cover on it.'

The Austin Jubilee on its way to a new home and restoration.

At the 2014 Classic Car Show at the NEC, the Austin 10 Drivers Club displayed on their stand a 1936 Austin 10 van, the restoration of which had only just been completed. For many years it was commonplace for manufacturers to offer van versions based on the standard car chassis, usually with beefed up rear springs and a lower back axle ratio to cope with the extra loads it would carry. These vans usually had a hard life with little sentiment attached to them and are now a rarity. Certainly, the Austin 10 Drivers Club know of only a few of this model remaining.

Owner Maurice Palmer of Birmingham is no stranger to car restorations and even though he is well into his seventies, was looking for a new project. VJ 8949 (a Herefordshire number) had been lying in pieces in a barn accompanying a Rover. After the death of its owner, the widow sold the Rover to Terry Preedy stipulating he must take the Austin as well. Terry told Maurice:

> It was last on the road in the early 1960s. It was purchased from a farm on the outskirts of the Forest of Dean and loaded onto a trailer. Having stood for many years under a canvas sheet out in the open, it was in a poor state. So rotten, in fact, that every bump in the road shook more and more of the wooden frame to bits.

Maurice's friend, Graham, heard about the Austin and went to see it. Graham reported

The restored Austin van – Maurice is still trying to piece together its history.

back, 'Well, it's all there, at least the bits the woodworm did not fancy. Too much work for me.' Maurice went to see it, describing it later in the Club magazine:

> The body had become a virtual flat pack, remaining bits of timber were present only because the woodworm were still holding hands. The scuttle had been separated from the cab roof. The area around the battery and tool box had more holes than a string vest. On a positive note, the wings and rear mudguards were sound and the rear doors could be used to establish the size of the rear opening, but they needed new ash frames.

In June 2012 Maurice bought it and started on the very complicated restoration.

Now that the work is finished, Maurice is trying to piece together its history. It still has a supplier's plate on the dash 'Watson's Motor Works Limited, Engineers, Leominster, Herefordshire, Tel. 60'. The last owner on the old buff logbook was E. C. Davies of Hillery Road, Worcester. The Austin 10 Drivers Club knew of its existence for a short while in 1972 when in the hands of V.A. Corbin of Barry, Glamorgan.

Nicknamed 'Octavia', an 8hp Austin 6 light saloon has been with Paul Isaac for over twenty-five years. This car registered EAX 168 in Monmouthshire was first owned by Mr William

Some of the parts of the 1936 Austin Ten van as purchased by Maurice Palmer.

Price. Its date of registration was 8 December 1939, three months into the war. When a teenager in South Wales, Paul Isaac worked for a garage owner, Mr M.J. Shord, the second owner of the car, who also had a collection of other cars. Some of these had to be sold off and the Austin 8 was offered to Paul, so in 1986, with the aid of £200 he borrowed from his parents, he was able to purchase. Since then, time has intervened. The car has been stored under cover, then moves to houses without garages made restoration difficult, and the latest move with his partner Georgina, to a house in Bath, has meant 'Octavia' is sitting at the bottom of the garden. Paul works abroad a lot and realises that he would not be able to restore the car and so it was sold on to another enthusiast.

In 1948 with an eye on the customer in the United States, Leonard Lord put on the market the Austin A90, also known as the Austin Atlantic. This had a highly styled body that was hoped would be appreciated by the American buyer. This was not to be the case. It is thought that approximately 8,000 were built and only 3,600 were actually sold in the United States.

Max Cain from Hoo, near Rochester, was a ship's captain and as such was able to persuade the powers that be that he should be allowed to purchase a new car when almost all early post-war cars were going for export. He purchased in 1949 a new Austin Atlantic convertible with the Birmingham registration number KOE 3. He still had the car

KOE 3 in its lock-up after leaves and spiders had been removed.

when he died in 1981. His widow kept the car stored until she died in 1996. Max's nephew, Roger Strong, was able to buy the car from the estate and took it back to his home in Richmond, Yorkshire. He recommissioned it for his own use but hardly used it and put it away in a lock up garage.

Recently, Roger decided to part with the car and contacted Alastair While from Gloucestershire. Now, Alastair already had two Atlantics, one under restoration and the other a project, so he was not looking for another! Roger persuaded him to come the 200 miles and have a look. He told me:

> The owner opened the door to the lock up, which was covered in spiders' webs and leaves from the last twenty Yorkshire autumns, inside was the Austin Atlantic covered in layers of dust. I released the hand brake and the Atlantic rolled out in to the light of day after twenty years. This car is quite special, not only because of it being an Austin Atlantic convertible, but the fact that it is a family owned car from new and from the first year of production, with many early features included being fully optioned when new, with the Ecko CR61 radio and power hood and windows.

Needless to say, Alastair bought the car. Until Alastair unearthed this car, it was totally unknown to the Austin Counties Car Club, which caters for Austin Atlantics.

'Octavia' has been sitting at the bottom of the garden since 1986.

'With Ecko CR61 radio and power hood and windows.'

In 1982 Austin Atlantic convertible FPN 717 featured on the album cover of *Watch this Space* by the Stargazers. The lead singer of the group, Ricky Brawn, was a fan of the Atlantic and suggested featuring one on their album cover. This album has been listed as Album Number Nine in the Telegraph's Top Twenty-Five Motoring Covers of all time. This actual car is now being given a new lease of life by David Whyley. The Atlantic was one of the last of the model built in December 1950. The car has a power hood and power windows as well as the optional Ecko valve radio.

David Whyley first met Vernon Cox at the 1984 Austin Counties Car Club Rally at Hagley Hall. Vernon was exhibiting a metallic green version. Vernon was the Atlantic Registrar for the Club. They became close friends. Over the years David pestered Vernon to tell him if ever he heard of a good Atlantic for sale. In the 1980s Vernon had bought FPN 717 for his own collection and moved it, with difficulty, to a lock up where he kept it safe for almost thirty years. Recently, Vernon said he was thinking of selling the car. David told me that he journeyed south with his daughter Alice. 'When we opened the door of the lock up Alice exclaimed, "Dad, this is just like Indiana Jones". There was the car, seemingly just disturbed from its long slumber.' After being transported back to Stourbridge a thorough restoration was started.

The full history of the car is known. It was bought new by a Mr Witts of Battle and by May 1953 it was with James Scott of Ringwood who kept it until 1967. In 1969 London Motors of Highbridge in Somerset advertised it for sale for £151 saying the all-electric power units worked and it had covered 37,000 miles. It is thought the garage resprayed it from its original rare metallic Cavern Green to white and fitted a non-original vinyl hood. The car was purchased by David Cropper who owned it at the time he was approached for it to be used on the album cover. This rare Austin Atlantic is being sympathetically restored after years of slumber in its lock up.

How far would you go to buy a classic unseen? In Australia you may have to travel hundreds of miles. Mark Yeomans of Austin Counties Car Club has been telling me about Chris Roberts whose round trip was 1,560 miles to bring back an Austin Atlantic. The story behind the car is

The Austin Atlantic on the record cover of *Watch this Space*.

'Dad, this is just like Indiana Jones.'

After standing in a shed for fifty-three years, the Austin Atlantic was rescued in a trip of 1,560 miles.

that the original owner died and the family put the car away in a shed where it stood for the next fifty-three years. It then had one owner for a short time who advertised it on eBay, which is where Chris's son Neil saw it. The collection in a Land Rover Discovery was not without its problems, including having to buy five new tyres en route. Loading was made more difficult by the car being stuck in gear, but by disconnecting the tail shaft, this obstacle was overcome. The car looked quite good when the dust was washed off. Restoration is underway.

The Barossa Valley in South Australia is famous for its wines. Garrie Hisco has, however, picked up a different vintage near Tanunda in the Barossa Valley. He was tipped off that there was an interesting car on a vineyard property. It turned out to be a 1951 Austin Dorset convertible. Peter Simmonds from the Austin Counties Car Club told us that a prototype convertible was produced in the UK in August 1948, but it never went into production. In Australia, however, a number of Dorset convertibles were built, some being marketed as the Austin Falcon or A40 Smart Set Tourer.

Garrie told me:

I motored up and found the location and in a vineyard building was the Austin covered in dust but in good condition for its age, with just a few knobs missing from the dash. The seats are remarkable in that the leather is excellent, as are the side screens and even the hood is perfectly serviceable. The car was originally painted navy blue with a blue or grey hood with red piping. It had been in store for thirty-seven years. I subsequently found out from the owner that he had bought it forty-seven years ago; it was his

1951 Austin Dorset Convertible which never went into production in UK; some were built in Australia and called the Austin Falcon.

Interior of the Austin Falcon.

first car and he had purchased it locally from its first owner. He had always wanted to keep it for sentimental reasons. Circumstances demanded some funds and I was fortunate to be able to purchase it.

It is believed that coachbuilders Harold Radford only built one shooting brake/country car on the Austin A110 Sheerline chassis. Built in 1952 its story is quite a sad one. In 2020 I heard about it from owner John Windwood:

No history has yet been traced of its early commission and owners. In the late 1990s it was acquired by entrepreneur Peter De Savery. The car, which had been sitting unused for some time, was mechanically overhauled and transported to one of his golf courses in Lincolnshire where it was used as a mobile bar on the ninth hole! It proved so popular that when he took over another golf course in Rhode Island, New York, he decided to ship it out there to serve the same function. A few years passed and the golf course changed hands. The car was containerised to be brought back to the UK for further use in its popular role. Unfortunately, during the voyage back across the Atlantic, it broke free in the container and was badly damaged. Presumably it was considered a loss and then changed hands a couple of times, finally being sold to Jaguar Land Rover as part of a collection they bought in 2014. They owned it for five years before selling it on. It then passed through another couple of owners before I bought it from a friend who I met through the Allegro Club! I am determined to restore the car. It is going to take a while as it has been very neglected over the years but is surprisingly solid.

The Harold Radford bodied Austin 110 Sheerline broke loose in its container.

The back end was worse than the front.

Some readers may remember Peter De Savery owned at one time Littlecote House, near Hungerford, at which he kept his collection of classic and other cars. The house and collection were opened to the public.

I have always had a passing interest in the Austin A40 Sports (produced 1950-53) as my father wanted one. My grandfather, who was head of the family firm, would not allow my father to have a 'sports car' as his company car. It was different for Joan, an 18-year-old lady living in Kent; she bought an A40 Sports third hand. She used it each day to travel to London to her job in the advertising industry. She progressed through her firm when one day her boss gave her a promotion. He promised a company car (a Ford Capri) on condition that 'I never see you driving the wreck again'. Fast forward to 2005 and Mike Greasby, Membership Secretary of the Austin Counties Car Club, had a tip-off leading to this lady's A40 Sports which had been kept in a dry barn ever since. She was down-sizing and very reluctantly had to let ODE 242 go, but happy to

sell to Mike for restoration. Mike was no stranger to these cars, having owned a number. He was used to underside rot but told me, 'One area of the under-chassis boxing was rusted through and on investigation I discovered the largest mouse nest I have ever seen, filling the entire boxed in area on one side. Clearly, the rot had not been due to water penetration, but mouse urine!' Early on in the restoration he was looking through Dave Whyley's book on the A40 Sports when he found a picture of ODE 242 being rallied by Brian Jenkins from Swansea. The Club put them in touch with each other and now Mike has a complete record of its club rallying career. Brian sold the car to Mercury Motors of North London in order to buy a Swallow Doretti. Joan, a young advertising executive, bought the car from Mercury, sales invoices for the A40 Sports and the Swallow Doretti survive. The discovery of the rally history explained some modifications which Mike had found on the car, such as 'engine mods, extra spotlights, map reading light, badge bar and headlight stone guards still in a box in the boot'.

Garrie Hisco has been out and about again, this time visiting a local auction. He had not intended to buy a car but was very taken by a 1954 Austin Somerset. He described it as having:

Original leather seats, some original paint-work, all badging and instruments complete, with invoices and insurance slips back to the first day of purchase. Although oxidised where the paint had fallen off in the warm, dry Australian sun, it was virtually rust free, with perfect floors.

Austin A40 Sports found by Mike Greasby in a dry barn.

The A40 Sports being rallied by Brian Jenkins.

1950 Austin Somerset had been stored since 1972.

A free Austin A35 offered in Cornwall.

The car was originally imported into Brisbane and then went to Adelaide. It was the owner's intention 'to keep it forever' and it remained in a lean-to alongside his home. At some time he had started to rebuild the engine and had obtained the necessary parts, which were still in their original packaging and stored in the boot. The owner had recently died, hence the auction, and Garrie bought the car still with the original key in the ignition and a final registration sticker of 1972.

I heard from Andy Ibbotson who told me, 'I worked for a lady at Cornwall College who, knowing of my passion for rusty old cars, asked if I would like a free Austin A35 saloon. It belonged to a friend of hers who had stored it in the garden for seven years and finally had to admit he was never going to do anything with it'. It turned out the previous owner had owned it for twenty-five or so years and it was thought it was last on the road in 1992. It was registered new in Bristol 934 CHW in July 1958. Andy goes on to say:

It does not have much going for it; the sills are rotten, the floor is full of holes, the headlining is ripped, the seats damaged and chewed by rodents (I found two dead rats in it), the petrol tank is holed, the rear bumper rusted away and there are no brakes. The bonnet is rusted through and there are massive holes in the bulkhead and inner wings … anyone else would quite honestly scrap it, but I don't see cars like that. It has survived all this time since 1958 so it deserves saving.

'Seats damaged and chewed by rodents.'

Andy collected it and moved it to his garden in 2014 and it has been sitting under a tarpaulin ever since. He is planning a sympathetic restoration.

In the Morris section of this chapter, you will find another vehicle restored from scrap condition by Andy Ibbotson, a yellow Post Office Morris Minor Van.

We now turn to stories of the finds of Morris cars. In 2012, H&H Auctions offered at their Duxford sale two vintage Morris cars, both with interesting histories and both from the same vendor. The 1924 Bullnose Morris PW 3580 was bought new by Cyril Case of Wells-next-the-Sea and quickly changed hands, again ending up with Mary Loads of Blakeney who licenced it as 'Hackney' with a quoted seating capacity of 'eight persons' (surely that eight was a three!). In 1929 for reasons unknown it was stored in an 'old fish shed in Sheringham' where it stayed unmolested for fifty years. In April 1979 it was sold by Sotheby's to the present vendor who has dry-stored it since then. There cannot be many cars of this age that have only been driven for five years! Though a front wing may need replacing, 'the whole car is a time-warp, even the tyres and battery appear original'.

The other car is a 1927 Flatnose Morris Cowley HH 3807. In 1934 it was owned by a wonderful lady, a writer from Carlisle, Daisy Washington. In the First World War she drove ambulances when in the First Aid Nursing Yeomanry (FANY) and lost a leg so doing. In the Second World War, she went back to France as Captain of a FANY unit. She gained both the French Croix de Guerre and the Polish Gold Cross amongst other medals. In 1950 she drove the Morris (known as 'Happy Henry' because of its registration number) from Carlisle to Oberammergau in Austria. She also owned a 1920s Austin and she would only tax one of these each year, swapping the tax disc when she changed over cars. An Austin tax disc is on the Morris to this day! After her death, the car was sold at Carlisle Auction Mart to the vendor in 1978 and was in use around Saffron Walden until 1983 when it was laid up.

Col Schiller from Toowomba in Queensland, a member of the Bullnose Morris Club, received a phone call from his friend, Steve, telling him that he knew of a man in Bararakula State Forest who

1927 Flatnose Morris offered by H&H in the same sale.

was keen to sell a 1925 Bullnose Morris. Ray Dove, the present owner, had bought the car from Steve some fifteen years before in an unrestored condition but had done nothing with it and now needed to raise some cash in order to repair his bulldozer. Col arranged with Ray to go and see the car, which was roughly a three hour drive away. He said, 'The Morris was hidden under several sheets of corrugated roofing iron and it has sunken into the sandy soil. This part of Australia is very dry, it only gets 300-500mm of rain each year.' After inspection, a price was agreed. This is a three door open four

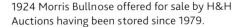

1924 Morris Bullnose offered for sale by H&H Auctions having been stored since 1979.

The 1925 Morris had 'sunken into the sandy soil'.

seater, the spare wheel being mounted on the running board alongside where the driver's door would have been. Amazingly, the body is almost rust free and the wood frame is solid. Even the upholstery seems intact. Col went on to say, 'It has a strange windscreen with the pillars mounted into a cast frame bolted onto the cowl. The front bumper also has cast holders and not the usual brackets. There are no identity plates on the body so it could have been a model sent out as a running chassis and bodied by a local Australian coach builder.' It has a period Royal Automobile Club Queensland badge mounted on the radiator cap.

The Royal Automobile Club of Queensland's badge mounted on the radiator cap.

Two seat Morris Cowley NT 8728 was registered in Shropshire on 6 July 1926. The first logbook has disappeared but a continuation one gives ownership in 1932 as Norman Glover living at the wonderfully named village of Ruyton of the Eleven Towns near Shrewsbury. There are no more entries and no other continuation book has survived. The present owner, Simon Harding, bought it from someone who had purchased from a local farmer. He knows that around thirty years ago the chassis, less body which had long been lost, was given to some children to drive around the farm. They

crashed it and it was repaired for them to continue to abuse! When you hear the dire mechanical state the car was in, it is surprising they could drive it at all! Simon surmises that as a hand throttle had been fitted to the top of the steering column, it may have been previously used, jacked up, to drive some machinery, a saw bench perhaps. He told us that amongst many other worn out parts:

> … the engine had broken up main bearings and at some point had run with broken piston rings on the original (still fitted) pistons which had almost worn through the top of the groove, but this did not seem to concern the person who fitted new piston rings later … the universal joint was still operating with about an inch and a half of backlash, the gearbox was quite spectacularly chewed up, in fact the inside of the first motion shaft and its gear were a fraction away from losing drive.

I am pleased to say that the car with a new body is well on the way to being restored.

Tim Dyer joined the Bullnose Morris Club and has been trying to find out some history of his car, a 1928 Morris Oxford (flat nose) saloon, registered VK 669. This is proving difficult because it would appear to have been in storage since 1952. He has been told that it was put into a tin shed in that year and over time the roof of the shed collapsed with the result that the weather has caused a lot of damage to the body. It came out of store in the 1980s when an owner decided to get some

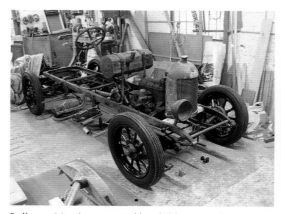

Bullnose Morris once used by children and driven around on a farm.

work done on it and rang his local repairer saying, 'I have a Morris Oxford needing repair and paint.' The garage assumed this to be a check over and paint on a Morris Minor! They got a shock. The owner then took fright at the price quoted and sold it to someone who lived nearby. He put it into a shed with the intention to restore but found he had too many projects. He had partly stripped it down and left it until 2017 when the site at West Coker in Somerset, on which it was stored, was to be cleared. It was then that Tim Dyer bought it. He would love to hear from anyone who might know the car. It is a four door saloon in black and brown, or it might be maroon. Here is a clue – it has a mushroom or toadstool painted on the inside of the radiator grille.

It is almost certain that the success of Herbert Austin's Austin Seven caused William Morris to consider making a small car. This car, called the Morris Minor, appeared at the 1928 Motor Show. By 1930 a quarter of the cars produced by Morris were the Morris Minor. The Morris Minor was fitted with Wolseley's lively overhead cam engine. Then prompted by the fact that it was known that Ford were producing a small car, Morris strove to get the price of the Minor down to £100, the first car (other than cycle cars) to reach this magic figure. This had a side valve engine, no bumpers, black radiator shell, new wire wheels, headlamp and sidelamp combined. It was widely heralded in the press, even making the front cover of *The Light Car*.

The very first car, registered JO 764 on 11 December 1930, was used by the press and then kept by the factory until 9 July 1931 before being

The Morris Minor now down to £100, a press release picture.

sold. At some stage various changes were made to this car including the wheels and radiator surround. Between 1932 and 1956 the history of the car is unknown except that Michael Strickland and then David Thorne owned it in Exeter; they are believed to have been students. I think Thorne later sold it to Patrick Pidler of South Molton, owner of a huge collection of farming memorabilia. In 1986

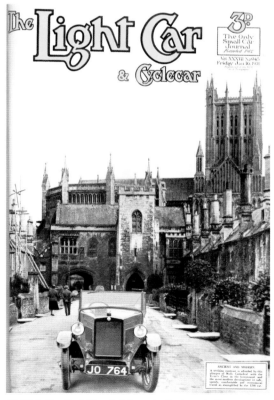

JO 764, the first Morris Minor to feature in the advertising.

1928 Morris Oxford has been in store since 1952.

this whole collection, including the Morris, was sold to Trevor and Christine Stanbury who were setting up a North Devon tourist farm at Higher Clovelly, near Bideford, called 'Milky Way Adventure Park'. In 1992 I had correspondence with that great Morris historian Harry Edwards about the car and I went down to Clovelly to see it. I wrote at the time that it 'is now in a rather sad state. It is lacking running boards and floor boards and still has a 1956 tax disc.' Also in the deal with Patrick Pidler was a 1936 Austin 7 Ruby CHU 54, last tax disc 1967; the Austin was displayed alongside the Morris.

Fast forward to 2012 when the Pre-War Minor Network website brought up the subject again and after a flurry of correspondence 'the owner confirmed that it was his intention to restore the car when his personal circumstances permitted'. Over the next few years, it cropped up occasionally, usually with comments about its deteriorating condition. In 2019 the Committee of the Morris Register decided that the car ought to be liberated and asked for a meeting with Trevor Stanbury. It was reported that 'the car's owner and adventure park founder was both courteous and hospitable to his visitors, the trip eventually proved to be a fruitless one as the Club's offer was deemed unacceptable'.

Mick Roberts, well known in the Morris Register as the restorer of two Morris cars including a 1932 Minor, had offered to assist the Club if the purchase had been made. Quite unconnected with this, Mick told me:

JO 764 'in rather a bad state' in the Milky Way Adventure Park.

I was visiting my son in Devon and thought my wife Judith and I would go and have a look at the car … I showed Trevor [Stanbury] photos of the restoration of my 1932 Minor and the 1934 Morris 25. He was very impressed … I think the fact that my wife was supportive about the car helped in the decision, but he needed to ask his family for their opinion first. Two weeks later while we were on holiday in Lancashire, Trevor phones saying he had agreed to sell the car to me. Great excitement …

The car is now in North London and restoration has started.

Mike Roberts about to start restoration of JO 764.

In 1929 a Morris Minor rolling chassis was sold to Australia to be locally bodied by Ruskin. It was purchased new by a jeweller in Brisbane who used it as his everyday car until he retired when he took it off the road. Its last registration was 1958. In 1964 the car was sold to Kevin, a great friend of Colin Schiller whose Bullnose Morris features in another story. Kevin had every intention of restoring the car, but somehow never got around to it. Recently, he sold the car to Colin who intends to put it back on the road. Colin told me, 'After removing decades of stuff covering the car, we then had to manoeuvre it around the side of the house, a tight squeeze.' A sad post script to this story is that a few months after the car was retrieved from Kevin's garage, his house was burned down.

In 1955 when David Bowman was fifteen, he was given a 1931 coach built Morris Minor for his

It was a tight squeeze to move the Morris Minor round the house.

TF 889 had been found in a disused quarry.

birthday. It had previously belonged to his uncle who had eyesight problems and could not drive anymore. It was in poor condition, but David restored it in time to take his test in it when he was seventeen. He used it regularly until it was sideswiped by a farmer's lorry and written off. The undamaged bits were given to his friend, Brian Barling, who was running a very scanty Morris Special. He also had an ohc Morris Minor saloon, registered TF 889 that he had found disused in a quarry and purchased it for £4. He used it until 1960 when he bought a Ford 300E van from a friend. David told me:

> During this time the two Minors were kept in his garage while the van lived outside … later the Sidevalve had its skimpy body removed and a 1½ hp Lister D Type stationary engine mounted on the back. It was then driven as and when required to power a saw bench which was located beside a wood pile at the far end of the garden … the saloon remained virtually untouched, although restoration was planned …

In 2019 David had a hankering after another car to restore and visited Brian, who by now was in poor health. He enquired about the Minor saloon. After a few days of deliberation Brian replied saying David could have the saloon provided he would restore it and that he took the other chassis

with Lister engine as well. In addition, he could have all the spares in the garage which included many parts of David's original Minor which he had received sixty years ago.

The Morris Special now with Lister engine removed.

David Wall has been telling me about a 1934 Morris Minor four door saloon, registration JH 6998, which his friend, Nick Le Neve Walmsley, found in a Norfolk barn. David told me, 'The owner had been willed it after looking after some land for the elderly owner. It had stood unused for at least twenty years. I think it must have been taken off the road when the flywheel came loose. It made an awful noise when first started up! It is now up and running again and being enjoyed.' I was recently told by an owner that there are around twenty-four Morris Minor saloons known of in the United Kingdom. This low survival rate is partly due to wet rot getting into the A posts which in turn support very heavy doors.

Morris 10/6 Special tourer thought to have been unused since 1968.

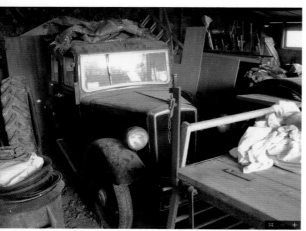

The 1934 Morris Minor four door saloon in store for at least twenty years.

Roger Bird is the motorcycle historian for Brooklands Museum and has four of his motorcycles on display there. He is a collector of pre-war Morris and was previously the editor of the Morris Register newsletter. A little while ago he was in the process of moving to a smaller house and had to part with one or two cars. Back in 2003 he was asked if he was interested in buying a Morris Ten Four two seater with dickey, which was part of a deceased estate belonging to Bill Dick of Watford. These 'ranged from a Jensen CV8 to a large number of Reliant Robins and a Marina estate'. He got more excited when shown two Morris Ten Six Special tourers, a two seat and a four seat. He was

able to buy both. He chose to work on the four seater on which restoration has started. He completed the wood frame but then got side tracked by more motorcycles needing restoration and did nothing more to the Morris. It is thought the car was bought in 1964 by John Hurst of Swindon who took it off the road to repair the wooden frame. He sold the car to Bill Dick in 1968 who never registered the change of keeper with the DVLA. The car would appear to have been off the road for over fifty years. The story behind the manufacture of the Special (only 361 were made) is interesting. It revolves around internal rivalries. Roger told me 'He [Leonard Lord] disliked Kimber [Cecil Kimber at MG] and the Special was intended as a rival to MG and is the only car Morris ever advertised as a sports car.'

The clearly labelled 10/6 Special engine in the Morris.

'Stored for many years under a pile of hay.'

Steve Knight from Box near Bath was attending a local Morris Register social meeting where it was mentioned that there was a Morris 8 looking for a new home – it had been stored for many years under piles of hay. Steve told me, 'I'd had a couple of pints at this point and was determined to buy it. The next morning, I thought better of it.' However, he relented a week later and contacted the owner. Steve was told that he had inherited his grandfather's cottage which used to be the local forge. There was a solid stone shed alongside in which his grandfather kept his Morris 8 and also lots of hay. The owner did not want to keep the car but felt it should be given a new lease of life, hence he had contacted the Morris Register. It had been described to Steve over the phone as being 'dreadful', but Steve thought quite differently. 'It was love at first sight and I agreed to buy it,' Steve told me. The logbook showed it was an early Series One Morris 8 tourer from 1935. According to the logbook it was last taxed in 1955 and a tax disc bearing this date was found in the car. It has covered 35,000 miles according to the speedometer. It appears to be basically very original. It has been fitted with a Series Two grille, there is evidence of a minor front end accident, and it has a replacement engine. Apart from the trim, which is rotten, the rest of the car appears to be very sound. Steve intends to restore the car sympathetically and retain as much of the patina (and hay?) as possible.

A 1938 Morris 8 sliding head four door saloon would appear to have had many owners in Scotland. Registered LS 4070, a Selkirk number, it has eventually ended up in the Outer Hebrides on the Island of Harris. The Morris Register helped

Removal of the 1935 Morris Eight Series One from long term storage.

John O'Hara 'just felt sorry for it'.

with the re-allocation of the number by the DVLA. The car has been bought by John O'Hara who found it in the hands of a dealer near Stornoway. He knew it was in a bad condition but 'just felt sorry for it'. John told me:

It has certainly been off the road since before the first V5 logbooks were issued in 1974. It was clearly left outside or in a leaky shed of some description and is extremely rotten … I get the feeling it has passed through umpteen people and used as a parts car for others. So much is missing from it. Inner metal, fabric and woodwork just crumbled in my hands when trying to remove it. Been sat outside for longer than I have been alive, I think. 90,000 odd on the tripometer. Running repairs are crazy on it. One cill is an old 2x2 bit of wood shaped, nailed on and painted to match. Bodged repairs everywhere in fibreglass and Polyfilla or some form of plaster. Someone kept it on the road as long as possible on a budget and skill level of not much … I reckon it's all saveable with work, a lot of it! … Restoration is underway, I say restoration but as so much is missing or beyond saving, I am doing a mild period custom rebuild.

It is thought that the oldest surviving Morris Oxford MO has recently been found, albeit in a poor condition. The MO was the first of a new line of medium sized Morris cars produced at Cowley after the war. Some say externally it looked like a blown up Morris Minor, but certainly the front grille was quite different. Bob Francis of the 6/80 and MO Oxford and Cowley Club has been telling me about an MO saloon which has turned up in Malang, Indonesia. It is thought it was built in late July or early August 1948 and was probably immediately exported so that it could be in the showrooms for launch date in October.

The owner of this car, Bambang Priy Utomo, does not speak English and so far he has not

The floor boards on the 1938 Morris are missing altogether.

provided any history or background. From the pictures it is quite obvious it's been unused for years. Except for the lack of an engine, it appears reasonably complete, with a few alterations from standard. The dashboard and glove pocket covers have been painted white which may disguise the original brown coloured crackle finish. Bob went on to say, 'The car would need to be thoroughly steam cleaned before any country would allow it to be imported due to harmful insects, disease, mould, fungus, etc.' The Club's historian, Nigel Anderson, says the Club records show an earlier car that was exported to Malta, but no trace of its present existence has been found.

Most will know that the early Morris Minors had their headlights in the front grille panel. But to comply with a new USA law, cars shipped to the States required new wings incorporating the headlights higher up. From January to June 1949 just 418 were built to this specification. They also had the trafficator slots blanked off as trafficators were uncommon in the USA and were fitted with twin Lucas round L488 tail lights on

From January 1949 exports to the USA of Morris Minors had to have their headlights in the wings and not in the grille.

The oldest surviving Morris Oxford MO built in early August 1948.

pedestals. John Voelcker from New York City, a member of the Morris Minor Owners Club, now has the oldest known USA-specification Minor tourer. It is, however, in a terrible state. He wrote about it in the Club magazine *Minor Matters*. It stood in a field in Texas before it was bought by Morris Minor owner Garon Wade, who realised that it really needed saving. However, he never got around to it and at last sold it, saying, 'I was tired of hanging on to everything and watching it rot.' He had owned it for thirty years, ten of which were undercover but twenty more in a collapsed shed. He was persuaded to sell it to Pat Allen of Joshua, Texas. When it arrived with him 'it was filled to the brim with leaves, dirt and rodent nests'. Allen had it partially steam cleaned and what he saw made him realise that he just did not have the skills to tackle the restoration. A year later he sold it to John Voelcker. John said, 'En route [from Texas to New York] over

'The dashboard and glove pocket covers of the Morris Oxford MO have been painted white.'

The oldest USA specification Morris Minor 'was in a terrible state'..

1,700 miles, the shaking and the swaying caused the rusty engine cradle and front frame rails to crack, dropping the front of the engine to a few inches above the ground. The bonnet flew off as well.' The engine turned over freely and had no scoring inside the cylinders and some pistons were date stamped 1957. From evidence on the car, it was originally maroon, a colour known to fade in hot sun, such as found in Texas. John is now collecting all the missing parts that will be required for this mammoth restoration. He is no stranger to looking after British cars as he still owns the 1961 Minor Traveller his father bought new in London, a 1958 Riley one-point-five saloon he had driven at college and his father's 1967 Sunbeam Alpine which again was bought in London when new.

Howard Johnson has a very soft spot for the 1950 Morris Minor convertible which he bought in the early 1970s from fellow student Garry Bullock for £15. Howard was a student in Brighton and regularly used the car for the journey home to Doncaster. 'Elsie' soon succumbed to this trip and was retired to his parents' garage. Writing in the Morris Minor Club magazine *Minor Matters*, he says, 'Elsie subsequently lived in a shed, a field, a polytunnel, a condemned garage, and a pretend restorer's workshop.' The restorer had stripped the car down but had done virtually no work on the car, nor had he done any re-assembly. Howard eventually got the car back in pieces, missing the driver's door and the original engine, amongst other parts. The car has become a running joke in the family as the children each looked forward to having the car for their weddings. The two granddaughters have

hopes … Howard is soon to retire and is not sure what to do as he feels he is not capable of restoring it and he assumes it will be very expensive to restore. Should it be sold as spares or even sold for scrap? Back in his impecunious post-student days he sold the distinctive number plate. The Morris Minor first appeared at the first post-war Earls Court Motor Show in 1948, so this is an early example of the MM.

Post Office Telephones had quite a love affair with the Morris Minor over the years. These green and later yellow vans lettered out for Post Office Telephones were a common sight. One such, YCY 795, entered service in 1971 and worked in the Swansea area (fleet no. U258342, later 71 300 8342). Does anyone remember it please? In 1977 it was sold off, painted blue and purchased by someone in St. Austell, Cornwall. A second owner in the area painted it black and cut windows in the side. It changed hands again and in 1986 it was laid up in a barn near Bodmin. It was found in 2014

'Howard is soon to retire and is not sure what to do.'

£15 Elsie and used as student transport.

'Should it be sold as spares or even sold as scrap?'

1971 Post Office Morris telephone van was laid up in a barn near Bodmin.

by Andy Ibbotson, a Morris Minor Owners Club member, who had been around old cars for almost thirty years, particularly Morris Minors, though he had never owned a van. He said '… I saw a sorry looking, badly painted, black rusty heap with four flat tyres, lots of rust and lots of filler.' Even so, he bought it. The start of the restoration was delayed whilst he finished restoring a Mini. The van was in a terrible state, for example, 'Almost the entire chassis from front to the rear axle mountings had received a second skin of metal. The gutters were plastered with filler and gaffer tape to "stop" the rust and the roof was held down at each corner with metal brackets to stop it flying off, the rust was so bad.' The restoration is now complete, most of the previous owners have been contacted, and it's just the South Wales working history that is wanted now.

'The gutters were plastered with filler and gaffer tape.'

Now fully restored, Andy Ibbotson still is unsure of its history in the Swansea area.

As was customary, they all stood around the end of the production line, managers and workers. It was 12 November 1970, and the last Morris Minor saloon was leaving the production line. Incidentally, Travellers and vans were made for a little while longer. After the ceremony was over, the car went for sale, no attempt was made to save it for historical reasons. It was registered FMT 265J, a Middlesex number. It would appear the first owner had an inkling of its importance as a letter survives dated 26 January 1971 from British Leyland certifying that this was the last saloon produced for sale from Cowley.

By September 1993 it was in the hands of South London motor trader, John Condon, who sold it to David Baldock of Goudhurst. He in turn part exchanged it with the Real Car Company in North Wales for a Rolls-Royce Silver Shadow. Ray Arnold of the Real Car Company realised this was an important car and tried to persuade the British Motor Industry Heritage Trust to buy it for display at Gaydon as well as the Morris Minor Centre in Bath. Both turned it down. Ray Arnold told me, 'It was just a typical used Minor at the time, scruffy, rusting in places, patched paintwork, etc. In 1994 we sold it to a guy in Altrincham … who was unfortunately unable to renovate it or care for it in the way that it deserved.'

In 2008 the Morris Minor Owners Club celebrated sixty years of the Morris Minor and Ray

The last Morris Minor Saloon leaving the production line in November 1970.

Newell, the Secretary of the Club, tried to locate it again. On the fortieth anniversary of the Club, contact with the car's owner was made and the car purchased by the Club. Ray Newell told me, 'We have made a start on some essential structural repairs and hope to return the vehicle to a roadworthy condition. Whether the restoration extends to a full concours style paint finish remains open to conjecture.' Then due to a generous legacy a group of Morris Minor Owners Club members got together and have restored the car to a high standard. The completed car in its 50th year has been loaned to the Mini Plant at Cowley for display amongst their own historic Morris cars.

The Morris Minor as purchased by the Morris Minor Owners Club.

# 6 | CLASSIC CARS 1946-1990

fter the war, the motor industry had a lot to contend with. Many factories had been bombed and there was a great shortage of materials. Some companies had been planning their new models in advance of the war ending. In the main, the first new cars coming off the production lines were revamped, pre-war models. The majority of the cars were to be exported to help pay off war debt, many to the United States. Those few cars that were released to the home market were very expensive in comparison to pre-war, partly due to high purchase tax. This resulted in a booming second-hand market where pre-war cars that had been laid up were being offered for sale at prices double that of their new price.

One of the first vehicles off the production line at Jowetts of Bradford were Bradford vans. These were based on the pre-war Jowett 8 and used the same 1,005cc twin cylinder engine. Very soon a Utility version was offered which had side windows and seats at the rear. Tim Brown from Congleton has discovered a 1947 Utility version. He heard about it through the Jowett Car Club grapevine. The vehicle had stood out of use in a leaking garage for over thirty years. Tim told me, 'The owner's late husband appeared to have been a bit of a hoarder, not throwing anything away. This was evident on first visiting the vehicle, which had to be unearthed to see it properly.' The car looked as if it was all there so Tim bought it. Unfortunately, the widow did not know much about the history of the vehicle. All that is known is that it was sold by Jowett agent Marriot's Garage, Broadwater Street, Worthing. It has the Sussex registration JPO 827. Restoration is now taking place.

1947 Jowett Bradford Utility JPO 827 – very little history is known.

Tim Brown told me about another similar model found by Alastair Gregg of Buxton. Tim describes this new find as requiring a 'heroic restoration'. ENV 36, built in 1948, was first registered in Northampton. In the 1960s the car was found bricked up in a garage minus its engine. The garage was about to be demolished and the car was retrieved and stored out of doors. The owner later moved house taking the Bradford with him and it was then left outside for another twenty-seven years! Alastair bought it in October 2017. An engine came with it, but it was in very poor condition. Alastair told me:

As you can see, there is very little bodywork on the chassis. However, there is a pile of

1948 Jowett Bradford Utility which has been left in the open for twenty-seven years.

body panels kept separately that should make some good patterns. The Jowett Car Club has dimensional drawings of the ash frame, so I have some skills to learn – carpentry, welding, spraying and lead loading, to name a few. I have run a Jowett Jupiter for ten years and have no intention of giving up.

Back in 1964 it is thought that a builder in Derby offered this van, then with a slipping clutch, to a Jowett Car Club member for ten pounds. The member could not afford it at the time and was unable to purchase it!

Thirty-seven years ago, David Wall was asked to estimate for repainting a Bentley drop head and was shown the car standing in a poultry shed at a farm near Wroxham in Norfolk. The owner never took up the estimate and then ten years later David moved his Toad Hall Motor Works into a purpose-built unit in Wroxham and the farm was on his usual 'test route' when trying out cars he had restored or worked on. He often wondered about the Bentley.

In 2010 a friend called in at the workshops saying that twenty-eight years earlier he had arranged three weeks' storage for his 1932 Singer at the same farm but never reclaimed it, and did David know if it was still there? They went to have a look. David takes up the story:

Both cars were still there. It was clear that the roof of the building had partly collapsed on the Singer. Being at the further end of the shed the Bentley [registered JLO 942] had escaped the collapse; it was covered in dust sheets and up on axle stands. The lady showing us round said they belonged to her brother living in London … Four weeks later the Bentley was mine and another friend, Nick Walmsley, bought the Singer.

Records show that the 1946 Park Ward drop head Mk VI Bentley was one of six to this design. This one had been built for Max Aitken – later Lord Beaverbrook. After a distinguished career in the

The 1946 Park Ward Bentley Mk VI which has escaped the collapse of the shed.

RAF, Max Aitken returned to civilian life and joined the family newspaper business, the Express Group. Nothing more is known about the Bentley until the mid-1970s when it was bought by the Norfolk owner from Frank Dale and Stepsons and put in the shed at the farm. David went on to say, 'The car was found to be in excellent mechanical health … now undergoing a considerate cosmetic rebuild and should look jolly smart in her Shell Grey over Garnet repaint.'

Nick Walmsley fell in love with the art deco design of the 1932 Singer, registered GY 826. This model had been designed by Charles Beauvais who had previously been art editor of *The Motor* before designing for various car firms including Star and Singer. The Club believe there are only three of this model surviving, with only one on the road. The Singer was surprisingly sound despite the collapsing shed, and

restoration – with David Wall, naturally – is proceeding as finances allow.

In 2018 an urban explorer and photographer, who wishes to remain anonymous, was tipped off about a textile factory in northern Italy that had been abandoned for more than thirty years. He didn't hesitate one moment and drove over to the place to find it as if it were left yesterday, with all the machinery still in place. In his own words, 'It was one of the best locations I ever came across, and I've seen quite a few of them over the years.' What he had not expected to see was an old Lancia tucked away in the garage belonging to the premises. It is an Aprilia of the second series, and a coach-built one too. The car was conceived as a 439 *autotelaio* with 100mm longer wheelbase and independent rear wheel suspension, finding its way to the workshop of Pininfarina in 1948 or 1949. Pininfarina was at that time building the factory saloons and convertibles but somehow managed to find the time to continue building special bodied coupes and convertibles also.

This Aprilia *Speciale* is possibly one in a series of just two or three cars, and it seems that it is the car that won a class prize at the 1949 Villa d'Este Concours. Before the war, Pininfarina had been responsible for a series of *aerodinamico* Aprilias, which were able to top 100mph. After the war, Pininfarina came with pontoon shaped and more elegant coach-built versions, inspired on the streamliners. Most of these specials used a very narrow version of the trademark grille, but this one is an exception. The lower side grilles with vertical slats are another typical Pininfarina

The 1931 Singer being removed from the collapsed shed.

Lancia Aprilia *Speciale* as first seen by our 'urban explorer'.

Lower side grilles with vertical slats typical of Pininfarina.

EDR 293, the Lanchester Woody being removed from storage.

feature, though, mostly seen on his Alfa 6C 2500s. The convertible appears to be in very original state, probably even wearing its original two-tone paint in a typical slate grey and light blue. For now it remains unknown what will happen to both the factory and the Lancia, as it seems the owner has no plans to do anything with either of them other than let nature take its course.

In 2014 the Lanchester Owners Club kindly drew my attention to a rather derelict 1948 Lanchester LD Ten that had been obtained by Ian Davison of Ryhope. This Woodie had been stored for fifty years under a blue sheet in a back yard in Roker, Sunderland, just five miles from Ian's home. It had deteriorated a lot in this time but even though some pieces had been taken off, Ian told me it all seemed to be there, though the engine had been left in the open with neither sump nor rocker cover in place – it had seized solid. Only sketchy

1948 Lanchester LD10 which has been stored for fifty years under a blue sheet.

history is known. It was registered EDR 293 in 1948 in Plymouth. It is not known if the Woodie body was built onto a new chassis or put on the car later.

The first known owner was Surgeon Captain Robert Etherington of the Royal Navy who was known to live in Devon. There might be a Plymouth connection here but we don't know if he was the first owner. He sold the car to his brother, William Etherington, in 1958 or 1959 and it was taken to Roker. Ian told us, 'In 1963 or 1964 the car was placed in the rear yard of the family house in Roker and the engine removed for repair.' On William Etherington's death the car passed to his widow and from her to her two step sons. They decided to sell the house and contacted a house clearance firm to help with its emptying. They knew of Ian Davison's interest in old cars and offered the car to him. Ian was Chairman of the Sunderland and District Classic Vehicle Society. He told me:

> At the present time I cannot find a coach-builder's plate or name anywhere but it appears to be professionally made as the windscreen surround and roof are one complete aluminium panel. The wings and bonnet are of steel … I have spoken to quite a few classic car enthusiasts around Sunderland … and no-one has any recollections or had heard any rumours of the car's existence.

UML 406 is a 1949 Triumph Roadster that was first registered in Middlesex. By 1961 it was with an owner near Woldingham on the Surrey/Kent border. In the next year it was bought by Robert Lewis who I believe used it until 1974 when he parked it up. On his death it was inherited by his son David. It was parked in David's aunt's garage and when she died recently it had to be sold. It was bought by keen Triumph Roadster Club member Bob Cakebread who was in the midst of a Roadster restoration and was looking for spare parts. Bob told me:

> The car was parked in a very interesting place. David's aunt had lived in a small cottage which was once in the grounds of an old Priory in East Farleigh in Kent. The garage was once the middle of three storage sheds which were built under the water tower for the priory. The garage roof where the car was stored still had the heavy cast iron base plate of the old water tank covering about a third of the roof, with the rest being timber that had rotted leaving a large hole in the roof … the fact that it had once been a water tower explains the height.

The garage built under the water tower contained a 1949 Triumph Roadster.

The car was parked very close to the left hand wall of the garage which had a very rotten wooden floor. The back end of the car was under a very rotten mezzanine level which, in turn, had heavy items stored on it. A health and safety nightmare. Because of the danger, David decided he did not want to work on the back end of the car. He was able to free the front wheels and hoped he could get his trolley jack under the car from the centre line to lift the rear wheels enough. At the first attempt the jack sank into the rotten floor. After a board had been placed under the jack, it worked. One back wheel was seized solid and 'after much hammering of the brake drum with a lead mallet, nothing moved. In desperation, there was nothing to do but to prise the brake drum over the shoes …'

Problems were not all over. 'Access was via a narrow gateway and a private drive serving several properties. After some manhandling of the trailer and tow car to get lined up for the exit, it was time to set the Roadster free.' David's father had also bought another Roadster for spares, most of which were the heavy bits on the rotten mezzanine floor. A few weeks later David turned up with all of these.

On the cover of *Floating Power*, the magazine of the Traction Owners Club, was a tantalising picture of a 1949 11B Citroen Traction Avant, which appeared covered in undergrowth.

Club member Peter Fereday, who lives for part of the year in France, remembers meeting, some twenty years ago, a lady called Renate from a neighbouring village and seeing she had a Traction Avant Citroen on blocks in her back

The Triumph was parked very close to the left hand wall.

garden. Recently, when he needed some spares for his Citroen, he thought of Renate and went to visit. He said:

> The Citroen was gradually being taken over by vegetation, but still performing useful duties as a garden shed. I discovered it had not moved since 1994; not surprising really as the wheels were stolen within a few months of it being parked up … Guarded by four *nains de jardin* (garden gnomes) … the traction was surprisingly complete.

It would appear the back axle had failed and it was Renate's intention to cut off the front end and use it as a bar in her house. She had done this once before in a previous house. She did agree to Peter taking a few useful parts. 'Renate seemed very content with a bottle of *Grand Cru St Emilion* that I offered in exchange.'

Sometime later when Peter returned to see if he could obtain the brake drums he found the car fiercely guarded by a new husband who would not allow any more parts to be taken off the car.

The Museum of English Rural Life at the University of Reading has possibly the best collection of rural artefacts anywhere in this country (more details on www.reading.ac.uk/merl). In 2013 they were steadily building up their collection of material for their new 'Twentieth Century Rural Cultures' gallery. One of their latest exhibits was a 1949 Series 1 Land Rover, MAE 397 last on the road in 1972. It was bought new on 29 April 1949 by Ivor Norris, a farmer from Avonmouth. He purchased it from Windmill and Lewis of Clifton, Bristol and traded in a 1.5 SS Jaguar. In the 1960s Mr Norris moved to a smaller farm in the Mendips, taking the Land Rover with him. In 1972 he developed glaucoma and was no longer allowed to drive on the roads. This was the last year that the Land Rover had tax and MOT until recently. However, Ivor continued to use the Land Rover on his farm, laying it up carefully

Ivor continued to use the Land Rover on his farm.

1949 11B Citroen Traction Avant covered in undergrowth.

'This is the first time I have been asked to unveil a car.'

each winter. He was helped in the recommissioning process by local enthusiast Chris Bachelor. In 1982 Chris found Mr Norris a good second-hand David Brown tractor to replace a worn out one, and swapped it for MAE 397 which, by this time, had done 45,000 miles. Chris carefully put it away in a shed until December 2010 when John Midwood was asked to carry out a sympathetic refurbishment on it. He found it to be almost completely original; all those little details that enthusiasts know about were there. The only thing that was wrong was the front bumper which had been replaced with a later one. The accident happened in Avonmouth docks when Ivor Norris was collecting biscuit waste for his cattle – the jib of a crane swung round catching the bumper. The good news was that the damaged bumper was still with the Land Rover and was restorable. I am sure that the museum was attracted to it due to its originality, the provenance of which was impeccable and it came with many photographs, much paperwork including most of the tax discs and MOT certificates, original guarantee, and original

invoice, owner's manual and log book. HRH The Duke of Gloucester was present to unveil the Land Rover when he next visited the Museum, quipping, 'This is actually the first time I have been asked to unveil a car.'

The Land Rover and its derivatives were soon popular with those people who wanted to make long overland journeys, whether that be to specific uncharted areas of land or long journeys even around the world. Sometimes the vehicles were left in the final country visited rather than have the cost of transporting it home. As an aside, it is also amazing the number of ex-(usually London) taxis or double decker buses which were used by students for long tours. They were nearly always left in some foreign country in a rather worn out state.

Keith Barrett from Plainfield, Ontario is the Canadian representative for the Land Rover Series One Club and owns no less than twenty of them. He saw an advertisement which caught his eye. 'Series 1 … old hulk … blown transmission … last registered in 1974 … drove half way round the world.' There was a picture of a yellow vehicle with writing on the sides. Keith's wife, Jane, loved yellow and as she had a birthday coming up, a deal was arranged. The snag was the Land Rover was 5,650 kilometres away in Whitehorse, Yukon, almost as far as you can get in Canada before hitting Alaska. Such mileages did not faze Keith. From details on the vehicle, it is obviously ex-military. The date of build is 1951, and under various coats of paint could be found the British registration NMH 927, which

The yellow Land Rover as given to Jane Barrett as a birthday present.

The '*Tour de Monde*' seems to have started in London and finished in New York. Does anyone remember the expedition?

The burnt out vehicle was placed outside in a farmyard.

is for 1963, presumably the date it was sold into civilian ownership. From here on it's a mystery. The '*Tour du Monde*', which is emblazoned on the vehicle, seems to have started in London and visited Istanbul, Cairo, Nairobi, Cape Town, Rio, Lima, Panama, Mexico, San Francisco and then New York. After the latter name there is an arrow pointing to 'home'. No amount of research has shown up any details of this tour. We do not know who did it, when or why. One can only presume that 'home' was London from where they had started and that the Land Rover was not, in fact, shipped back to the UK. How or why it went to the Yukon is yet another mystery. It had been found in a scrapyard in Yukon in 1988 and put into storage.

The removal of the Volkswagen Cabriolet was extremely difficult.

At the moment Keith intends to get it back into running order, but wants to conserve the panels and the lettering exactly as they are.

We all know the Karmann-built Volkswagen Beetle Cabriolet, but there was also the two-seater Hebmüller Cabriolet. This was a pretty roadster built by coachbuilder Joseph Hebmüller of Wuppertal, Germany, as commissioned by VW. Originally, plans to build 2,000 of the two-seaters were made, but a fire plagued production and eventually just 696 left the coachbuilder's site between 1949 and 1952. About 100 survivors are known.

When Volkswagen enthusiast Bjoern Schewe heard of a car unknown to the Hebmüller Register, he was eager to find out more. It turned out that an owner in Switzerland had brought his Hebmüller to a local garage for repair many years ago. Unfortunately, there was a fire in the workshop and the burnt-out vehicle was placed outside on a farmyard. When the owner died, some fifteen years ago now, the rare Volkswagen fell into oblivion. Schewe told me:

But then, this summer, a hiker accidentally discovered the car and posted a photo of it on a walking forum, where it was seen and sent over to me. Next, my friend Christian Grundmann contacted the local community of the Swiss village, of which the mayor himself was kind enough to help. He managed to get in touch with the heirs of the car's old owner, who lived in Germany.

Soon after that a deal was struck and the purchase was completed, but due to the free accessibility of the car on an uninhabited farm, collecting it had to be organised quickly and Schewe and Grundmann promptly went to Switzerland in order to salvage it. Schewe said, 'Initially, it was intended to leave the car in its condition "as discovered", but a restoration is possible despite the fire damage.'

When you think of the great coachbuilders of the past there are a few who stand out and they are mostly European. Mexican businessman Ruiz Galindo established a coach building company in Mexico and named it *D.M. Nacional*. Here he tried to emulate some of the best from Europe. From 1950 to 1955 he made a series of stand-out bodies on mainly American chassis. I am not sure how many were built but it is thought only one survives and that is in a parlous state. This is a 1950 Chrysler Imperial 'Sedanca Deville'. It was originally finished in yellow and black with a green interior. The original owner is unknown but around 1987 it was bought by an owner in Connecticut who, for some reason, left it out in the open. It is now in dire condition and in 2017 was offered for sale by Dragone Auctions at their Lime Rock sale. The auction catalogue said, 'It would be an incredibly interesting and wonderful car to restore and bring back to its original magnificence. Any concours would be enamoured to have it present … and possibly the only *D.M. Nacional* left today.' I do hope someone took up the challenge.

Darren Bell was so enthusiastic about a 1952 Ford Anglia E49A his father had laid up in the garage that he joined the Ford Sidevalve Owners Club in 1985 at the age of 14. At that time, he was taken by the hot-rodding fraternity and had

Headquarters of D.M. Nacional with 1950 Chrysler outside.

Left out in the open the Chrysler 'was in a dire condition'.

many plans for the Ford including 'a huge Ford V8 engine'. He now says, 'I am so glad it never happened'. The first owner of RMV 730 is thought to be the dentist whose practice was below the Bells' flat; the Bells bought the car from him in 1963. The car was used by Darren's father, Douglas, and his sister Moira, who is thought to have painted the chequered radiator grill in true 1960s fashion. In 1971 the car failed its MOT on a handbrake fault and was duly parked up in the very garage in which she now resides. Darren told me, 'As my father was a working blacksmith in the local brick works at the time he acquired the garage, he decided to line the floor of the garage with firebricks which I believe have absorbed any dampness and kept the old girl in pretty good shape over all these years'. The future is quite different from hot rodding; Darren intends to 'do some light cleaning up of her, although my ultimate intention is to do an oily rag style of recommissioning, just getting her road worthy as she is in full original patinated glory'.

Next door to my sister-in-law in Gloucestershire lives Peter Bowen who, in 2014, bought a fine looking 1937 Riley Kestrel Sprite. When talking to him about it I found out that he had just rescued his late brother's 1953 Bristol 401 from storage near Hull. In 1970 the late David Bowen had bought YMH 192, a 1953 Bristol 401, originally in maroon but by then painted green. It cost him £110 and was in good order; in fact, it won a concours event that year! No previous history is, however, known, though there exists a photograph of it competing in the sixth 'Rally of the Sun'. David used it regularly in conjunction with his company car and he

The 1953 Bristol 401 competing in a hillclimb at Prescott.

and Peter competed in a number of Bristol Owners Club events (or invited events) with it. They took it to such places as Prescott and Gurston Down hillclimbs, Curborough Sprint and one sprint on the perimeter track of what was then RAF Gaydon.

David was an engineer and he changed jobs a few times, always taking the car with him. It was last taxed in 1989. At one stage it was left outside and suffered at the hands of some vandals. David took the engine and gearbox out with a view to fitting a 110hp engine he had obtained from the late Leonard Setright. He started to strip out the car as well. In May 2010 he died; his ashes being scattered at Prescott. Peter Bowen inherited the car and is determined that he will restore it. He has rented an industrial unit on a local farm and has bought a two post lift to help him. It would appear that David had stripped another Bristol of useful parts as many spares came with the car. David had

This 1952 Ford Anglia E49A was laid up in this garage in 1971.

Peter Bowen inherited the car and is determined he will restore it.

The 1955 Messerschmitt KR200 lying uncared for in a French barn.

done just one bit of restoration; the boot lid had been beautifully repainted in dark green.

In Messerschmitt Owners Club circles Nick Poll is very well respected as a restorer. He also has a collection of Messerschmitts as well as a British built Nobel 200, a German Fuldamobil built under licence in the UK by York Nobel Industries in Bristol. For some years now Nick has known of a 1955 Messerschmitt KR200 lying uncared for in a French barn near where he lived in the French Pyrenees. The owner seemed unwilling to sell. In 2012 he was out for a run in the Nobel with his sons and decided to call in on the farmer. Perhaps it was the presence of the Nobel, who knows, but the farmer changed his mind and sold the car to Nick. When he had trailered it home, he had a very good look at it all round. He found out that it was the third oldest of the model known to survive and was a new one to the Club. In fact, the model was still evolving when 50213 (the 213th to be constructed) left the production line. Nick found many of the smaller fittings were quite different from the later models. He told me, 'Although quite tatty, the car is very sound so my plan is not to restore the car but just improve it'.

S.E. Opperman Limited of Stuart Works, Boreham Wood, Hertfordshire, developed a tractor or mobile cart called the Opperman Motorcart. It had three wheels, front wheel drive and could carry 30cwt. The firm commissioned Lawrie Bond (of Bond Minicar fame) to design a car with 'Big car comfort and small car economy'. The result was the Opperman Unicar which appeared in 1958 which was fitted with an Excelsior 328cc engine capable (they said) of 60mph. The two rear wheels were

placed inward of the body sides, so doing away with the need for a differential. They could be bought assembled or as a kit and around 200 were sold.

*RumCar News*, the magazine of the Register of Unusual Microcars, wrote about Hans Bodewes from the Netherlands who has bought one which he believes has been out of use for some thirty years. It was registered NHM 338 in May 1958 at East Ham, though its first tax disc did not seem to be issued until 30 October 1962. Its first registered owner was Daniel Gurt from Bocking in Essex. It then went to Eccles in Lancashire, followed by a stream of owners in Yorkshire. It was bought in 2000 by Herman Hensen and taken to the Netherlands. Hans bought the car in 2014 and started a complete restoration. Nearly everything possible seemed to be wrong with it. This is part of what he told me. 'The doors were just stuck to the body; the hinges were missing. All cables, rubber and loose things were missing or broken. The fabric of the seats had collapsed. There were no headlights … the tyres were all different sizes and had punctures.' He persevered and it received its Dutch registration in October 2016.

NHM 338 is an Opperman Unicar which had been out of use for thirty years.

The hinges were missing and the door was sealed shut.

The Armstrong Siddeley Heritage Trust had some unusual photos sent to them. They had received a letter from Signor Giuseppe Carusi who was, in 2016, in Nigeria on business. He stumbled across the remains of a 1956 Armstrong Siddeley 346 limousine part stored in the open and in a dilapidated condition. Giuseppe gave me more details:

It is in the Lagos Port area. A friend of mine remembered seeing this car many years ago when it was still in good shape. He had also

The restored Opperman received its Dutch registration in October 2016.

'We found it [1956 Armstrong Siddeley 346] dumped in a corner behind buildings covered in trash.'

When new, the Armstrong Siddeley was delivered to the Governor General of Nigeria in Lagos.

known the owner, who had passed away a few years back. We went to the last place where he had seen it, but it was not there, so we started asking around. Finally, we found it dumped in a corner behind the buildings covered in trash. Had it been in better shape I would have bought it and taken it to Italy to try and repair it.

He said that as the licence plate on this car was LAS 1, this must have been the car used by Her Majesty the Queen when on her first Royal Tour of Nigeria in 1956. Research in the Trust's archives reveals that chassis 346406 was delivered to the Governor General in Lagos and it's almost certainly this car.

Though there are clubs for them, I get the impression that the caravan and camper van are often overlooked by mainstream enthusiasts. That is strange as many have experienced at least hiring them for holidays, and if you are involved with motor sport, many are used by competitors to live in and tow their racing cars. The Commer 15cwt 2500 was a very popular basis for conversion into camper vans. One such written up by *Autocar* was the Commer Hadrian converted by Motor Caravan Bodies Limited of Dunstan, Gateshead. Autocar liked it as it used a coach-built body which was bigger than the standard van and gave much more room. Patrick Collins from the National Motor Museum, who used to be in the motor trade, helped me with some research and told me, 'One common factor through all the brochures I have looked at is they manage to make the interior space look huge. Now I remember working on Commer vans and campers and there was no way they were that roomy inside.'

Mike Evans from Exeter has found a 1962 Commer Hadrian which has been in a local barn since 1978. It is an early model bought new by its only owner, Mr Pemberton, and registered JJK 707. He used it for many holidays including at least one trip to Spain. Shortly before it came off the road it was fitted with a 1,725cc replacement Gold Seal engine and gearbox with overdrive. Mike told me, 'The camper was lying next to the remains of an Armstrong Siddeley Sapphire.' The interior appears to be very complete and original, though damp has got into the plywood which has delaminated. The Classic Camper Club told him that only two others were known to the club.

1962 Commer Hadrian in a Devonshire barn where it has been since 1978.

'The interior appears to be very original and complete' but has suffered from the damp.

The Mini was such an innovative design and so successful in all its forms, it really deserves a chapter to itself. Jerome Booij from the Netherlands, who often contributes to 'Lost and Found', has written no less than three books on their derivatives. The success of the BMC Mini led to two factory commercial versions, the van and the pick-up. The pick-up was built on the slightly longer Minivan platform with open cargo area and tailgate. They all had stamped steel slots in place of the car's chromium plated grille. It could be bought in a very basic form in which nearly everything was an extra, including a laminated windscreen! Also, a tilt and supporting bars were available.

1961 Mini pick-ups are very rare. Expert Bill Best knows of only nine worldwide and he has acquired the oldest, a Morris variant. The launch date was June 1961 and the one he purchased was built on 15 March. It was seen recently on a Portuguese website by Dieter Deschacht who noticed some distinguishing features which denoted an early example. It was owned by the proprietor of a Mini restoration shop in Lisbon who had stripped it, sand blasted it and then stored it in the open on the back of a pick-up truck. It had, of course, become completely covered in red rust. The owner had intended to customise it with big wheels, big engine and other mods. It is now back in the UK where it will be fully restored. 58,179 examples of the Mini pick-up were built between 1961 and 1983.

Bill has done some research at the British Motor Museum at Gaydon. It would appear that there were restrictions on certain goods coming into Portugal from other than Portuguese colonies. This car was exported new to Angola (then belonging to Portugal) and to Portugal in 1969.

The Mini Moke was developed as a possible light go-anywhere vehicle for the Ministry of Defence. One of its snags was its low ride height, even with larger wheels and the idea was not taken up. It was then marketed as a fun vehicle and soon became a cult. It was manufactured in the UK from 1964 until 1968, after which manufacture shifted to Australia and then to Portugal where the last one was completed in the mid-1980s.

Longbridge did experiment with a Mini Moke with two engines known as the 'Twini'. This had a 948cc engine at the front and an 848cc version at the rear. Three were built; a prototype given the number SPL 578, a hand-built model SPL 921, which is now at the British Motor Museum at Gaydon, and SPL 935 which was left hand drive and fitted with twelve inch wheels and sent to the USA. Here it was tested at the Army Tank Automotive Centre at Warren, Michigan. When the testing was over, the Moke was bought by Army Reservist Merle Taylor. He used the Moke locally, taking part in parades with it. In December 1988 it was sold to Ervin Baer, who bought it for his grandson to drive around their farm. When it stopped running, it was put away at the back of a barn where it attracted all sorts of lumber and other junk.

Grady Shaner runs a truck garage in St. Mary's, Ohio, and in 2013 was out at the Baer farm working on a vehicle when the front end of the Twini was pointed out to him. He later owned up to never having heard of a Mini Moke, let alone a Twini.

The Mini Pick-up has been sandblasted and then stored in the open.

It was originally purchased for a farmer's son to drive around on the farm.

Eventually he bought it and took it to his garage where it was seen by Ned Lawler. He and his wife are Anglophiles and love visiting meetings such as the Goodwood Revival. They have a collection of British cars including a Mini Countryman and earn their living photographing cars (Shamrock Motoring Images). Ned knew immediately what it was. He knew all the right people to contact, including the British Mini Moke Club and soon a full restoration was under way. It took a year and Grady told me:

One thing we could never get to work was the clutch system to run both motors together, and I doubt if it ever worked properly from the original prototype. The problem is you have a master cylinder trying to function two slave cylinders and there is not enough fluid volume to do that. To overcome it, we fitted shut-offs on the slave cylinder so we can just run one motor at a time now.

Crayford Auto Developments was founded in 1963 and over the years built a wide range of conversions on all sorts of vehicles, ranging from estate cars, bullet proofing and stretched limos. They are possibly best known for turning saloons into convertibles. 1963 saw the launch of their first Mini convertible. They were approached by Heinz foods to make fifty-seven convertibles for a competition. The final decision was for fifty-seven Wolseley Hornet convertibles with the proviso that Crayford did not make any other convertibles on this model. The competition was a great success with over a million entries and these vehicles have become a cult with forty-two believed to be still existing.

One such, which only just survived, is LLH 824D and is owned by Nick Belton. A June 1966 car, it was won by Mrs S.K.H. Thurman of Leicester. After a stay in the Midlands, it went to Keighley and Haworth before transferring to Liverpool and

A full restoration of the Mini Moke was undertaken.

An unusual view, the Mini Moke when restoration was completed.

then to Torquay. In the 1980s it was badly damaged in a workshop fire. Nick went on to tell me:

It had a burned roof, boot, wings, and blistering of the paint. Luckily the car was pulled out before the building was gutted. I do know that it was then left outside in all weathers, sometimes uncovered, leading to it filling with water and rotting the floor away.

Nick bought it on eBay in 2008, but had only relatively recently started the restoration. He had the unrestored tub on show at the Heinz 57 Reunion event at Gaydon in 2016.

Barry Priestman of the Heinz 57 Register has been in touch about another car from that event that was present in a very unrestored state. Owned by Lisa Furness, it has a sad story. No-one is sure who won it in the competition but its third owner was Mrs Betty Nichols of Westcliff-on-Sea who drove the, by then, light blue car every day to her place of work, the crazy golf course at Southend.

Barry Priestman visited Betty Nichols in 1991 and saw LLH 859D which by this time was badly rusted having been exposed to the Essex salt air for many years. He convinced Betty to get it restored. She sent it to a restorer who stripped the car but never did any work. He was then closed down by Trading Standards and the garage contents were cleared. The remains of the car were found in a

The Wolseley Hornet Crayford Convertible when owned by Betty Nichols who ran a crazy golf course.

'Skippy' on show at the Heinz 57 reunion at the British Motor Museum, Gaydon in 2016. 824D is in the background.

skip by a Mini fan who recognised the car and rescued it. Since then, it has had the name 'Skippy'. It
has had a number of owners since, none of whom
did anything with it. In 2004 it was bought by Lisa
Furness who was involved with the Elf/Hornet
Club, hence her interest.

A conscientious Registrar of a one make car
club will try and trace and record every existing
example of the models covered by that club. Barry
Priestman is that man in the Crayford Convertible
Car Club. Over twenty years ago, someone handed
him a cutting of an advertisement for a BT prod-
uct that featured the rear end of a classic car in a
garage. The car was a Crayford converted Cortina
Mk 2 registered UGT 640F, a car unknown to the

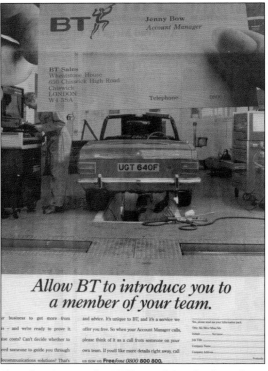

The advertisement for BT illustrating a classic car in a
garage.

Register; Barry duly noted it in his records. In
October 2017 a car dealer contacted Barry saying
he had taken in a Crayford Cortina, which was
outside his normal expertise, and would any club
member be interested in buying it. It was registered UGT 640F. The dealer said it had been off
the road and badly stored for twenty or so years.
Barry arranged to go and see it. He told me:

The car had been T cut and polished and was
bright and shiny, but twenty years in a damp
lock up had taken its toll. The hood was
in bad shape and the whole of the interior
stank of damp and mould. The whole of the
brake system and clutch had rusted solid..

The car was, however, being prepared to be auctioned by Barons later in the month. It went to auction but failed to reach its reserve. Barry is also Club
Secretary and a few weeks later received a letter from
a long-time member saying that he would not be
renewing his subscription as his Crayford Cortina
had been stolen from its lock up some time in the
last few months and had disappeared. The car was
UGT 640F. The police were called. Over a year later,
the case came to court and the dealer was found
to have faked his proof of purchase and the Club
member got his car back, well sort of! The DVLA
claimed that as the car had been stolen, the owner
was no longer the owner, even though the car had
been returned to him by the police. The owner has
now done a deal with a very enthusiastic Cortina
owner who will recommission the car. Back to that
advertisement, the member did say that he had previously owned a garage and MOT station and that
many years ago he had been approached by BT who
used his facilities as a set for their advertisement.

If ever a car needed some TLC, it is this 1975
Cortina GT with Crayford conversion. Its owner,
Marc Powell from Liverpool, is a fan of the Ford
Cortina, owning five in a row for everyday use. He
then strayed to an Escort RS Turbo, a Morris Minor
Traveller and a P6 Rover 2000SC. He went on to
tell me, 'I also fancied a Mk 2 Crayford Cortina but
the ones I saw were scruffy … this made me look

'The hood was in bad shape.'

for a Mk 3 as they were easier to identify.' In May 1993 he eventually found GOV 218N in Margate. It had been side swiped but a new offside rear quarter panel had been fitted. Marc drove it back to Liverpool and used it regularly until 1998. He then took it off the road with 93,000 miles on the clock, intending to restore it when he retired. He garaged it locally but had to move it to a friend's house when the garage was needed for other purposes. He applied to go on a local car restoration course, but it was full. However, it was agreed the car could be worked on by the course students. 'The car was stripped of its seats, etc, and braced all the way round inside to keep the car's shape and strength together.' The course finished and the building and land was sold so the car had to be moved. Marc found that the car had received some side damage whilst at the college and some items had gone missing. A friend of a friend in the Midlands ran a restoration shop and said he would do it, so the car moved to the Midlands. No work was done so it came back to Liverpool, this time minus its seats. In 2007, 'I knew of a lad who was interested in doing the work'. He took it to his premises but due to business expansion, they eventually had to put it outside with a sheet over it. Marc retired in 2019 and went to retrieve the car for restoration:

> When the covers were removed I did not expect what I saw. Initially I was shocked as well as disappointed to see how much the car had deteriorated since I last saw it. I would be OK with the mechanicals but the task of welding the car is not something I could do.

He now feels it needs a good home. He told me that 400 were made originally, around twenty-five are known to the Crayford Owners Club, with ten only being on the road.

When friends of Nick Hills inherited a house of an uncle they hardly knew, they didn't realise there was also a car hidden in one of the four garages on the property. They asked Nick to come over to Kent and see it, and he was much surprised to find an early Ford Capri Mk 2 with the desirable three-litre engine and just 26,000 miles on the clock.

Mk 2 Ford Capri found in a garage that was about to collapse.

Braced all the way round to keep the car's shape and strength together.

Nick told me:

Their uncle owned it from when it was six months old and several people have suggested it was a demonstrator from Ford. The garage was locked and we were just in time as it was literally falling in on the car. The foot wells were covered thirty centimetres deep with nutshells as squirrels had found access to the place, so the interior is not the best. But the car itself is in a great condition. One of the tyres was still holding a healthy 20Psi pressure.

The Capri turned out to have been parked there twenty-six years ago, but the reason is a bit of a mystery. Nick said, 'We don't know why he stopped driving it as he did carry on driving for years.' Nick has now agreed to buy it and get it restored. It's not his only classic Ford. 'I'm not particularly brand loyal to be honest as I have all sorts of cars, but

when it comes to the Capri, everyone prefers the Mk 1 but I really think the Mk 2 better.'

It is interesting where you pick up clues which result in you purchasing a classic car. Adrian Howe from Somerset was attending the annual car show put on by Thornfalcon Cars just outside Taunton. He was in a queue for a coffee and a pork roll when the person behind asked what car he had come in. He replied, 'I have come in a Mk 2 Cortina with a V6 engine.' The reply was the shock. 'Ah, a Savage. We have one of them rotting away in our yard.' Adrian did not follow this up immediately, but kicked himself for not taking contact details. Quite by chance the two met again the next day in a local builders' merchants; this time he took some details and eventually ended up buying PHJ 959G, a Saluki Bronze Savage Estate. The history of this 1968 car is a little vague. The first owner we know about lived at Banwell, near Bristol, in the late 1970s. The seller had bought it in 1991 after it had been parked up on a farm unused. It had not

The Capri leaving the garage for the first time.

PHU 959G Ford Savage bought after a chance remark in a queue for a pork roll.

run since. Adrian in turn did not start work on the car immediately but in 2015 he was asked to take it to the NEC for display on the Ford Cortina Mk 2 Club stand. He had carefully retained the thirty years of dust and grime on the car and was worried about spoiling this on the journey to Birmingham, but that's another story …

Jeff Uren of Race Proved Performance and Racing Equipment Limited converted over 1,000 Mk 2 Cortinas by fitting the V8 Essex engine and other modifications, of which approximately 100 were estate cars. Jeff also worked his magic on a variety of other cars, mainly Fords, over a period during the 1960s and 1970s.

Reliant had been making three wheel vans since 1935, later a four wheeled version. In 1958 they started providing a 'packaged motor industry' to countries where there was little industry. The first, an estate car, was built for Autocars of Haifa, then the Mebas pick-up for Greece and the Sipanai Dolphin for India. For Otosan Industries of Turkey they built the Anadol A1 saloon, a right hand drive version of which was purchased by Jim Pace of Sunderland in 2018. Jim is a Registrar within the Reliant Sabre and Scimitar Owners Club. The bodywork of the Anadol was the work of Tom Karen of Ogle Design, whilst David Page of Reliant designed the chassis. The mechanical parts came mainly from a Mk 1 Cortina 1200 with Triumph Herald front suspension. It is thought that Reliant built three cars themselves and Jim's is the only one in right hand drive. The original owner had worked at Reliant and bought this pre-production car when he left. It had probably been a factory hack prior to this. It was last taxed and on

the road in 1989. In 2006 it was advertised on eBay and bought by Paul Molynaux who stripped the car down and did a substantial amount of restoration work on it. He later passed it in incomplete condition to an owner in Leicestershire who did little to it. Jim is a keen member of the North East Restoration Club who have excellent facilities for members who wish to work on or restore their own cars. Jim had his name down for such a restoration bay, but until now had no car to restore! As a postscript, there was to be an Anziel Nova built by Reliant for the New Zealand market. This was, in fact, an Anadol in right hand drive form. A prototype Nova with two door saloon bodywork was tested, but it never reached production. According to a press cutting I have seen, this car survived in New Zealand twenty years ago.

The 'Quasar Unipower Cube' has to be one of the more peculiar cars having found its way to the public. It was a square vehicle dreamt up by the

Built by Reliant for Otosan Industries of Turkey.

The Anadol emblem.

Parisian duo of Emmanuelle and Nguyen 'Quasar' Khanh. She was a fashion designer, he a Vietnamese born industrial designer. The Mini based vehicle was originally meant for promotional purposes of Emmanuelle's fashion consortium, but eventually thirteen were made and marketed by Universal Power Drives of Perivale, who had also been responsible for the sleek Unipower GT. One of the Quasar cars went to Triplex Safety Glass Limited to promote their new Spectrafloat glasses and it was the star of their stand at the 1968 Earls Court Motor Show.

It is that particular car that was hidden in a South of England barn for decades. The owner doesn't exactly know how long he has had it but thinks he must have had it from somewhere between 1984 and the early 1990s, until when it was taxed and given an MOT. He used it only locally up until 2002 before it was taken off the

road and put in storage. When the time had come for a renovation, it proved to be quite a challenge to reach the barn with a Land Rover to tow it out, but not for Wolfgang Buchta, Editor of the Austrian magazine *Austro Classic*, who has a fascination with quirky vehicles. Buchta cut away some trees and bushes and hitched the cube car on his trailer to drive it back home to Austria. He said, 'Now we have agreed to put it back on the road, which hopefully is going to happen shortly.'

Steve Peel runs CMS Porsche from Horton, near Telford, but has a soft spot for the Ford RS Turbo series. For some years he had heard rumours of a Ford Escort S1 RS Turbo lurking in a garage in the Telford area. All the avenues he explored had led to nothing. Later he was contacted by a friend who had been asked to remove an RS Turbo from an overgrown garage – was this the missing car?

Steve told me:

> Yes it was. This car was truly buried [at the bottom of the garden] in a lean to shed cum barn, and of which, to be honest, I'm amazed that the building had never fallen over in the wind, and parts of it were rotten and actually had branches growing through the walls and roof. We entered through a side door, which then fell off its hinges, and clambered our way into the main space. There she sat covered in dust and dirt sitting on four flat rotted tyres looking a bit sorry for herself, but complete.

Getting the car out was another matter. They had been warned to 'bring along chain saws and tools

The Quasar Cube used by Triplex Safety Glass as a promotional vehicle for Spectrafloat glass.

The Cube had been hidden in a South of England barn for decades.

Ford Escort S1 RS turbo lurking in a garage near Telford.

It had to be retrieved from the other end of this building.

to cut down trees, hedgerow and bushes that had grown up in front of the main doors'. Steve was able to purchase the car, so stopping it going for auction. He found out it had been bought new in 1986 from a Bristol dealer, who had it registered for four months, so possibly it had been a demonstration car. The first and only private owner had used it for 27,409 miles when, in 1994, it was put into store. The owner passed away and differences in the family resulted in the car staying in the barn. Steve was well pleased with his purchase:

Inside it's still in fantastic condition with no damage to the interior and no cracks in the dashboard. On the outside she has minor rust blisters … has all the original Ford stamped factory body panels and production body stickers and no evidence of accident damage or body repairs.

He believes it is very rare to find a D registered car which was to 'non custom' specification, meaning such items as the windows were wind up, not electric, and there was no electric central locking.

James Wade has recently completed a six-year rebuild of a 1986 Rover SD1 V8 Police car. James told me that previously he had owned such a car but 'due to an inability to weld, and no money, I scrapped it and I always regretted it'. The car he bought in 2012 was first registered to the Lancashire Police in September 1986, possibly the last of the genuine V8 Police cars. It was sold at public auction in 1989 to Mrs Jan Knox of Broadstairs. Later it went to an owner in Surrey who lent it to his brother who used it until the late 1990s; the last tax disc still in the window was for 1998. It was then parked up in a council-owned lock up garage. We do not know why it was taken off the road. James told me:

Unfortunately, the roof of the council garage leaked so water was pouring in over the car, particularly the driver's door area. Ultimately the metal frame that held the driver's door

The last tax disc on the Rover SD1 V8 was for 1998.

glass up rotted through and the glass dropped down. This allowed the water to get straight into the car which rotted out the driver's door card and seat base. The car had been advertised on eBay and it failed to sell. Not surprising really as it was in such a bad state. It got relisted again and I bought it for £350.

On the journey back from Surrey, James stopped to check the ratchet straps on the trailer and noticed the trailer bed had turned orange/brown from all the rust which had fallen off the car. Many people who saw the car at this time thought that it could not be restored.

The restored car looks magnificent and draws a lot of attention wherever it goes.

Before I came to work at the Montagu Motor Museum in 1963, I had earned most of my living from motor sport photography. I was, however, always quite happy to take on other assignments. I was asked by Bertram Mills Circus to visit the circus when it was in Gloucester and take a series of very natural photographs of circus life and the circus acts. I cannot remember now how I got the job, but I do remember having a very interesting time. Unfortunately, the act I describe here was not on the programme at the time of my visit.

Ever since it was first produced people have been adapting the Land Rover for specific tasks, but none so unusual as a 'one off' manufactured in the workshops of Bertram Mills Circus in the 1950s. This 80in 1951 Land Rover registered LLY 920 was adapted to carry Kam, one of the circus elephants. In the act Kam appears to drive the Land Rover into the circus ring, and circle the ring, when suddenly there is an explosion under the bonnet and the vehicle stops. The elephant gets

The restored car looks magnificent and draws a lot of attention.

out and pretends to crank the starting handle, gets in and drives out of the ring.

The special Land Rover was built with a three foot extension to the chassis and all the suspension modified to carry the extra weight. Though it looked as if the elephant was steering, the wheel was not connected to the steering. All the driving and steering was done by a man secreted in a wooden box structure mounted on the back with all the controls extended by rods. Quite a number of bits for the conversion came from a Rover P3. The whole vehicle was painted grey.

It was sold when Bertram Mills Circus closed down and was bought by Roberts Brothers Circus who painted it red and yellow and used it with a similar act. Later it spent around thirty years in the open in a hedge. It was then bought for spares and never stripped but it was stored for another fifteen years. More recently it was offered for sale on eBay and was bought by the late Phil Bashall of Dunsfold Land Rover, who have restored it to full working order and have sourced a plastic elephant to sit on it, unfortunately it is not a full sized one. Phil also made the comment, 'We understand from talking to the original driver that the loaded vehicle was, not surprisingly, very heavy to drive but also had a tendency to be very wet and smelly.'

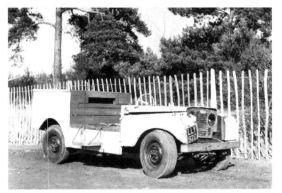

The modified Land Rover built by the workshops of Bertram Mills Circus.

Not quite sure if this is legal.

Kam driving the Land Rover in the circus ring.

After thirty years in a hedge the Land Rover was saved by the late Phil Bashall.

# 7 | SPORTY CLASSICS

After the war as car production increased most manufacturers were concentrating on the more traditional cars that could be sold abroad. MG had the MGTC in production in 1946 and Healey, a new producer, had his first car on show on 1 January 1946. As we will see in the next chapter, the 1950s was an era when the special building craze started. Some of these individual cars were so successful that other owners wanted one and so companies like Lotus, Dellow, Fairthorpe, Ginetta, Marcos, Turner and many others came into being. Another trend was the firms starting up to make speed equipment for a wide variety of cars. For example, your humble Austin A35 could be turned into a very effective and fast sports saloon.

It is not so commonly known that soon after the war when Morgan was getting back into production again, they sold fifty-six chassis to different garages or coachbuilders who went on to put on coachwork to customer specification. One such car sold with all running gear but 'less wings, head lamps, panels, windscreen and bonnet. Radiator block only supplied'. This rolling chassis went to Motourist Limited of Great North Road, London N2. They in turn passed it to Leacroft Sheet Metal Works of Egham that was owned by racing drivers Gordon Watson and Robert (later Roberta) Cowell. Leacroft built a number of bodies for sports racing cars for HWM and others. Their speciality was using steel tubes for the frames, rather than wood. I have no idea who the customer was for this Morgan or who actually designed the body. The car was registered SMX 474. It took part in the 1949 BARC Eastbourne Rally with possibly Jim Wimborne driving.

The Leacroft bodied Morgan.

SMX 474 taking part in the 1949 Eastbourne Rally.

A duplicate logbook gives the owner in 1952 as Basil Jones of Rugby. He apparently bought the car on impulse after seeing it on public display somewhere, even though he did not have a driving licence at the time. He used the car until 1967 when it was taken off the road with a broken push rod. No further work was done on it. The car was inherited by his nephew Damien Romano in

The car was inherited by Damien Romano.

The Standard engine badged as a Morgan.

Morgan 4-4 of 1950 registered KYN 113.

2008. Roy Padgett of the Morgan Sports Car Club is still trying to trace the history of the car during the years it was on the road. Damien has started a restoration, helped by the fact that the car is complete.

It's not often that a 'barn fresh' Morgan 4-wheeler comes on the market. Richard Edmunds Auctions of Chippenham included one in a sale in 2013. Sadly the early history of this 1950 Morgan 4/4 four-seater, registered KYN 113, is lacking. Its mileage of 45,000 is thought to be genuine. The post-war Morgan 4/4 was similar to the pre-war model. Production got underway in 1946 and like most other firms many went for export. Whilst the 4/4 pre-war mostly used the Coventry Climax engine, post-war cars used a special overhead valve engine of 1,267cc made by Standard but badged Morgan. This car was supplied new to Naylor and Root of Wandsworth. Then there is a gap until 1970 when it is known to have been taken off the road. It was dry stored until 2003 when it was sold

to an enthusiast with a number of cars. It was his intention to restore it, but he then realised that this was unlikely to happen and so put it in the auction. It came with its original sales brochure and handbook.

In the 1960s the Swiss importer of Morgans was Rolf Wehrlin from Basel. He had received a number of enquiries from potential Morgan owners for one with a hard roof for use in bad weather or in the Swiss winters. Morgan did not seem to be interested in making such a car, so he took an old 1954 Morgan Plus 4, restored the chassis to as new condition and fitted a Judson supercharger. For the body he fitted an Ashley Laminates Sportiva 2+2 coupe body. The Sportiva was announced in 1960 and the later versions, of which this was one, had a revised rear end with a boot lid. This car was exhibited on Mr Wehrlin's stand at the 1962 Geneva Motor Show as 'Morgan Gran Tourismo'.

I was told that Peter Morgan was furious when he saw it and demanded that it be taken to pieces

'The Morgan Gran Tourisimo' on Rolph Wehrlin's stand at the 1962 Geneva Motor Show.

and scrapped or he would not supply any more new cars to this importer. The car was partially dismantled and left. Mr Wehrlin continued to sell Morgans. It stayed in this part dismantled state for over 40 years until it was bought by Markus Tanner who owns the Classic Car Connection restoration shop in Lichtensteig. Markus told us, 'The car is still in pieces and I am struggling to find time to work on it. When taking the car apart Wehrlin stuffed the full Judson supercharger kit back into the original box with the original fitting instructions and stored it with the rest of the car.' Mr Wehrlin said that he had many enquiries for the car at the 1962 show and is convinced it was this car that caused Peter Morgan to build the closed Morgan Plus 4 Plus which, as we all know, did not sell very well! Most Morgan owners did not like a fixed roof.

Later I showed this story to Charles Morgan who said:

Rolf Wehrlin was a great dealer, a good engineer who did much to help Morgan overcome various rather specific Swiss regulations around noise, etc … I am not sure my Dad's reaction would have been too strong but I suspect he was already working with EB Plastics [on the Plus 4 Plus] when he saw this car and would have tried to stop an Ashley Laminates competitor.

'The car is still in pieces and I am is struggling to find time to work on it.'

Colin Chapman started his competition career as a trials car builder and driver. By the time he came to lay down the first chassis for the Lotus Mk VI, he was really only interested in racing, though early adverts for this new car kit stated that it

The top chassis tube was expertly reshaped to take the twin carburettors.

could be built to comply with the new RAC trials formula. Only one was modified and built for trials. Registered HEL 46 this was one of the first five kits built in 1953 and was purchased for trials use by Horace Sinclair Sweeney. To comply with the trials regulations, the engine had to be mounted higher in the chassis and further back. In so doing, the air intakes for the twin SU carburettors of the Aquaplane modified Ford 1,172 engine fouled the top chassis tube which was expertly re-shaped accordingly. After one season with the car he sold it to Arthur Hay who ran an electrical business in Alton. Between 1954 and 1964 Arthur had an extremely successful career with this car with many wins to his credit. He entered thirty of the MCC long distance trials, retiring from one only and winning an award in all the others, including three of the much coveted 'Triples' for clean sheets on their three main events (The Exeter, Lands End and Edinburgh trials). He was a great supporter of events run by the 750 Motor Club. Whilst he was competing in these events, he also found the remains of both the Lotus Mk II LJH 702 and Lotus Mk IV LMU 4; the former had been Chapman's very successful trials car. In his own quiet way, Arthur was the saviour of these very early Lotus cars. HEL 46 was kept in very good mechanical condition and, although during its competition career it suffered from the occasional contact with trees or other solid objects, he never thought to take out the inevitable dents in the bodywork. When he retired from trials in 1964, he just put the car away in his garage exactly as it had been run in his last trial. In the storms of 1987, the roof of the garage collapsed, but friends removed the car to other storage. Arthur died in 1996. His daughter,

Arthur Hay driving HEL 46 in a 750 Motor Club trial.

Elisabeth Telford, who had been his passenger on some of the trials, kept the car in dry storage. Enthusiasts saw the car for the first time in many years when, in 2002, it was trailered to Brooklands to take part (with the Mk II and the Mark IV) in the centenary celebrations of the MCC.

Martyn Halliday, founder of the Historic Sporting Trials Association, bought the car in 2010 and has only recently got it back to running condition, though he had taken it to Race Retro where it was possibly the most unrestored car present, but always drew the crowds. Whilst most of the history of the car is known, Martyn would very much like to get in contact with any relatives of Horace Sinclair Sweeney, its first owner, or anyone with trials memories of this car or Arthur Hay.

The chassis on the Mk VI Lotus, Colin Chapman's first production car, was also the basic chassis for the Mk VIII, IX and X. For the latter three there were outriggers fitted to take all enveloping streamline bodies. Announced in 1951, the Mk VI was supplied as a kit for home build

and some 110 were delivered. Chassis 81 was registered for the road (URO 80) by John Harris in May 1955, and is believed to have been one of only three to have been sold as a Mk VI with Mk IX modifications fitted. It had a Coventry Climax 1,100cc FWA engine, Lotus Mk IX Elektron brake drums with steel liners, and a De Dion rear axle. Other details included hydraulic brakes with master cylinders on the bulkhead and the single

The Lotus VI awaiting restoration by Martyn Halliday.

John Harris at Druids at Brands Hatch in the Lotus VI.

large fuel float bowl for the twin SU carburettors was mounted on the chassis. John Harris used it in competition before selling it to George Jasberg in September 1956. George was a United States serviceman based in this country; he shipped the car back to the States on completion of his tour of duty. He sold it in 1958 to Kenneth Hartley of Garden City, New York State and by 1961 it was with Wayne Goldman of Vermont, still with FWA engine and its other Mk IX derived parts. Ownership after this is uncertain until 2018. The car was then found in a barn in Connecticut where it had been resting for thirty years or more. The finder realised that the task of rebuilding this by now dilapidated wreck was beyond him and it passed into the hands of UK-based Lotus restorer Mike Brotherwood. Over the years, a number of changes had taken place, I am not sure who by, changes such as the replacement of the Climax engine with one from a standard Ford Cortina, the De Dion axle had gone, replaced by a standard

Ford live axle, Dodge disc wheels had replaced the original wire wheels at the rear and the Elektron brakes were missing. The bonnet and rear wings were also missing. Mike's American friend, David Belden, collected the car for him and with Lotus pals stripped it of all the incorrect parts and those

The Lotus was found in a barn in Connecticut.

Many bits were missing when found.

The Lotus XI purchased from Lotus by Puerto Rico Auto Club.

parts of the chassis which were too rusty to be rebuilt. The resulting pile fitted into quite a small wooden crate for shipment.

When Mike opened the box at his workshop he declared, 'It is better than I expected, not at all bad. I have 50 per cent of the chassis, most of the panels, and the front suspension are all there and it has a stamped chassis number, which is unusual.' Mike is possibly the only person making and stocking Mk IX spares so it will not be too difficult for him to rebuild the car back to original specification.

Nigel Fox from Wiltshire has been a Lotus enthusiast for many years but always hankered after an aluminium-bodied car. Now nearing retirement, he has one, a 1957 Lotus XI, ex-works car, which competed and finished the Sebring twelve hour race in 1957. When looking through the Club Lotus magazine, he saw a small ad for a Lotus XI with racing history. It wasn't until he telephoned the owner that he found it was in Milwaukee, USA. The history sounded interesting, and the condition was described as good having been stored under cover and unused since 1991. Nigel, along with Mike Brotherwood, the Lotus restoration expert, flew to the USA to have a look. The car was as described and had a lot of spares with it. Nigel bought it complete with the trailer on which it sat for twenty-six years.

Colin Chapman looked to the USA as a market for his sports cars. In order to afford to enter works cars for races like Sebring, it was his habit to pre-sell the cars and only let the owners take delivery of them after the race! Sometimes if the new owner was an experienced racer, the owner was entered as Team Lotus. This was the case with Nigel's car which had been purchased by the Puerto Rico Auto Club and driven by Victor Meriono, Luis Pedrerra and Rafael Rosales. It finished thirty-second in the race and third in the class. The car competed in other races, including winning the Nassau Speed Week in 1958 and was brought back to mainland USA in 1962 where it had a number of owners who all raced it. In 1980 it was bought by Dave Dunn for historic racing and fitted with a 1,200cc Coventry Climax engine. Dave last raced it in 1991 after which cracks were found in the frame and it was put into store. In 2018, he sold it to Nigel Fox.

It arrived in the United Kingdom in November 2017, with no problems importing the car, but customs did not seem to have a class for historic trailers! Nigel was determined to drive the car to Historic Le Mans and be part of the Historic Lotus Register gathering. Mike Brotherwood gave the car a full chassis up rebuild. The crack in the frame was not serious. Bob Dove of Motorsport rebuilt the engine. Mike was amazed how original

Mike Brotherwood testing the car during restoration.

The car made it to Le Mans with virtually no problems.

the car was with a number of racing additions he had heard of but never seen. The car made it to Le Mans with virtually no problems at all. No attempt has been made to rectify various repairs in the bodywork. He is in two minds as to whether to leave it green or repaint it red which was its colour at that Sebring race.

A rare BMW 328 lightweight racer with a post-war Veritas rebuild was unearthed from a barn in the farm town of Villisca, Iowa some time ago. The car was locked up there in December 1971 by a local corn farmer who had towed it inside with a tractor, only to leave it untouched for the next forty-five years or so. When he tipped off local repair shop owner Dereck Freshour about it, Freshour was interested immediately. He buys and sells classics regularly with his high school buddy Heath Rodney, who owns a number of Harley Davidson dealerships. Despite not knowing what it was, the duo agreed on a sale and pulled the car out. The 1966 registration told them it was a 1950 BMW Veritas.

They managed to get in touch with Veritas authority Jim Proffit, who found out it wore chassis number 85031. Next step was BMW's Classic department in Munich, who eventually certified the car was the real deal. Its history turned out to be interesting to say the least. The car was built in May 1937 as a high-spec'd lightweight racer – one of sixty-one. It was raced at Le Mans that year, entered by the NSKK – the National Socialist Motor Corps. Just months later the car had made it over to the UK, where it was raced by Prince Bira and next entered in the 1938 Mille Miglia, where it came eleventh overall. After that the history gets muddy, but it must have been converted by Ernst Loof of Veritas fame in 1950, receiving a coupe body made by Authenrieth of Darmstadt.

It also turned out that a member of the US Air Force stationed in Germany took the car to the

BMW 328 lightweight with post-war Veritas coachwork stored since 1971.

Prince Bira driving the 328 BMW.

US in 1957. Just one more owner followed before it was sold to the Iowa farmer in 1971. Now that Freshour and Rodney had found out more about the car's intriguing history, the question became how to tackle the car's restoration. Eventually they decided to restore it to pre-war factory lightweight configuration, taking it back to its glory days. They will place the Authenrieth body on a rolling chassis and keep that in its as-found condition.

The Mercedes-Benz Classic Center at Irvine, California, have recently purchased a 1954 Mercedes-Benz Gullwing that has been in store since 1965. Its discovery was filmed with Tom Cotter (author of the fascinating book *Cobra in the Barn* – Motorbooks International, 2005) on Hagerty's YouTube spot. This is the forty-third Gullwing built. Its last registration plate is for 1965 (though there are claims it was last used in 1956). The odometer stands at 33,308. It was stripped for a repaint and coated with primer. The repaint never happened, all the chrome parts which had been removed were put inside the car, and it went into store in Ponte Vedra, an upmarket beach resort in the north-east of Florida. There is a fine coating of surface rust on the exterior and the interior is complete but filthy. The Mercedes-Benz Classic Center took it to the Amelia Island Concours in 2019 exactly as it was, without cleaning it up at all. Here it was shown alongside the Gullwing number 44, a fully restored car. Constantin von Kageneck, marketing and communications specialist for Mercedes-Benz Classic Center, said, 'To see it in its original state is a phenomenal experience.'

When William Lyons launched SS Cars, which was to become Jaguar, he kept Swallow Coachbuilding and continued to build sidecars.

This 1954 Mercedes-Benz Gullwing has been stored since 1965.

The interior needs a very thorough clean.

He sold this company in 1945 and it later became part of Tube Investments. When there was a drop in demand for sidecars, Swallow turned to car production in 1954, making the Swallow Doretti two-seat sports car which used Triumph TR2 running gear. This proved a very popular car, especially in the USA. They were making ten a week when production suddenly ceased in 1955 due to 'changes in company policy'. It is known that one car had been sent to Ghia in Italy for a coupe body to be built. This car arrived back after the company ceased trading. Frank Rainbow, the Swallow designer, gave orders that it be scrapped.

Richard Larter from Scotland is a fan of the Citroen Light 15 but also of Swallow. He had restored one Swallow, only to sell it to buy a Light 15. He did, however, go out and buy the remains of another Swallow in 2004 which he believes to be the Ghia car. It is almost certain that it was not scrapped because it was advertised by both Performance Cars of Brentford and Mayfair dealer, Simmons, in 1961.

Richard Larter told me:

When I got the car it was badly stored in an open shed on a mushroom farm in Wokingham. The owner had found it in a scrapyard in Reading in the 1970s and thought it was restorable and started stripping it down. He then ran out of steam and there it remained until I bought the car in 2004 from the deceased's estate. [The previous owner] had shown pictures of it to Frank Rainbow in the late 1970s who said it looked like the Ghia car but insisted he had given instructions for

it to be scrapped … The front end is pure Swallow, but someone has crudely grafted on a grill surround from another car … The rear of the car, roof and windscreen surround are fabricated in steel … The roof is a compound curve and the pillars have a complex structure so not an amateur construction; Ghia made their prototypes in steel.

Richard has restored the chassis and running gear which was displayed at the NEC Classic Car Show in 2015.

Stanley Howard 'Wacky' Arnolt sold British cars before going into car production with a car of his own name based on the MG TD with a body designed by Bertone. He made 100 of these before designing a more powerful car, the Arnolt Bristol – 257 of these were manufactured and many went into motor racing. Daniel Rapley has found one from c1956 in a garage in Chicago that appears to have been raced. There were other race cars there as well including an Elva Formula Junior. The Arnolt Bristol had been purchased by George Adamek in the late 1950s and laid up with the engine out in 1964. The engine was still there awaiting a rebuild. Daniel went on to tell us:

We started ferreting through the garage and finally discovered a corner with Arnolt parts and a lot of debris from a rodent. When removing these parts, we disturbed a skunk. I had to beat a hasty retreat. I was due to fly back to New York in a couple of hours and the last thing I needed was to get hosed down by a skunk!

The Ghia bodied coupe Swallow found 'in an open shed on a mushroom farm in Wokingham'.

C1956 Arnolt Bristol found by Daniel Rapley.

Daniel told me that George when he was racing 'had trouble beating the AC Bristols. They had longer legs, but there was one track, Willow Springs, which was a short track and it was the only one where he had an advantage … He relished telling me the story of the first time he beat them. One day he also beat one of the Factory Arnolts. Wacky Arnolt walked over and congratulated George and offered him factory support.'

Mike Waller from Hampshire raced a Kieft Formula Junior which he enjoyed very much. He admires the engineering and the man behind the South Wales make, Cyril Kieft. For around ten years he has been looking for a Kieft Sports Car. Incidentally, that is what Cyril Kieft called it, hence capital letters, it never had any other name. Recently Mike found one advertised in *Classic and Sports Car* magazine and followed it up. Kieft made six 1,100cc Sports Cars between 1954 and 1956. Two were raced at Le Mans in 1954 and 1955. The 1956 car that Mike Waller went after was the last of the six made. It was sent new to Bill Bowman in the USA. This model Kieft is believed to have been the first production car to have been fitted with a one piece fibreglass body. The car in America was, in fact, aluminium bodied; Mike believes it went out with the plastic body and an early American owner changed it. It is believed that one of the Le Mans cars may have been bodied in aluminium.

Once in America the Coventry Climax engine was soon replaced by a Chevrolet V8. This has resulted in a lot of modification to the chassis, causing it to bend. Soon after this, that engine in turn got changed for a Ford Consul Mk II. The history

In Mike Waller's garage with the body in the foreground and the chassis top middle.

from circa 1958 until circa 1993 is unknown and Mike would like to hear from anyone who recognises the car. In 1993, the now rusty car was bought by collector Howard Banasak Junior. He took the wheels off and painted them but did little else. Recently he decided he just was not going to restore all his cars and it was offered for sale.

When I saw the car, the body was off and the chassis was back from sand blasting which showed up many imperfections in the welding that had been done to the car since it left the UK. The two main chassis tubes were rusted through in places underneath, and if you looked at the chassis from the side, the bend in it was very obvious; in fact, it was bowed by two and a half inches. Mike has now rebuilt it back to as near original as possible – a correct Coventry Climax FWA engine came with it.

The first Turner sports car was announced in 1955 using the 803cc Austin engine. Older readers will remember the publicity pictures for the car featuring singer Petula Clark. When in 1956

1956 Kieft Sports Car as recovered from the USA by Mike Waller.

The car has now been rebuilt with its correct Coventry Climax FWA engine.

Austin's announced the 948cc engine, this was soon adopted for a new model for Turner called the Turner 950. At first this was outwardly similar to the previous model but with most sales being in the USA, an American agent suggested the addition of fashionable fins, which were soon adopted. An early 950 model with rear sloping tail bodywork and no fins has recently turned up in Bluffton, South Carolina.

This car was sold in 1958 and an early owner is known to have raced it. In 1967 it was bought by Don Guscio who used it for some time before leaving it out in his yard. It has now literally sunk into the yard where it has been for many years.

In 2015 Russell Filby of the Turner Sports Car Register described it to me:

> The car is very complete but had deteriorated with the exposure, the windscreen frame is there and the car is on wire wheels, as expected the floor pans as well as the steel doors are rusted through. The fibreglass body is in good condition, the engine [Morris variant] looks original and complete other than missing a distributor cap. The seat frames are there as well as the steering wheel but in a poor condition … the large framework at the front is some form of roll-over bar which has been removed from the car. Of this early body style only fifteen are known to the Turner Register to have survived worldwide.

The Morris engine of the long-stored Turner.

The Fairthorpe Electron Minor was available either in kit form or as an assembled car. Around 500 were sold as kits and one of these was bought in 1960 by a young Alan Green. Alan, with two friends, each with their own cars, went to collect the kit from the Chalfont St Peter factory. He told us:

> It was transported to my home in Enfield in and on three cars - body and chassis on a roof rack, engine and gearbox on the rear seat of an Austin A40 and the remainder of the components spread between the three. The car was completed and registered [5398 MK] in 1960. I joined the Fairthorpe Sports Car Club in that year and am still a member.

The car, driven by Alan and his wife Shirley, was a great success covering over 200,000 miles before being laid up in 1982. It had travelled all over the continent on many holidays, was used every day to go to work and the 948cc Triumph Herald engine averaged some 48 miles to the gallon. The car was eventually laid up as it required some work; having two daughters meant that a larger car was required for regular use. Whilst some restorations get delayed through having to build a garage, Alan and Shirley, with the help of a bricklayer, then spent the next few years building their own energy conservation house, fitting it out and making a garden.

Alan started a restoration of the car which is progressing slowly. He mentioned an incident when travelling to Norway. 'When Norway and Sweden drove on opposite sides of the road there

1958 Turner exported to the USA and then left in a yard.

The 1960 Fairthorpe Electron Minor was laid up in 1982.

was a chicane built in the road at the border. It was rather like the Musical Ride of the Household Cavalry at the cross over, when we went through!'

In 1989 Mark Hyman was at the annual Hershey meet. Here he met a man who told him about a 1962 Facel Vega II he had bought in 1971 and had never used. It was, however, not for sale. Mark was keen to buy it and made an annual phone call to the owner. Mark told me, 'In 2013 I convinced the owner to let me at least see the car which was stored in a building in Minneapolis. Upon inspection I found that it was totally complete and as it was when purchased in 1971, it even had the 1971 licence plates on the car.' At long last he was able to purchase it. This is a car of which the Facel Vega Club had no knowledge, having had it listed as 'being destroyed'.

Silas Cook from Portland, Oregon in the USA, tells me, 'On the eve of my 50th birthday the phone rang and I was told that if I still wanted the car I could have it. I headed over the very next day.' The story starts with a Portland, Oregon owner laying up a 1962 Ginetta G4 in 1978 alongside his house and covering it with a bright blue tarpaulin. In 1999 Silas Cook first heard about it and tried to buy it, but it was not for sale. He dropped by twice a year for the next fifteen years, he even regularly checked on Google Earth to see if the blue tarpaulin had been moved. He told me:

> Underneath the tarpaulin was indeed a very early Ginetta G4 albeit in a very sad state. The entire car, cockpit, engine bay and rear trunk area was one enormous rat's nest. Were I a person of sound mind I would have politely thanked the owner and walked away, but given my rather limited brain capacity I whipped out the cash and paid the man.

Trevor Pyman of the Ginetta Owners Club has been helping trace some of the history. This was the eleventh G4, completed at the very end of 1962 and registered 377 HOJ in Birmingham in January 1963. The first owner is unknown but the second was Bob Crutchley of Kings Heath, Birmingham. He sold it to Mr D. Nehl of Portland, Oregon who kept the car briefly, then sold it to the last owner. Silas went on to tell me, 'The car has many interesting features including a rare Martin valve assembly and other period Martin speed parts, very extensive drilling on the door hinges, foot pedals, door

This 1962 Facel Vega was laid up in 1971.

1962 Ginetta G4 'albeit in a very sad state'.

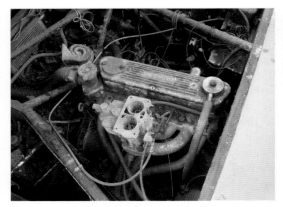

The car was fitted with a very rare Martin valve assembly.

The MGB which took part in the London to Sydney marathon was, in 2015, found in a scrapyard.

handles, etc. It also has recessed front directional unlike any other G4 I have seen.'

The 1968 London to Sydney Marathon was devised by Sir Max Aitken of the *Daily Express* over a lunch with Jocelyn Stevens and Tommy Sopwith. It was designed 'to raise the spirits in the country'. It attracted a great deal of publicity with 100 entries with works teams as well as privateers taking part. The only sports car to finish was an MGB (UMD 534F) driven by Jean Denton and Tom Boyce in forty-second place (out of fifty-five finishers). This car had help from the Special Tuning Department at MG, Abingdon, but was a private entry, the car being built up by Tony Denton, Tom Boyce and Pete Smith. It was sponsored by *Nova* magazine which was for 'a new kind of woman'. It is said the magazine had more male readers than female ones!

After the rally the car disappeared from sight, though it is thought to have been on the South Coast in the early 1990s. In 2015 it turned up in a scrapyard where an employee saw the London to Sydney badge on the dashboard and contacted the MG Car Club. Chairman of the MGB Register, John Watson, and others, went to view the car. Whilst the car was not in very good condition, it still had an amazing number of the rally modifications for the Marathon. The Register have bought the car and will be restoring it to Marathon rally condition. Already it has appeared at a Marathon Club event at Gaydon where it caused great interest. Jean Denton, who died in 2001 at the age of 65, had an extraordinary career. Not only was she a professional racing and rally driver for a few years, but she rose to the top in the motor industry

The London to Sydney marathon badge on the dashboard was spotted by a scrapyard employee.

before becoming a Director of a number of government bodies. She was made a life peer in 1991, becoming Baroness Denton of Wakefield. She was later made Parliamentary Under Secretary of State at the Department of Trade and Industry, then headed by Michael Heseltine.

Tom Boyce, who helped with the build of the car, died in 2015 but not before he had given the Register a lot of information. Pete Smith came forward after hearing about the car and became a Special Advisor to the project.

It caused quite a stir at a marathon club event at the British Motor Museum at Gaydon.

It is well known that when Sir William Lyons produced the first of his new sports cars in 1950, the XK120, he had only intended to build a few. However, the demand for them was such that they had to go into full production. The initial batch of 242 all had aluminium bodies; after that they changed to steel and the early ones are very sought after.

In 2017 Gary Seraphinoff of Seven Gables Motor Garage in Bloomfield Hill, Detroit received a phone call from a guy who was buying a Jeep from an elderly lady. He said she had an old sports car stacked away in a barn. When asked about it she replied, 'That's my 1950 aluminium Jaguar.' She had said that she bought it in 1969 for $75 and was going to restore it.

Gary was interested to know more but the finder would not give away the location. The finder telephoned the lady three or four times a year, but she would not sell, until one day four years later she said 'yes'. Within a few hours Gary was travelling to Wisconsin to meet the lady. It sounds as if the owner was as interesting as the car. She had been described as having white hair with a purple stripe, an Annie Oakley style six shooter strapped to her right leg and a sheathed ten inch Bowie knife strapped to her left leg ... she had

been married to a biker and had been a pin-up in the 1960s, appearing as a centrefold in *Easy Rider* magazine.

Gary said the description was very accurate and a cash deal was done, counting out the notes on the bonnet of the Jaguar. It would appear that a previous owner had sold the engine and dashboard for use in a speed boat. A Chevrolet engine and automatic box had then been fitted but it had never run like this, and the Chevrolet engine was no longer with the car.

The eccentric owner of the 1950 all-aluminium bodied XK120.

I received the following email from Rodney McDonald:

A local newspaper advert in Fairhope, Alabama, USA, for a clearing-out sale included a 'Jaguar XK-E' in the list of items to be sold. My friend and I were early arrivals at the water front home that was the site for the sale, and we were told that the owners for the estate were asking $2,000 for the old Jaguar, with removal required within forty-eight hours. The 1969 E Type coupe was complete, but had been under seawater twice during the onslaught of Hurricanes Ivan and Katrina that struck the American Gulf Coast. The seller also stated that, in the event no-one had purchased the car by 2.00 pm, the price would be halved. They took a chance on the fifty percent discount and departed. They returned promptly at 2.00 pm and, to our delight, the E-Type was unclaimed. We wrote the seller a check just as another chance-taking buyer arrived.

The old Jaguar was loaded on a recovery truck and delivered to my friend's garage where we gave it a close inspection. All of the opening panels had to be gently prised open due to the corrosion from the salt water. The interior was a total loss and the boot and floor panels had been mostly eaten away. Water had risen to the top of the dashboard, making the instruments almost useless. We decided that the car's highest calling was that of a spares donor and we set out to remove as many useful

The engine compartment of the E-Type.

mechanical, body and trim pieces that we could and offered them to restorers of other E-Types. To date, we have shipped parts of the Jaguar to buyers all over the USA, as well as UK, Germany, Italy, Australia and Argentina.

Sadly, my friend and partner in this endeavour passed away recently, but this project (along with the restoration of his own 1964 Jaguar E-Type coupe) brought us close to the comradery that our hobby creates.

One of the founder members of the Cornwall Vintage Vehicle Society is Tony Barfield and over the years he has owned all manner of cars including a Rolls-Royce, Rileys, Morris Tens and a 1932 Austin 7 Saloon called 'Felicity' which he bought in 1966 and still owns. As a child his son Adrian was taken round to all sorts of motoring events and one of his vivid memories is seeing an open MG in 'cream cracker' colours of chocolate and cream. In recent years Adrian has been rebuilding a Cornish cottage and passed the time of day with a neighbour who was rebuilding an old chapel. In the course of conversations, it became apparent he had an old MG in an outhouse. Adrian told me:

The car was placed in a concrete block shed, put on blocks and carefully covered with heavy duty tarpaulins with everything being held in place with stout chicken wire, but due to the magnitude of the building work required on the chapel, that was where the car stayed for the next thirty years. Unfortunately, during that time the owner never found time to put a roof on the shed!

This E-Type had been underwater when hurricanes hit the Gulf Coast of the USA.

Adrian had tried to buy it on a number of occasions, but when the neighbour reached eighty, he realised he would never get round to it and offered it to Adrian. This 1948 MG TC, registration NWL 248, has now been completely restored in green (not chocolate and cream!) and used on recent suitable Club events.

In 2015 Adrian heard of another car laid up locally, owned by an elderly widowed lady. He takes up the story:

We opened the barn doors and there in front of me was the chassis and body of an Austin 7 box saloon covered in dust and cobwebs. Although I was assured it was all there, the rest of the car was completely dismantled. The car was identical with father's 'Felicity', in fact they were just 200 numbers apart. The Austin 7, registered KX 8676, has no known history until purchased in 1966 by the lady

MGTC stored in a shed without a roof.

The Austin 7 taken off the road in the early 1990s.

when she and her husband used it regularly until the 1980s, taking it off the road in the early 1990s for restoration. He died before he could complete the work. In order to find all the parts that were scattered over the barn, it had to be cleared of rubbish, two trailer loads going to the tip before they could look for Austin 7 parts. All of this was accompanied by much tea provided by the lady, whose parting words to them were 'I do have another old car if you are interested'.

Tony followed her around the paddock to another barn which contained a tractor and various items of farm machinery. He said '… tucked away in a corner I could just discern a car shaped object covered with a very grubby and torn dust sheet which, when pulled back, revealed a 1969 Jaguar E Type FHC.

VBL 363G had been owned by the family since the early 1980s. When later they moved to Cornwall and bought a farm, the car was laid up for a few years, later in favour of a Land Rover which was more suited to a farmer's requirements. The owner's late husband had done some restoration work on the car, including the engine, but never finished it before he died, in fact the rear axle was off the car when Adrian saw it. An offer made by Adrian for both cars was accepted. The Austin 7 is now well on the way to being restored, whilst the E Type, with back axle refitted, has been cleaned up and carefully stored, and will be the next in line for work.

The weather at the 2013 Hershey was at times rainy and cold, and Adolfo Massari from LBI also added

When the covers were pulled back a 1969 E Type Jaguar fixed head coupe was revealed.

'miserable'. The rain caused the collapse of their tent onto one of their cars; they were not amused. The sun came out and along came a gentleman who brightened their day. He told them of a Jaguar E Type he had seen locally to him in Lancaster, PA. A few days after Hershey he rang again with an appointment for them to meet the owners.

Back in the 1970s Flo had been a great fan of the E Type Jaguar. In 1972 her husband, without telling her, bought a one owner low mileage 1967 E Type coupe and casually left it in the drive for her to find on return from work. She loved the car but there were two problems. 'She did not know how to drive a stick shift and the British Racing Green over tan was a colour scheme that she hated.' However, she learned to drive the stick shift and in due course the car was repainted dark blue with parchment interior. In 1988 after 56,000 miles, the car needed some minor engine and body work repairs which were never completed.

Flo's once glorious E-Type after many boxes had been removed.

Adolfo told me his first reaction on seeing this car. 'The sight was absolute heaven. Right in front of our eyes was Flo's once glorious E Type surrounded by boxes, cobwebs and covered in 25 years of dust. A very solid body, matching numbers and with the 1972 original purchase receipt.'

Dave Forshew from Bristol contacted me as follows:

It all started with an email that simply read 'Do you know anyone who would be interested in an E-Type Jag currently sat in a garage that needs to be demolished?' To which I simply replied 'Depending on price and condition, I would!' This led to my

greatest piece of motoring good fortune and the realisation of a long term dream.

On Friday 13 January 2012 (lucky for some) 'a price was agreed. Within four hours there was air in the tyres, the brake pads had been removed from the callipers and the car was rolling free and ready for its first light of day for twenty-five years'.

Dave's friend, who sent the email, was a carpenter and was carrying out renovations on the house of the son of the owner of the E-Type. The son wanted 'the car moved in a short time scale with the minimum of hassle.' The garage, which was due to be demolished in order that three new garages could be built, was situated adjacent to a house in a private road in an urban area between Bristol and Bath and ironically Dave told me, '[it was] next door to my employer's house where we had held a party only two months before and had actually been talking about barn find cars!' The car had come off the road due to the owner's health problems and the fact that a vehicle had backed into one of the garage pillars at the front and completely jammed the door. Access at first had to be gained through a damaged side panel of the building. Later the door 'had to be unbolted from the wall and physically carried away'. Incidentally, Dave was given the garage as part of the deal.

This Series 3 E-Type V12 2+2 coupe was first registered UMT 789M by Loxleys of Bromley in August 1973. The first owner was that great motoring enthusiast Victor Gauntlett of Pace Petroleum of Farnham (and later Proteus Petroleum) who, through his companies, sponsored many motoring events and was the personal sponsor of Nigel Mansell for his first two years in Formula One. He

The garage door was jammed shut and entry was through a damaged side panel.

was also Chairman of Aston Martin. The car has only had one other long-term owner. The mileage on the clock reads 38,052. The last tax disc was for 1987. At some stage, and probably in the 1980s, this car was changed from its original azure blue with biscuit interior to red, both inside and outside. Mechanically the car is sound, the engine runs well, but the brakes need a complete overhaul.

The first owner of UMT 789M was Victor Gauntlet.

The Porsche 901 after removal from the barn.

Studio picture of the Porsche before cleaning.

The restored Porsche now in the factory museum.

No welding is required, though a complete respray is needed.

Many Porsches were exported to the United States and more of this make than any other European car seem to have survived, many it would appear in barn find condition. This first one, however, was found nearer to the factory. In September 1963 Porsche showed a pre-production 901 at the Frankfurt Motor Show. In September 1964 the production model made its debut at the Paris Motor Show. Almost immediately Peugeot sent a letter to Porsche advising that they had the French copyright on the use of the '0' in the middle of an automobile numeral. Though this only applied to France, Porsche quickly decided to change their model name to 911. Porsche built 235 911s in 1964, the first 82 of which were designated as 901. None of these were officially sold to the public as 901s but a few made it out of Porsche's gates with 901 tags. These are very rare and until recently the factory did not have an example in their collection.

300#057 was purchased by a Porsche enthusiast from its first owner many years ago. After a time, marriage and children meant the family no longer fitted into the car. It was side-lined.

The factory heard a rumour from a film crew of this 901 standing at the back of a barn on a former farm at Brandenburg. They found it in very poor condition with both front wings missing and there was much rust damage. The interior was in a very poor state. However, many of the little details only to be found on the 901 were still there. They purchased the car and after three years of restoration it is now featured in the factory museum as a special exhibit entitled '911 (no 57) a legend takes off'. I was told that one of the most difficult parts to repair and restore was the original ash tray!

I have been in touch with Frank Sajjad of MB Vintage Cars from Brook Park, Cleveland, Ohio. He was recently tipped off by a member of a family that the car was coming up for sale. It is possibly the most rusted out Porsche I have ever seen. Frank told me:

The car was purchased from an estate sale of a gentleman who passed away leaving it behind in one of his barns. I was told this car was his daily driver from 1967 when he purchased it new, until 1974. Since then it has

sat in his barn until a few weeks ago [2017] when we pulled it out …

As he was a family man, I assume other priorities must have taken over. We know he was a busy man and had many cars, so maybe another one became his favourite, and as you know people tend to hold on to these cars with the intent to restore or sell in the future when the value of the car has increased, and often never get around to it … Unfortunately, the barn was not climate controlled, so the car declined as opposed to being preserved.

'It is probably the most rusted out Porsche I have ever seen.' (Frank Sajjad)

The rusted out Porsche - no doubt someone will love it.

All the numbers are correct. It would appear everything is frozen and there are no floorboards on the driver's side. One of the stickers on the car rather ironically points out that the car is (or was) Ziebart protected!

Not many Ferraris are lying about unused; however, Christopher Gardner and his friend Allessandro Bruni seem to have a knack of finding them.

A few people had heard about this 1955 Ferrari 250 GT Europa body by Pininfarina with just 8,400 miles on the clock. Very few had been able to locate it, and no-one had been able to purchase it. Most Ferrari experts doubted its existence and thought it was a scam. I can assure you it's real and does exist. Ferrari built twenty-two of this series and this one is a three litre V12 with the desirable Colombo V12 engine. Mr Raffaele Lacarbonara had bought this car from its first owners forty-eight years ago. It was placed in his small Volkswagen dealer showroom in the mountain village of Taranto in the Puglia region of Southern Italy. About twenty years ago he moved it and stored it at his house.

Allessandro Bruni, often known as the 'Alfa Doctor' or 'Truffle Dog' because of his ability to root out barn finds, was holidaying near Taranto, heard about the car and went to investigate. I was told there is a certain dishonour to selling such cars in that part of Italy, but the main hurdle was that the car had become part of the village folk-lore and could not be moved without permission of 'Capo di tutti capi', the 'Don' boss of the village, and his permission was not forthcoming. When asked what would change his mind, the Don said, 'Only an order

The interior is all original, though the carpets are slightly moth-eaten.

from the Pope could over-ride my decision.' I was told that 'this goes back to horse-drawn days; you never sold your horse and cart, they were a status symbol. If you sold it, it showed you were broke – it was much like the last thing you did in life.'

At this point, Bruni called in his friend, Christopher Gardner, a car hunting sleuth based in Switzerland, who has helped me in the past. Christopher's brother is a Canon with the Institute of Christ the King in Firenze, Italy. A member of this order is a First Class Chaplain in the Sovereign Order of Malta, an ancient order which defended pilgrims to the Holy Land during Crusades. It still has appointments and acts under instruction from the Pope. His connections prompted a particular request of chivalry, a special favour directly delivered to the Don's Church that had been in bell-ringing distance from the 250 Europa for five decades. Once the 'Don' had received the nod from Rome, the Florentine police department escorted the Ferrari out of the Sicilian hills for destination Suisse.

It would appear that all the occupants of the village turned out to wave at the departing Ferrari chanting 'Ciao, bella macchina'.

It is now owned by Christopher Gardner and he told me:

> With 13,700 kilometres on the clock, the Ferrari is a time capsule bearing all original paint, original interior, carpets (moth eaten), complete tool kit and a pile of period photos … it runs and drives like a new Ferrari … the Ferrari will not be restored, it will be carefully preserved with attention to forensic detail, nothing will be changed, this is the ultimate bench mark.

Ferrari 250 GT '… he moved it and stored it in his house'.

Swiss based Christopher Gardner appears again here when he bought what was reputed to be the last Ferrari 212 of the eighty built, a Pininfarina low profile coupe. He tells me that finding accurate documentation on the early Ferraris is very difficult, if not impossible. He had an inkling that this car had been wrongly described. He found out that the first owner was Tom Marchese, a prominent United States car dealer in the 1920s and 1930s who also regularly raced, including a finish at Indianapolis in 1929. He later changed to being a major motor sport promoter, winning several 'Promoter of the Year' awards.

Christopher told me, 'A newspaper article provided by the family gave a written account of how Marchese visited Enzo Ferrari to take personal delivery of his dream car … the article also mentioned that Marchese had bragged that the car would do 150mph.' Christopher felt that it was unlikely that Marchese would have travelled to the United States on the *Queen Mary* and to return on the *Andrea Doria* (with his new car) to buy an 'old model', much more likely an early edition of the new 250MM of which the Europa was the road going version but even so was capable of over 150mph, which the 212 was not. He went on to say:

The car was very fast and far more agile than any 212 that I had driven over the years, this car just seemed better for some reason. Measuring the capacity of the cylinders I came up with 3,000cc, a far cry from the 2,560cc of the 212 … along the way, starting in the 1960s, the Ferrari was misidentified as the last 212, when actually it was one of the first two 250 Europas.

He spent a year trying to get some confirmation from Ferrari, but they were being very tight lipped. Then he had an invitation to a Ferrari sponsored dinner and sat with some important people from the factory. A deal was done and a few days later came a photocopy of the appropriate Ferrari ledger. '250 Europa Prodotta. 1953. Cillindrata 3,000 coupe. Chassis 0297EU Pininfarina consignation a. Tom Marchesi USA, Thiensville 2 posti.'

This is a very shortened version of the huge amount of research that went on to trace this identity. Chassis 0297EU was with a Mr Seider in Chicago in 1961, later passing to the Brook Stevens Museum in Wisconsin. It stayed in the

This is reputed to have been the last Ferrari 212 built.

USA until 1996 when it came back to Italy with Luigi Mancini in Pisa. The total mileage is 54,000 kilometres, and the general impression of the condition of the car, especially the all-original interior, backs up this figure.

The Ferrari was missing all the chrome trim that had been removed by the owner to make the car look more aggressive. The trim had been stored tied to the rafters of the owner's barn near Pisa. When removed it was discovered that every piece had the Pininfarina job number stamped on it. The recent discovery of a colour photo taken in 1960 showed the original colour that matched the paint remains under a glossy American re-spray in the late 1970s. That photo has allowed the Ferrari to be repainted in its original livery.

I received an email which started with:

Funny fact: in 1982 a man went into a Ferrari dealership [in Belgium] to enquire about a Ferrari 308. He was not taken very seriously but did walk away with a brand new Berlinetta Boxer. Attached you will find a teaser picture of this one owner 1982 BBi, fully original which has been in storage for almost twenty years, it still retains all its tools, tool bags, booklets, invoices and its Ferrari radio.

Of course, I had to know more. The story was told to me by Dieter Vandenbroucke:

The car belongs to a friend of mine whose father, now a retired baker, only drove the BB in his leisure time and on dry days [36,000 kilometres on the clock]. For the rest of the time the Ferrari slept in the back of a bakery and every time he wanted to drive it, all the baking equipment had to be moved. For a while it kept company with a Lancia Stratos, but that got away some time ago. After years of non-activity the Ferrari was covered in dust and flour but was always kept warm by the oven.

The car has seen the light of day again and is in the hands of his son Enzo (he was born a year after the car was bought!). 'For now, he is keeping the car dusty because you can wash it only once!'

The general impression of the condition of the car, especially the interior, was that it was all very original.

**Above:** 'You can wash it only once.'

**Left:** The Ferrari Berlinetta Boxer stored in the back of the bakery.

**Below:** The Ferrari was covered in dust but it was kept warm by the baker's oven.

# 8 ONE-OFFS AND SPECIALS

This chapter covers a wide variety of one-off motor cars. Most specials were of a design built for the satisfaction of its constructor or for a specific purpose or a competition formula. Older readers may well remember the special building craze of the 1950s and 1960s. Many of these usually open cars were based on the pre-war Austin 7 or Ford 10 chassis. There have been quite a variety of vehicles, for example, built for advertising purposes. I know that the National Motor Museum at Beaulieu has a Daimler in the form of a beer bottle, and a Mini-based vehicle shaped and painted like an orange for Outspan.

There have been many attempts to make a motor car that looked like a yacht. One of the most striking was built by the French coachbuilder Henri Chapron for former automobile engineer turned fashion designer Louis Reard. Reard's main claim to fame was as the inventor of the bikini swimsuit in 1946, named after Bikini Atoll, the island in the Pacific where the United States conducted their first atmospheric atomic test. Reard claimed he named the swimsuit after the test island as it was 'small and devastating'. It was the first swim wear to expose the navel and was a real breakthrough.

Back to the car! Reard wanted an appropriate advertising vehicle on and around which he could show bikini dressed models. He decided it should represent a yacht, originally the coachwork was placed on a post-war Hotchkiss 686 chassis, but this proved to be under powered and so it was later changed to fit on a 1937 Packard Super 8, at the same time the driving position was changed from right to left. The coachwork had a real bow, a boat cabin with port holes and a rear deck plus a searchlight on the roof.

The coachwork had a real bow and cabin, rear deck and portholes.

The bow showing air intake for the radiators – Louis Reard looked on.

The car was taken to many French holiday resorts as well as following a number of Tour de France cycle races. Everywhere it went the car caused a sensation, as did the swimsuit wearing models.

The history of the car after Louis Reard stopped using it is scant. It did appear at Retromobile in 1987 and then disappeared into a private collection in France where Hans Veenebos more recently took colour pictures. It is a pity it does not come

The car now in a private collection.

out more often as it would be a winner at almost any show with or without the models.

From boats we go to aeroplanes. It has always been the dream of some automotive designers to build a car that could easily be converted into an aeroplane and which could fly. A lock keeper on the French canals called Fernand Maratuech was an inventor in his spare time. He had designed and built a steam-driven sewing machine (!) and a gas powered motorcycle. He turned his ideas onto the car which could fly but came to the conclusion that on his limited salary that would not be possible. Instead, he made a car that looked like an aeroplane, though it was missing wings and a propeller. It was powered by a 350cc BSA motorcycle engine. Known as the Maratuech, it was run regularly in the early 1920s. In the 1930s it was stored. In 1990, Fernand's widow gave the car to the Automobile Club du Sud-Ouest. With financial help from *Fondation du Patrimoine*, which helps to protect all types of French heritage, and the oil company Motul, it has recently been restored to running order by Pierre Arnaud. It can now be seen exhibited on the premises of the Automobile Club du Sud-Ouest in Marseilles.

Having dealt with a boat and a plane, it would seem natural to follow it with a train! When I learned that an unrestored 1929 'Trackless Sound Train' was being offered for sale in Oregon I had to investigate. H.O. McGee Manufacturers of Special Automotive Equipment of Indianapolis, in the early 1920s, built onto a car chassis a reproduction of a locomotive adorned with all the accoutrements of cow catcher, bells, whistles and so on. This in turn towed a reproduction of a Club Car carriage and was sold to MGM who used it for publicity purposes. One such did come to Britain whilst on a 'world tour', and pictures of it in London did appear in a retrospective article in *Antique Automobile* in 1976. That same article also told us:

The Maratuech, the car that looked like an aeroplane.

The method of expelling smoke through the funnel is to drop crude oil into the exhaust manifold and the smoke is conveyed by way of a small pipe to the smoke stack. In the stack are revolving blades which cause the smoke to be emitted in puffs instead of a steady stream. This operation is controlled from the driver's seat from which too, the whistles, wireless apparatus and bell may also be worked.

This reminds me of the famous 1910 Brooke Swan Car, once owned by the Maharaja of Nabha, in the Louwman Museum in the Hague:

The swan's beak is linked to the engine's cooling system and opens wide to allow the driver to spray steam to clear a passageway in the streets. Whitewash could be dumped on the road through a valve at the back of the car to make the swan appear even more lifelike.

Later in the 1920s, Paramount Pictures were looking for ways to publicise their films and their Publix chain of cinemas and later of course 'talkies'. They went to H.O. McGee for a simpler version of their original concept. It is thought that some 16 of these later versions were built mainly on Graham- Paige chassis, certainly the one I saw offered for sale is on a 1929 Graham - Paige saloon. In this latest form the front part of the large saloon was converted to look like a railway locomotive, much of the interior of the saloon was kept and a balcony built on the back. A very powerful sound unit was included which could broadcast music, advertising and interviews. In this way the 'train' could tour a town or district to publicise a recently released film, stars or celebrities could appear on the back balcony and they could wave and move about whilst talking to the audience or when the 'train' was stationary could be interviewed live. It is thought that five or six of these vehicles still exist.

Based on a 1929 Graham-Paige saloon and converted to look like a railway locomotive.

'Stars or celebrities would appear on the back balcony.'

The original buck was built from plywood and chicken wire moulded to shape.

The one for sale looks as if it has been rather badly stored for a long time, most of the roof is missing and much of the interior. The original 8-cylinder engine has been removed and a Studebaker flat-head 6 with manual box has replaced it. Sounds as if it might be a 'slow train'.

In 1960 Forrest Robinson from Keene in New Hampshire started to build a special. It was based on a 1956 Oldsmobile chassis and running gear with a V8 Oldsmobile engine. The body was home-made and, apart from trying to look futuristic with a triangular fin at the back, was not based on anything at all. The present owner George Albright, a Society of Automotive Historians member from Florida, told me:

He built the mould for the body out of ply-wood and chicken wire moulded to shape. Then he dipped burlap bags (coarse woven

The body was home made and had a futuristic triangular fin at the rear.

sacks) in plaster of paris and put them over the chicken wire to harden and to give the mould its shape. He then produced a fibre-glass body from the mould ... the doors are meant to slide into pockets in the leading edges of the rear fenders. It is not obvious how the rear tyres are meant to be changed.

No sooner had Forrest finished building it than he was called up. In 1966 he was approached by Green Acres All Star Dairies who wanted to hire the car for two years to promote their Batman themed dairy products. They had the rights amongst other things for 'Batman and Robin' ice cream. They rented the car and painted it purple with Batman stickers on the side. On its return, Forrest sold the car. It then sat for 30 years in a New Hampshire barn, was then left outside, bought by a Chicago collector, stored inside again with no work being done, until George Albright bought it in 2011. He will be restoring the Batman car back to its orig-inal form and colour scheme. He thinks the only things missing are the seats and the windscreen which is from a 1954 Buick mounted upside down.

More commonly, ordinary people, for whatever the reason, decided to build a car to their own design. Take Charles Godsal, for example. He was the son of an engineer and inventor. He inherited some of his father's inventiveness and in 1935 he decided to build a sports car, though in this case he contracted out much of the work. He teamed up with Stewart Daniels who had previously been working in the Competitions Dept at MG. They contacted Research Engineers Ltd of London who made one-off prototypes but had not built a complete car before. The chassis was built by John Thompson Pressings of Wolverhampton. It had special Godsal designed sliding pillar front suspension, more sophisticated than either Morgan or Lancia. The engine was a Ford V8 mated to a Riley ENV gearbox reputedly bought from racing driver Whitney Straight. The back axle was from a 1923 Bentley obtained from Dorothy Paget. The very stylish body was built by Coachbuilders Corsica of Cricklewood based on designs submitted by Godsal in the form of a model. It was registered NJ 9183 (East Sussex) on 4 June 1936. Not much more is known of the car except that after the war an owner made a lot of changes to the bodywork at the front including cycle wings which very much detracted from its appearance. In this form it features in the 1969 film *Mosquito Squadron* starring David McCallum (the Man from UNCLE). In 1972 it was offered for sale amongst a group of sports cars and its lines intrigued Anthony Sidgwick from Cirencester, an eccentric antiques dealer who had a side-line making dolls houses in the style of the child's home. He bought it, researched its history as best he could, and asked Ashton Keynes Vintage Restorations to return it to its original outline. Keith Bowley, who founded Ashton Keynes Vintage Restorations, told me, 'I remember the job which we had to do with the aid of just two photographs of the completed car. After a lot of searching, I have found that picture as well as one from before it was bodied.' In 1977 it was offered for sale by Paradise Garages and it went to Jerry Old in California. He used it very little but did take it to some shows. He moved in 1993 to Kansas City on retirement. He tried to get it running but failed and had a local firm achieve this for him. The car was then put up for sale. In

A clip from the film *Mosquito Squadron* showing altered coachwork and wartime white edged wings.

Ashton Keynes Vintage Restorations later rebuilt it back to original outline.

2021 it was looking very smart and was about to be offered for sale at an Amelia Island auction.

Barrie Carter and his friend Neville Heath would often ask the question, 'What happened to Ashley Cleave's Morris Special that they both remembered competing in trials, hill climbs, sprints and circuit races?' I also remember the car in the long distance trials and wondered the same. Ashley Cleave was a partner, then Director, of Callington Motors in Cornwall, who had been Morris dealers since 1926. Pre-war he took an accident damaged 1936 Morris 8 saloon and used the frame and the engine to make a very potent all round competition car registered CCV 952. Pre-war it was supercharged but later, and still before the war, he fitted an MGTB XPAG engine. Between 1938 and 1973 when he retired from motor sport, this car had won well over 400 trophies (many for circuit racing) and is possibly this country's most successful competition car ever. He drove it on the road to every event he competed in. He took part in an MCC meeting at Brooklands pre-war and then all over the West Country and often much further afield. At race meetings he usually

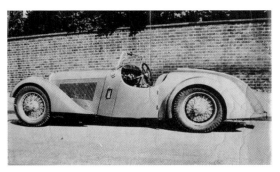

The body of the Godsal was built by Corsica.

Ashley Cleave in the Morris Special at Twengwainton hill climb.

managed to compete in at least three different classes and entered as a racing car by removing the wings. The Morris 10 engine was highly tuned, he even had two sets of pistons so that different compression ratios were available. He was able to get a 12.5 to 1 ratio and running on dope was able to obtain 6,400 rpm with reliability as well!

In 1989 Neville Heath was driving his Dellow in Tavistock when a lady came up to him saying her brother had a car like that. It was Ashley Cleave's sister who, incidentally, still has all of his trophies. After his death in 1979, the car had passed to a nephew who did a few events in it and then stored it away. Barrie Carter was able to obtain it in 1992. He used it on the road for a few miles and found it to be 'very dilapidated'. Various things got in the way of progress on the restoration, including a serious illness. Barrie is now in the process of restoring it. He told me, 'It is eligible for more series and special events, including Brooklands meets, than any other car I know.'

Special builders often would take an existing chassis and design their car to fit that.

Alan Staniforth is possibly best known for his Terrapin, designed primarily to compete in sprint and speed hill climbs. Designed by Alan Staniforth and Richard Blackmore, approximately 100 Terrapin chassis were made and sold. There were Staniforth specials before that and one 'SUG 55' has been rescued by Rhys Nolan.

Barrie Carter obtained it and 'used it for a few miles but found it to be very dilapidated'.

SUG 55 'built on a Mk V Buckler chassis' being raced by Alan Staniforth at Brands Hatch.

SUG was built up on a Mark V Buckler chassis, fitted with a tuned 1,172 engine and for a body used either the first or a very early Rochdale Mk VI body. 'The body that would fit almost anything. Price new £75'.

Amongst the paperwork that came with the car, Rhys found the logbook and only then did he realise he had bought a Staniforth special, possibly his first. There was also a letter from Alan Staniforth to Peter Silverthorne dated March 1954 giving a potted history of SUG. To fund the costs, he sold 'LM9, the 1932 ex-works Aston Martin for £200'. It took 'nearly two years to build. No lathe, no electric drill, no welding gear or knowledge, and no heat in the garage. Finished in Spring 1954 just in time to find the first Lotus VI on the same grids'. It took part in at least 12 events, most race meetings but one speed trial and a rally! It was also taken on a holiday in France. Alan had no trailer so drove to and from all meetings. One such return trip from Oulton Park to Leeds was

undertaken with a broken crankshaft. The car was sold in the winter of 1955. Alan said: 'The new owner drove off in the snow and vanished with the car from my life totally, until you [Rhys Nolan, the present owner] rang.' In the 1980s the car passed from two brothers into the hands of a

The remains of SUG 55 being removed for restoration.

Buckler enthusiast, John Gough, who has recently died. Rhys Nolan heard about a Buckler for sale and went to view. He said:

Seeing the car surrounded by brambles and weeds, it was obviously still saveable, but it would be no small task. But after much deliberation I decided to purchase. So here we embark on a journey, from where it is now surrounded by brambles, to perhaps close to how it was when he used it for everything, rallies, races, hill climbs, and even on office duties in his employment as a journalist – also trips to France.

Someone who preferred to design his own chassis was Peter Whitaker who, whilst still at Nottingham University, built a most unusual special in the garage of his parents' home in Lincolnshire. The basis was a home designed and built tubular steel chassis. The suspension, steering, brakes and wheels came from an Austin 7. The engine was a 742cc Raleigh V twin air-cooled unit, formerly in a Raleigh Safety Seven three-wheeled van or car. The bodywork is unusually made out of sheets of Tufnol and there is not a curve on it. It was painted bright red and known as the PDW Special, or more usually 'The Red Car'. It was registered in Lincolnshire ECT 370. It had a top speed of around 45mph. Peter's son, Jeremy, can just remember having a ride in it, but it is thought by the family to have last run on the road in the early 1960s. Whenever the Whitakers moved house after this, they had to have a double garage with the PDW taking up half under cover of a tarpaulin. Peter died a few years ago and Jeremy has put the car into store.

Known as the PDW Special or just 'the red car'.

Soon after the war, a couple of enthusiasts were keen to get local motor sport going again. They were Harry Hopkinson, a garage owner from Eversley in North East Hampshire, and local engineer Jim Perry. On 10 January 1946 a meeting was held in Harry's local pub. Amongst those who were soon to join up were Bill Boddy who had guided *Motor Sport* through the war years and vet Holly Birkett, who was also involved with the 750 Motor Club. The now well-known Hants and Berks Motor Club was formed. In 1949 Harry Hopkinson decided to build a special, no doubt helped by Jim Perry, who was an expert welder. He chose an Austin 12 chassis into which he placed an 1,172cc Ford engine fitted with a Garrett supercharger. Garrett had started in business in 1936 and during the war made many cabin blowers for aircraft; this may be one of these. They are now famous for turbocharger technology. The car was known as the Ausford.

David Atkinson first saw the car 40 years ago, out of use. Harry told him that he would give him the car later. The 'later' was 20 years ago. It has been in store again ever since. Sadly Harry and his son John have died and as all paperwork has been lost, we know very little about the car except that it had been in store since 1954. David said he heard it had been raced but trialling was what it was best at, and it gained a number of trophies from 1950 to 1954. Whilst Harry drove it in trials, his daughter Molly did a few driving tests in it. There are two Club badges on the front, one for North West London Motor Club and the other the Hants and Berks Motor Club. David did say, 'I think it used to have double wheels at the rear and they were from an early Land Rover, but I do remember someone borrowing them and not returning them.' Now after 66 years of storage the car has been sold.

One of the problems with Specials is that the builder often does not write up his experiences and the background to the Special. Many years later when these cars turn up in the proverbial barn, it is very difficult to find out about their ancestry. Even more frustrating is finding a photograph of an interesting looking vehicle and knowing nothing about it. In this next case, as far as I know the car does not survive, but some very interesting drawings and a photograph do.

Austin Twelve chassis 1,172 Ford engine with a Garrett supercharger.

After forty years in store KNN 234 sees light of day.

The car gained a number of trophies in events between 1950 and 1954.

Motoring art collector Tony Clark has a fascinating pair of drawings plus a Polaroid photograph of a mystery sports car that he would like to identify. The drawings are dated 1957, from the Joseph Lucas styling department, and show a two-seater with headlights mounted on the bonnet, much like those of the Austin-Healey 'Frogeye' Sprite. These were bought at an H&H auction, and in the same lot was the small Polaroid print dated February 1958 and credited to Keystone Press Agency. The car in the photo has similar headlights but the rest of the design does not follow the drawings. It looks like a glass-fibre special, but the number plate is not legible and it is running on trade plates. Does anyone recognise the car? So far no one has come forward.

Unusual design feature; the headlights mounted on the bonnet.

Another view from the same batch of drawings.

Has the polaroid image any connection with the other two?

GN 312 is an Austin Seven Special with no history.

The 1950s and 1960s were the heyday of the home-built special. A whole industry quickly sprang up to supply those who wanted to build their own, usually sports, car, based on the Austin 7 or Ford 10 chassis. The builders were greatly encouraged by the 750 Motor Club and their very popular and successful 750 and 1172 racing events. Firms made modifications for the chassis, suspension and braking, many 'go faster' modifications for the engine and gearbox, and bodies in many styles made from aluminium or glass fibre. These specials were all homemade, often by people who made few, if any, notes of how or why they built them. Now some 50 or so years later some are coming out of the woodwork, and nothing is known about them.

Matthew Mason soon found this out after he bought such an Austin 7 Special at the annual 750 Motor Club's Austin 7 Rally at Beaulieu in 2016. All the dealer could tell him was that it came from the estate of a deceased owner in Scotland. Faintly discernible on the rear is the registration number GN 312, a London number from 1931 – presumably the original number on the Austin 7 road car that had been sacrificed to build the special. His special has the front wings bolted on to the brake drums so they swivel with the wheels, the engine has only a few go faster parts and has only one carburettor. The body is made of aluminium or Duralumin, the panels of which are crudely rolled around the steel tubular frame. The dashboard is made from an old road sign. No sooner had this story been published in *Classic and Sports Car* magazine than Matthew Mason received the following email from John McGrath:

The Austin 7 Special was part of my Uncle's estate. I sold three Austin 7s to Nigel Snow trading as Yorkshire Austin Seven Specialists in November 2015. As far as I know the special and a seven saloon were acquired by my Uncle some time in the 1980s. There was no paper work for the special. The saloon and the special were acquired when he lived in Ringwood in Hampshire. He moved to Blackpool in 1990…The cars were put into his very large garage and they never moved until I had to sell them.

Not all specials were sparse open two-seaters. Here is one that was built as a closed car. Peter

The Austin 7 Special being stored in Blackpool.

The car had been standing in the open for 25 years.

Not all specials were two seat open cars as can be seen by this one found in Belgium, which had the British registration number VTN 569.

Moens has come across a very unusual special in Belgium. It is an 1,172 Ford engined special which had the British registration VTN 569. This car, presumably the donor car, was registered on 22 February 1955. The continuation logbook from September 1970 records it as 'Rebuilt Ford Special [type] Hermes'. The keeper at the time was Christopher Wood of Glinton, Peterborough. We do not know when it was taken to Belgium. Peter Moens told me:

> The present vendor bought the car a few years ago with a view to restoring it. When he bought it, it had been standing in the open for some 25 years. He put it into dry storage in his own garage. He had other projects and it has stood there for some years. He now has an unseen move from his current house and this has made him put the car up for sale.

We do not know who the builder was, but he has not used one of the many body shells that used to be on the market. He has built the entire closed bodywork without incorporating any curves using just rivets and screws for fastening. It has certainly suffered during its time in the open.

It may surprise some people that an early special, when found in pretty poor condition, was deliberately not restored. On 7 June 1939 the Wiltshire War Agricultural Executive Committee took delivery of a new Morris 8 van registered CAM 325. No doubt this had a hard life during the war encouraging farmers to produce more food.

It was sold off in 1950 and an early owner was Alastair Stewart; it cost him £7. He really wanted an MG but could not afford one, so he decided to build the worn out van into a special. This was a very home-made special using panel work from a Chevrolet lorry for the body and also the instruments. It was completed in 1951. It was called 'Jamie' after a character in the film *Whisky Galore*. Alastair was now a young officer in the Highland Regiment and the car travelled many miles both in this country and Europe. On one occasion he had a head on crash with his Commanding Officer's Jeep which resulted in a redesign of the body to make it a little more rakish. In 1954 he got married to Donina and a more suitable car was acquired and the special was 'pushed to the back of a barn and forgotten about'. Alastair's son Lachie, with his father's

This Special, built in the early 1950s, was revived again in 1973.

help, got the car running again in 1973 so that Lachie could learn to drive on the farm land. It then went back into the barn again. For Alastair's 90th birthday in 2016, the car was retrieved, put into running order as a surprise for his father. Lachie joined the Morris Register and obtained a lot of help from them with the re-registering of this car with the DVLA. He has decided to just conserve the car as much as he found it. In this condition it has caused quite a stir at local rallies. This must be a very early example of the type of vehicle that started the post-war special building craze.

Not all specials were sparse. This one even has its own ventilation system. A one-off special, believed to be designed in 1967, has found the owner it deserves after so many years of languishing. Based on an Austin 1100, the Chambers Special was the brainchild of engineer Michael Chambers. It's an interesting car with some unusual features, among them rear seats that face backwards, a heating and ventilation system made to blow air through

eyelets in all four of the seats, doors with built-in armrests, safety locks and strengthening for side impact, plus a very clever adjustable steering column. The car was first registered in 1969, using the front and rear hydrolastic subframes of an Austin 1100, which were bonded into the one-piece

Based on an Austin 1100 the Chambers Special had some unusual features.

Now in fully running order and restored as an 'oily rag' Special.

bodywork. Even the heated seats came from the same mould. The 1,100 engine it originally used was equipped with used twin 150 Stromberg carburettors, although it comes with a 1,275cc unit now. The car was on the road until 1997 after which time it became derelict. It changed hands several times before Simon Pike bought it in December 2018, finding it needed some love. Unfortunately, the company which transported the car from Kent to Simon's place in Cheshire lost its rear hatchback door in transit. Simon, nevertheless, persists in believing that the Chambers Special deserves to be brought back to its former glory, and now plans to have a new rear door made.

The heating and ventilation system blew hot air though the seats.

After a production car had passed its first lease of life a few got converted into something else, the most common being the removal of aging bodywork and converting the car to a pick-up or flat back truck. This 1925 Morris Cowley had been converted into a tractor type vehicle many years ago and ended up with John Keeley at Knowle Hill where in 1985 it was spotted by Chris Acock who asked if it was for sale. It was not. Over the next twenty years he asked the same question and got the same answer. John Keeley died in 2004 but still his collection did not come up for sale. On the death of his widow, Cheffins held a grand sale which included the 'Cowley Garden Tractor', which Chris bought.

Quite a number of bits had gone missing since Chris had first seen it. It was missing the scuttle, radiator, and the cylinder head was loose. The pistons were seized and there was no magneto,

Quite a number of bits had gone missing since Chris Acock had first seen it.

carburettor or exhaust. An old gentleman came up to him after the sale and asked if Chris actually knew what he had bought! He told Chris that it had left the factory as a car in 1925 and for some reason was bought back by the Morris factory at a later date where it was used as a general tug towing trailers around the site. After the war it went to Lord Nuffield's estate where it was used to tow gang mowers to cut the grass. Later it passed to a scrap merchant called Passey from Wallingford and was sold to John Keeley. The first thing Chris did was to join the Bullnose Morris Club and through them found some very interesting and knowledgeable people to advise him on the rebuild. The tractor is now restored (Chris calls it a 'rustoration') and is road legal (BF 8146) and has attended a number of rallies where it caused great interest.

At the annual rally of Austin Sevens at Beaulieu in 2016 there was one which really caught my eye.

The Bullnose Morris tractor on its way to a car rally.

It was a 1932 Austin 7 saloon (originally) that had been converted into a pick-up/tipper light truck. This may not sound so different from any number of cars converted for agricultural use once their useful road use was over. In this case, however, it had been engineered in such a way that the driver sat over the engine facing backwards, or so it would seem. However, the whole car had been reversed. The back axle was now the non-steering front axle and supported the tipping pick-up section, whilst the front wheels were now at the back, but were still the steered wheels, i.e., the car had rear wheel steering. Very little is known of the history of the vehicle other than it was converted for use on a market garden on Mersea Island on the Essex coast, south of Colchester. It had been brought along by the Austineers of Bradford-on-Avon.

Another Austin Seven conversion I was intrigued by came from New Zealand whereby a pick-up type

Very unusual Austin Seven converted for agricultural use.

of vehicle had been made from an Austin Seven but it had been converted to four-wheel drive. Ken Cooke of the 750 Motor Club told me:

It is definitely powered by a late-model Austin Seven engine with an angled manifold, enabling a downdraught carburettor to be fitted. It also has a much-modified chassis. The hubs and the wheels are Austin Seven and the driveshafts are enclosed. The swing-axle front suspension is on coil springs with telescopic dampers. The rear suspension

Probably unique, an Austin Seven with four wheel drive.

features a kind of subassembly that is suspended on large inboard coil springs. I have never seen anything like it.

The only thing that was missing was a slogan sticker on it which should have said 'The smallest 4x4 by far'.

Large old cars are the most popular for rebuilding as commercial vehicles. Such conversions these days are nearly always rebuilt back to original form with reproduction coachwork. In the USA a 1929 Packard 645 with straight 8 motor in the form of a tow truck was offered for sale. It came complete with crane. No details were given of its history, but it is assumed it was converted in the late 1930s or the 1940s. It is lettered out for the Centerport Auto Service of Long Island. It is known to have been stored for some 50 years. I do hope that this is restored as a breakdown lorry – it would cause a great stir on the rally fields as these conversions are now so rare.

When constructing a two-seat sports car special you had the choice of making an ash frame and panelling it yourself or buying an off-the-shelf body which was often made of aluminium or fibreglass. The four Walklett Brothers were agricultural engineers from Woodbridge in Suffolk. After building a Wolseley Hornet special, they experimented with

1929 Packard 645 converted into a breakdown truck.

a car of their own. From this beginning grew the Ginetta Car Company we have today. Very early on they started experimenting with fibreglass and one of the first bodies (1958) they offered for sale was called a Fairlite. This was made to fit the Ford 8 and 10 chassis. Later, this body was developed into the Ginetta G3 and the G4. It is thought that more than 25 Fairlite bodies were made and only one is currently known to the Ginetta Owners Club.

Ginetta enthusiast Scott Baillie from Kinghorn in Fife, a G21 owner of 30 years and previous G32 owner, and one time Club representative for Scotland, was looking for a retirement project and found one only ten miles from home. It was a very derelict Fairlite bodied special on a Standard Light 12 chassis with 1,608cc Standard engine as was eventually marketed to William Lyons for use in his Jaguar SSII sports car. The donor car KS 6969 was registered in Roxburgh on 13 February 1936. It then had a number of owners in Scotland before reaching James Craig of Buckhaven, Fife, who appears to have owned it at the time of the conversion in 1959. It is known to have been taxed in 1960. Scott told me, 'The lady who owned it until about a year ago is the daughter of the last registered keeper and cannot remember the car ever being on the road.' She said she remembered it

'being used as a firewood store for 30 years'. There are some pictures of it when on the road, presumably in 1960, which clearly show the radiator as being cut into the front of the car and the bonnet missing, which Scott told me 'was still missing'! He went on to say that the engine had sat for 40 years with no plugs having obviously suffered from frost damage to the aluminium head.

In more modern times, specials have become more sophisticated. Here is an unusual example which had reached the running stage in 2002 but

Ginetta Fairlite body shell on a Standard Light twelve chassis last taxed in 1960.

still awaits completion. After Reliant took over Bond in 1971 they had ideas for a four wheeled sports car based on the Bond Bug. Ray Wiggins of Reliant approached BRM to ask if they would design a new ohc aluminium cylinder head to fit on the Reliant engine. It was found it could not be of cross flow design because of the positioning of the studs in the Reliant block. The cylinder heads were made by Coventry Climax Ltd. BRM modified six engines for a sports car that was never produced. Presumably because they did not get paid, BRM directed these engines to be destroyed and four were, but two remained in store. Here they stayed until around 1982 when a Mr Parker (navigator Mr Newby) approached Reliant with the idea of running a Reliant Kitten in the Monte Carlo Rally. The possible publicity attracted Reliant to the idea, and they gave him a new Kitten and the two BRM engines. In the 1983 Monte Carlo Rally, the Reliant retired when a con rod came through the side of the engine.

In 1992 Mike Webster of Braishfield in Hampshire bought the rights to the Bond Bug (and the Bond name) and reproduced it in four wheel kit form as the WMC (Webster Motor Company) or Webster Bug. He had open and closed versions. When exhibiting at the 1993 International Kit Car Show he met a man who told him he had one of the Reliant BRM engines and the unique BRM

parts of a second, asking if he would be interested in purchasing. This man also owned the Monte Carlo Kitten. Mike was able to buy the two engines and the Kitten as well. At this time Mike had been trying to purchase the Berkeley Bandit prototype, but it was not for sale so he decided he would make his own Bandit based on a Bond car and call it a Bond Bandit. After all, it was Lawrie Bond who designed the original Berkeley cars. The body shell was based on a slightly lengthened and slightly widened Berkeley 4-wheeler to fit on a Bond chassis. Into this car was fitted the Reliant BRM engine and it got to the stage where the car was running and driving but needed finishing. Then in 2002 he was able to buy the Berkeley Bandit prototype, and work on the other Bond Bandit stopped. He still has the car with the BRM engine in store. The

The very rare Reliant/BRM engine.

The Bond Bandit Special made by Mike Webster with Reliant/BRM engine.

second engine he built up using a new block and crankcase, together with the original BRM parts, and sold it some years later. It was last heard of in a Tempest kit car.

Mike Webster's name crops up again in this story. In the 1950s, Berkeley's of Biggleswade were one of the largest producers of caravans in this country. They were pioneers in the use of fibreglass in their construction. Lawrie Bond approached them to produce a new four wheeled front wheel drive car of his design. The idea of car manufacture appealed to the Directors as it meant they had full employment in the summer, when caravan building was slackest. When the Austin Healey Sprite appeared at the 1958 Motor Show Berkeley knew it would be strong competition, so they commissioned John Tojeiro to design a fibreglass sports car to rival the Sprite. Tojeiro planned to use the new 997cc 105E Ford engine. With a rush the first prototype of the car, now called the 'Bandit', was shown at the 1961 Show and registered 700 CNM. But it was too late as the caravan business hit recession which dragged the car company down as well. Two prototypes had been made; number 2 has we think been lost, but number 1 survives. This car has never been fully completed as it has no hood or side screens. I have been told that John Tojeiro was not happy with the rear suspension he had designed, but he had no time to alter it. The car which survived has been crashed twice, possibly it is thought due to a suspension fault. After the first crash it was bought from a scrapyard and rebuilt. It crashed again in 1965 and was restored again in the 1980s by Bernie Pearson, some new panels being made in a film company's special effects department. In 1998 it was sold to Neil Berber of Bristol who completed the restoration. Mike Webster, who was then running an Anzani engined four wheeled Berkeley, bought it in 2002. It has been stored in the back of his garage since then. It was last taxed for the road some 20 years ago.

Not all sports car specials were small. Sir Thomas Sopwith was Chairman of Hawker Siddeley; his son Tommy worked within the organisation at Armstrong Siddeley. Tommy built a hybrid sports-racing special at the factory. The chassis was from an Allard JR and had De Dion rear suspension and was fitted with a hot 3.4 litre Armstrong Siddeley Sapphire engine. It had a very modern looking body, somewhat like the

The interior of the Berkeley Bandit.

The 1960 Berkeley Bandit prototype in store with Mike Webster.

Aston Martin DBR1. Racing under the 'Equipe Endeavour' name, Tommy Sopwith had a number of successes with this car in 1954, racing it at 17 different events. At the end of the season, he turned to saloon car racing. In the late 1950s the car, less engine, was sold to Privateer Brian Croot who fitted a race tuned Jaguar 3.8 litre engine. He competed successfully with this car, a C type Jaguar, and also an Allard. He stopped racing around 1970. Croot sold the Sphinx to Paul Weldon who planned to race it. He brought it to the Allard Owners Club concours held near Newbury on 14 September 1980. The Club magazine reported on the fully restored Sphinx '… very

Tommy Sopwith had a number of racing successes with 'The Sphinx' in the 1950s.

well restored with smart navy and white paint-work … it won best open Allard'. It later disap-peared and was rumoured to be in France. Later it appeared at Dragone Auctions at Westport, Connecticut, USA.

One of the saddest cases I have written about in recent years was the fate of the Timbs Special. I am grateful to Geoffrey Hacker for drawing my atten-tion to Norman Timbs who was a prolific engineer. He had worked on numerous Indianapolis race cars including the Blue Crown Spark Plug specials which had won the famous race three years run-ning. He became an expert on ground effects in America. In the late 1940s, just for his own amuse-ment, he had built an astonishing-looking road going special. Into the chassis was fitted a 1947 Buick straight 8 engine, mounted behind the cock-pit. Front suspension was simple Ford beam axle whilst at the rear it was independent swing axle. Inspired by the pre-war Auto Union streamliners he constructed a two-seat roadster body that had no interruptions to the sweeping body line. The 17.5ft body was in aluminium, made and welded by Emil Diedt. The paint finish was a gold flaked maroon. For its time it must have been a real show stopper.

By 1950 it had been sold and was used in an advertisement for a restaurant, later passing into the hands of a film prop buyer. By 1997 it was owned by Stan Carter, a collector living in the Dry Lakes area and storing his cars in the open as there was little rain. Soon after he died, the car was offered for sale at a Barrett-Jackson auction at the Peterson Museum in 2002. It was in a dilapidated condition with many parts missing.

The plywood buck for the body shell of the Timbs Special.

The car was stored in the open in the Dry Lakes area.

It was bought by Gary Cerveny of Malibu. Gary managed to trace Timbs' son who had a scrap-book of articles and photographs. Custom Autos of Loveland, Colorado, made a magnificent job of the restoration and the car appeared at the Amelia Island Concours in 2010 and Pebble Beach two years later. In November 2018 a forest fire swept through parts of Malibu and one house that was destroyed was that of Gary Cerveny, along with his collection of 76 one-off custom cars, race cars and others. Gary has since decided to restore four of the burned cars including two Rolls-Royce Silver Ghosts and the Timbs streamliner. As the previ-ous restorers had gone out of business, Gary had recruited Rex Rogers who had previously worked for them on the streamliner's first rebuild. When completed I am sure it will again wow the onlook-ers at the shows.

By contrast this car really ought to be included as an example of coachbuilding but it is so bizarre I have termed it as a special. Immediately after the war, three friends, all with previous connections to BMW, got together to found Veritas, whose cars were at first all sports racing cars and in those early post-war years, very successful. Customers asked them for road cars and these were made from 1950 onwards with BMW running gear, lightweight tubular chassis and coupe, roadster or cabrio-let coachwork by Spohn of Ravensburg. Pre-war Spohn (founded in 1920) had mainly built bodies for Maybach and some for Mercedes-Benz. After 78 had been built Veritas, even with full order books, could not raise sufficient cash, and went out of business. Servicemen based in Germany with their American cars started taking them to Spohn to be customised. Spohn interpreted American trends in a particularly extravagant manner

Custom Autos of Loveland, Colorado, made a magnificent job of restoring the Timbs Special. Eight years later it had been all but destroyed in a forest fire.

displaying great fins, vents and layers of chrome. Halwart Schrader, writing the Spohn entry in the *Beaulieu Encyclopaedia of Coachbuilding*, wrote '… which they [the owners] got in the form of baroque caricature of one of the best names German coach-building once had to offer'.

The first owner of the 1950 Veritas SP90 chassis 5089 ordered his car with a cabriolet body in blue. Within a year or so an owner took it back to Spohn for a complete rebuild which featured extensive modifications including huge fins and a rebuilt front end. A returning serviceman shipped the car to the USA in the 1950s and kept it until 1965 when he sold it to R.J. Mrofka. The new owner could not get the inline 6 cylinder engine to run properly, gave up and sold it to his friend, Lee Hartung of Glenview, Illinois.

I had been introduced to Lee Hartung c2004 by friend David Kerr of Chicago. Lee Hartung, then in his early 80s, was a heavily bearded eccentric

1950 Veritas chassis fitted with a Spohn body.

'Huge fins and a rebuilt front end.'

who had been collecting for over 50 years. I wrote this collection up for *Classic and Sports Car* in June 2003. He had around 100 cars on show. The problem was some of them could not be seen for the amount of interesting stuff piled on top of them. In this collection was the Veritas. It had not run since he had obtained it in 1965 and was almost invisible, only those distinctive tailfins sticking out. Hartung knew all about Veritas and its Spohn

body and told us it was 26ft long, but we had no means of estimating as we could not find the front! This was one of the most interesting collections of unrestored cars I have ever seen. Sadly, Hartung died and his collection was sold in 2011 in a three day auction. At the time of writing, Mark Hyman of St. Louis is the temporary custodian of this car having been asked to sell it on behalf of the collector who had purchased it at the Hartung sale. It had joined a collection of mainly unrestored cars, the owner only getting it roadworthy, leaving the bodywork as bought, still with some Hartung dust on it!

The eccentric Lee Hartung.

When in the Hartung Collection this is all that could be seen of the Spohn car.

# ROLLS-ROYCE

Even Rolls-Royce cars wear out and something has to be done with them at the end of their life. Most Rolls-Royces have been owned by wealthy people who may have surplus space where they can just park up the old Rolls and it stays there until the estate is eventually sold up. It was not unusual for the more formal bodied early versions to have a body changed later in life. Perhaps the original body needed repair or was just looking out of date, but the car was mechanically sound. There were companies such as the Southern Motor Company of London who advertised new bodies to refresh old Rolls-Royces. During the Second World War, many were donated to the war effort or were requisitioned, and were turned into vehicles such as ambulances and NAAFI wagons, and then came back on the market after hostilities were over; some, as we shall see, being rebuilt as shooting brakes. From the historian's point of view, many of the Rolls-Royce build records have survived and are in the hands of the Rolls-Royce Enthusiasts' Club. Every time a spare part was bought from a Rolls dealer or repairs were done at the factory, these facts were noted, and because of this it is often possible to find out the names of many of the previous owners.

John Fasal is probably the world authority on the 40/50hp Rolls-Royce, particularly the Edwardian ones. His book, written with the late Bryan Goodman, *The Edwardian Rolls-Royce* (self-published in 1994) lists every chassis produced in this period at Derby, with a history of each. When he wrote the book, he did not own one of the cars – he just dreamed of owning one. On 19 May 1994 he received a phone call from Michael Sapsford of Pevensey. 'I thought you might be interested in a

project.' He had for sale a farm trailer consisting of a Rolls-Royce Silver Ghost chassis, front axle and front wheels. It had no markings on it – but John knew that as it was a ladder frame it must be pre-August 1911, so he bought it. Then started a massive hunt, first for clues that might determine which chassis it was and then for the parts required. The chassis had many holes drilled in it as evidence of a number of changes of specification and body. The rusted torque tube bracket told him it was post-1400 series and before 1500, the positioning of the radiator mounts narrowing the field down to 150 chassis. Holes in the cross members showed it had a 'C' rake steering column, so it was from an open car. More research revealed it could have only been chassis 1419. This chassis went on test in September 1910 and was retained by the Derby factory as their demonstrator car, known then as a 'trials' car. This carried a side entrance 4 seater body, very similar to the London 'Trials' car which has Barker Roi-des-Belges coachwork. John made the interesting comment that whilst many of the Rolls-Royces sold in this country were closed examples, those customers coming from warmer

Previously used as a farm trailer, this chassis proved to be from a unique Rolls-Royce.

This picture from a Rolls-Royce brochure shows the London trials car which was very similar.

climes wanted an elegant open car and the Roi-des-Belges style was ideal for them, hence the fitting of this type of coachwork on the 'trials' cars.

In February 1912 the factory sold the car in chassis form to Charles Braun whose address was *The Car Illustrated*, 168 Piccadilly, London W. This was the offices of the society motoring magazine edited by Lord John Montagu, the grandfather of the present Lord Montagu. Charles Braun was the Director of the Publishing Company in 1912 and 1913. He had Holland and Holland build him a 4 seat tourer body and the car was re-registered LD 4740. In 1917 it passed to Captain Beresford Horsley of Chislehurst. It was known that soon it had been rebodied and was now licenced LL6348. Between 1929 and 1933 it passed through a number of members of the Horsley family in Kent. There is then a complete gap in its history until 1988 when Frank Bates of Smarden sold it as a trailer to Kevin Town of Egerton. Rolls-Royce Enthusiast Club member Brian Thompson recognised it as a Ghost chassis and bought it for £50 in May 1994, selling it on to Michael Sapsford and then to John Fasal. This is not the place to tell the story of the long and very detailed restoration save to say it took some fourteen years. John has kept a very detailed record of the restoration, every detail being photographed and the date of the picture noted. Throughout the reconstruction, John has paid particular attention to using as many period parts as possible or remade items to the same specification. He told me, 'It drives you nuts to be

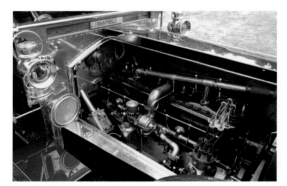

A detailed record of all the work was kept.

a perfectionist.' When I first saw the completed car John pointed out a small plug under the switch box on the dashboard. He said it was for a sat nav! He explained why. 'With the amount of petrol this car uses you cannot afford to get lost.' I am so glad he retains his sense of humour after 14 years of restoring what is thought to be the fiftieth oldest Rolls-Royce 40/50.

In Poland, Zbigniew Krystowczyk owns a 1926 Rolls-Royce Phantom 1 chassis which has not been on the road for 40, or maybe more, years. It was bought new by Ernest Broadhurst of Tootal, Broadhurst and Lee, cotton, silk and wool manufacturers of Newton Heath. Tootal is a name that is still well known in the trade and is now part of the Coats Viyella Group. The Broadhurst family were good customers of Rolls-Royce before the last war, owning five from 1910 onwards. Chassis 56SC was fitted with an enclosed drive limousine

The restoration of a 1910 Rolls-Royce Silver Ghost took fourteen years.

body by Hooper. Unusually for this date, it had steel artillery wheels. In 1936 it was bought by dentist William Croll of London W1, and later in the 1930s it had joined the funeral fleet of A. Cain of Hanwell. It is believed that at some later date the car was converted into a hearse.

The history hereon is unknown until 1967 when it was owned by David E.C. Roberts of Teddington. At some stage the car was partly rebuilt with a tourer frame, and it was in this state when seen by Andre Blaize at the Rolls-Royce Enthusiasts' Club rally in Kelmarsh Hall in June 2009. Andre Blaize has done much of the research on this car. Zbigniew purchased the car much in this condition in 2015. He told me:

I have a theory [that] the frame was made of some tropical hard wood and had never been completed. The wood was only roughly finished, it would not have been possible to fit aluminium panels on it … when I got it in 2015 it was critically rotten and in my opinion has never been finished. And moreover, the chassis had been badly stored out of doors and suffered from exposure to UK weather.

Zbigniew is a keen Rolls-Royce enthusiast and had every intention of restoring the chassis and building a body for it. However, his other car is a Brewster bodied Phantom II which he has found required much more work than he at first thought, so the P1 chassis has to go to pay for these repairs.

The Rolls-Royce as seen by Andre Blaize in 2009.

1926 Rolls-Royce stripped ready for a rebuild.

As is well known, pre-war Rolls-Royce chassis were sent to outside coachbuilders for their bodywork; in this way very few are exactly the same. One such coachbuilder was Hill and Boll of Yeovil, Somerset. They were a typical provincial coachbuilder founded c1838. The first car they bodied was the Petter of 1895 - some say this is Britain's first car. Petter were well known as engine manufacturers but decided not to get involved with the motor car and the rights were transferred to Hill and Boll who made around 12 cars, some of which were electric. They made car bodies until 1930.

In 1928, Hubert J. Lawrence of West Lavington in Wiltshire, a local landowner who owned West Park Farm and dairy, purchased a 1928 Rolls-Royce Phantom 1 chassis. He sent this to Hill and Boll and had a Coupe de Ville body built on it. It is known he used it sparingly. It is believed he still owned the car in the 1940s, but its history is lost until bought by William Cross in Oakland, California, in 1971. With him it only had light use and was put into storage. Recently it has been removed from hiding. It is in a lovely used condition, almost all original, even down to Barker style dipping headlamps and the original Wiltshire registration plate MW 5172 front and rear.

Who on earth would buy two absolute top of the range road cars and insist that they came without headlights? The answer is Frenchman Armand Esders who made his fortune in the ready to wear clothing business with shops all over Europe and beyond. He claimed he did not want to drive at night. He is best known as the owner of the second Bugatti Royale to be built whose roadster coachwork was designed for him by Jean Bugatti – a later owner had it re-bodied as a Coupe de Ville by Henri Binder, with headlights.

The other car was a Rolls-Royce Phantom II chassis which he ordered from the stand of the coachbuilders Letourneur et Marchand at the Paris Salon in 1931. This company had been founded in 1905 by two former craftsmen from the firm of Henri Binder. They tended to specialise in top of the market cars. Armand Esders ordered a very

Unusually, the coachwork of this 1928 Phantom One is from Hill & Boll of Yeovil.

This turned out to be a very original car.

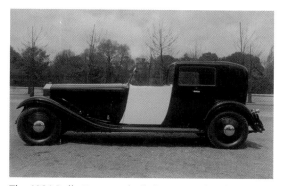

The 1931 Rolls-Royce as built for Armand Esders.

special Coupe de Ville coachwork. The car was of perfect and discreet elegance. It was in polished black paint with ivory driver's door. It had no headlamps, no visible door hinges, no outsider door handles or windows on the driver's doors. There was a central handle on the passenger door (a Letourneur et Marchand patent), no chrome, no bumpers and no spare wheel and no mascot was ordered. The inside was discreet luxury. The car took part in a few Concours d'Elegance events in the 1930s. It was sold in the late 1930s to an owner who had it modified into a four door limousine by

As rebuilt in 1938 in a more conventional form.

covering the driver's compartment. This modification is thought to have been done in 1938 as this is the date on the windscreen glass. By chance the original door locks were reused and the original low roof was covered by a slightly higher roofline. It is known to have been owned by the same family from 1965 until 2004, when it was discovered by French enthusiast Mario Montanaro. It had not been used for decades and failed to sell at an Osenat auction in 2004. Recently Christoph Grohe from Switzerland had the opportunity to acquire it and soon started to rebuild it back to original specification. The lower roof of the original cabin was hidden under the higher roof of the limousine. This renovation was completed in time for the car to appear on his stand at Retromobile in Paris.

The lower roof of the original cabin was hidden under higher roof of the limousine.

Malcolm Richardson from Perth, Australia, already has two Rolls-Royces but has now added a third. This is a 1933 Rolls-Royce Phantom II limousine which was recently sold at a Shannon's Auction in Sydney. It has an interesting history. It started out as a demonstrator for Car Mart Ltd of Park Lane, London. The car had been bodied by Thrupp and Maberly with an elegant sports saloon body complete with twin spare wheels at the rear taking up much of the boot space. It was registered in London ALB 900. It was bought by Lady Rachel MacRobert, an American who had married wealthy Sir Alexander MacRobert, a Scottish businessman. In 1920, he had founded the British India Company which made textiles for both civilian and armed forces use.

In April 1940 a replacement logbook was issued to Eduard Knox of Merton, London SW19, which

1933 Rolls-Royce Phantom Two with elegant sports saloon coachwork.

clearly stated that it was by now a hearse. Knox kept the car until 1964. The logbook shows that the body was later altered to that of a saloon, but unfortunately the date is not clearly stamped. It is recorded that Rolls-Royce checked it over in 1964 prior to it being sold to its most recent owner who was then living in Bangor, North Wales. There is a record of the cost being £350 and the seller was Alpe and Saunders. This firm, previously Wylder of Kew, as well as selling Rolls-Royce and Bentley post-war, was better known for making bodies for hearses. It is almost certain that they re-bodied this car with the rather sombre limousine style that it has at present.

The Wales-based owner then moved to Sydney in 1969 taking the car with him on the SS *Alaric*. He went to live in Randwick in Sydney and he had the idea of running a wedding hire business with the car, but this came to naught. By the 1980s it was placed on axle stands in a purpose built brick garage and there it stayed until his recent death.

In 1922 Rolls-Royce introduced the 20hp model to be a cheaper, simpler car more suitable for owner drivers. It was very successful and in 1929 was improved with a larger capacity engine to become the 20/25. One such chassis of 1934 is listed as going to Barker and Co. for coachwork for a Miss Mills. The first owner recorded in the car records held by the RREC is that of Mrs Griffiths Hughes of Battle, the only other recorded owner being G. Crump of Holland Park Avenue, London W11 in July 1961. The car was registered AYO 402 and the coachwork was a Barker Sedanca de Ville. I have heard from Peter Sorensen from Denmark. He told me:

In 1972 my father heard about a Rolls-Royce 20 which had been imported into Denmark from England in 1965 by a young man who was studying in Hjoerring, northern Jutland. The car was stored in a garage in the city. When the young man travelled back to his

It is thought the car was rebodied by Alpe & Saunders.

home in Zealand he left the car in Hjoerring. My father had contacted him asking if he was interested in selling the car. Unfortunately, my father died before he saw the car.

Peter decided he would buy the car in memory of his father. He was at the time in no position to repair and run a Rolls-Royce so he: 'placed it in [a warehouse] on blocks – and the engine was preserved'. It has been there for 45 years. In 2017 he decided to part with it and 'with new tyres, new exhaust and mounting of indicator lights, the car was MOT tested and registered on Danish plates.'

A quick look at the pictures of this 'barn find' condition Rolls-Royce might give the impression that restoration might not be too complicated but that is not the case! This 1938 Rolls-Royce 25/30 chassis left the works in January 1938 and was driven to their London dealer H.R. Owen. It was not uncommon for body-less chassis to be driven from the factory to the dealer or coachbuilder. The delivery drivers were a hardy bunch sitting high up on a bare chassis with virtually no weather protection and certainly no seat belts. After delivery they were often to be seen hitching a lift back to the factory clutching their trade plates. This chassis was then sent to J. Gurney Nutting

1934 Rolls-Royce 20 in store in Hjoerring in Jutland.

The car was finally taken out of store in 2017 after forty-five years out of use.

of Chelsea who built a very striking 2-door fixed head coupe body on it. In May 1938, it was sold to Sir Herbert Smith of Witley Court in Worcestershire, and quickly passed to A. Harley of Southport five months later. He kept it throughout the war passing it to Clifford Martland of Rufford in 1945 and ten months later to J.W. Jeary of Birmingham. The rest of the history is a most interesting mystery. It has a Puerto Rican licence disc on it for 1976 and we do not know when it went to that country or when it came back. Hans Compter from New Zealand, well known for sending many old car finds to Europe and the UK, has bought it. He told me:

It is in very original and complete condition with the exception of the seats which I suspect could still be in use in somebody's beach house in Puerto Rica. What is most remarkable about the car's condition is that all the aluminium body panels and mudguards are in near mint condition without any corrosion but that the structural wooden frame has been almost totally gobbled up by the larvae of very hungry and voracious longhorn beetles. I have never seen anything like it in my nearly 60 years in the hobby!

The car is now at Hans Compter's European facility at Eibergen in the Netherlands.

I know from my own experience talking to a number of frame makers and coach makers that one of the most difficult jobs is to make a frame to fit existing panels, even on an open car – on a closed one, even harder. Here is a real challenge for

somebody. This is not the first time I have heard about woodwork being eaten away by termites. On the island of Tortola in the British Virgin Isles, Tony Robinson went exploring at Smugglers Cove whilst the rest of the family went swimming. He found a derelict Rolls-Royce 20 standing in a dried-up swamp. I wrote at the time, 'The amazing thing about the car was that termites had eaten every scrap of the woodwork so that all the body panels had fallen off. This included the dashboard which resulted in the instruments hanging on the end of their wires or cables.'

Adolfo Massari of Luxury Brokers International commented to me, 'The most interesting and unusual finds tend to come when you least expect it.' They had recently moved their operation to a new facility in Philadelphia. One morning a stranger pulled up, obviously having seen the activity of moving all the cars from the old warehouse. He asked if they (Adolfo Massari and Andrew Mastin) wanted to see an old car. Andrew takes up the story:

We followed him for two blocks where he stopped in front of a 1950s warehouse, walked in, shook a few hands, and were then blown away. In front of us, stationary for 30 years plus, was a dusty old 1937 Rolls-Royce Wraith Sedanca by Windovers, reportedly one of only three made … the car was owned by the warehouse owner's father since the 1950s when he purchased it from Inskip in New York [Rolls-Royce importers] … unfortunately, later he fell ill and the car was put away.

Whilst this 1938 25/30 Rolls-Royce just looks like a barn find, its wooden frame has been entirely eaten by wood-boring beetles.

Thirty years of storage for this 1937 Rolls-Royce Wraith, body by Windhover.

We turned to Philip Hall of the Rolls-Royce Enthusiasts' Club to see if they knew anything more. Philip told us:

> WKC1 is not a 1937 car but one of the very last Wraiths to be built in 1939. It was shipped to New York in October 1939 [after war had been declared] and sold via the agent J.S. Inskip, to Mrs Marie K. Schofield of 930 Fifth Avenue. No subsequent change of ownership was recorded by Rolls-Royce, but Bernard King's book shows it being owned by someone named Andrews in 1997.

The advertisement for the stock of the Real Car Company of Bethesda, North Wales will be known to many readers. They specialise in selling Rolls-Royce and Bentley. They have a very efficient agent in the United States who finds quite a number of cars for them, and not all of them are left-hand drive. After the Second World War there was a spate of selling old Rolls-Royce cars from this country to the United States and I suspect some of those coming back went out at the time of this selling spree. A new 1925 Rolls-Royce 20hp chassis was ordered by Mrs F. Eleanor Dixon, a wealthy American lady living in a large Tudor style mansion. She sent it to Brewster and Co. of New York for a handsome landaulet body to be fitted. In 1912 she had married Fitz Eugene Dixon, a wealthy banker and captain of the USA Davis Cup Team. In that same year her father and brother had both been lost in the *Titanic* disaster, whilst her mother was rescued in a lifeboat and survived. The Rolls-Royce records show that she still owned the car in 1938 but nothing more is known of the car until 1964 when it was owned by Joseph A. Benoit. He sold it in 1969 but there is no record again until 1976 when it belonged to William Higgins Jr. He is known to have run the car for a few years before selling it to a dealer in South Carolina. The dealer decided it needed a restoration and I was told that 'he dismantled various parts and removed the body causing quite a lot of damage, including breaking the frame at the A-posts around the windscreen'. At this point, he sold the car in pieces in around 1980 to Douglas and Mary White, who had every intention of restoring the car properly. However, the Whites, who were members of both the Rolls-Royce Owners' Club (of America) and

1925 Rolls-Royce 20 with Brewster coachwork as sold to Douglas & Mary White.

the Rolls-Royce Enthusiasts' Club, got side tracked by Silver Ghosts. The 20hp was then stored at the back of their heated garage for some 40 years. In 2018 they sold the car to The Real Car Company. John Milan from Devon purchased it from them and has sent the car to Ben Smith Engineering of Okehampton for a restoration back to original condition.

Brewster of New York can trace their carriage building back to 1810 but started making car

The car about to leave for Ben Smith Engineering.

bodies in 1905. When Rolls-Royce of America was set up in 1919 Brewster was one of their favoured coachbuilders. This car was the only Brewster landaulet fitted on a 20hp chassis and one of the last bodies built by Brewster before they were taken over by and incorporated into Rolls-Royce of America.

Another car that the Real Car Company shipped back to this country was a 1937 Rolls-Royce 25/30 3-position drop head coupe by Barker. According to the Rolls-Royce build cards, this car left them in March 1937 for the coachbuilders. The first owner was Miss Monica Soulas in Buenos Aires. However, the car returned to the United Kingdom in June 1939 when it was bought by Mabel Mlinaric of Twickenham and registered DUL 592. It was last taxed in 1971 when Ms Mlinaric sold the car to William B. Duff Jr. of West Redding, Connecticut, for £6,000. Its use in America is not recorded but relatively soon after it arrived the engine was taken to pieces and has never been re-assembled. It is unusual to find fine

coachwork in this configuration and its overall originality makes it a very desirable car. It would appear to still have its original interior and paint. It came with its original guarantee and the receipt from Ms Mlinaric as well as the 1971 tax disc still on the car.

October 1971, the last year in which the car ran in the UK.

The 1937 Rolls-Royce 25/30 drophead as purchased by the Real Car Company's agent in the USA.

1928 Rolls-Royce 20hp being prepared by Chris McPheat for its first run.

Here is a car that fits in the 'oily rag' description. In October 2013 auctioneers H&H included in their Duxford sale no less than 13 Rolls-Royce and Bentley cars which had come from the collection of Ken Britton from Leicestershire. For many years most of these had been stored in the open, stripped of some parts, and had deteriorated badly. Some were just chassis. Even so, they brought in £290,000 in total. One at least had been kept undercover, a 1928 Rolls-Royce 20hp Weymann style body by Hooper. The first owner was Sir Bruce Thomas of Rutland Court in London who took delivery of it on 24 December 1928. From this we can deduce it was a Christmas present. It was first registered XV 9146. On 18 November 1953 it was bought from the original owner by Shane Chichester. He was previously an Inspection Engineer at Rolls-Royce. He had joined the company in 1913. At this time, the number was changed to EOC 888. Ten years later it passed to his son, Oscar.

At the H&H sale there were many people looking around the car, but few bidders in the afternoon and it was bought by Chris McPheat for a customer who had seen the possibility of it being used as an 'oily rag' car. Since the sale, Chris has

been right through the car and believes it is very original. All the oiling nipples (except one) were there, which he told me was very unusual. It came with a trunk mounted on the luggage rack in which are three fitted suitcases. The original upholstery was all there. The fabric of the roof had been neatly repaired in a couple of places. The fabric body was sound and paint patinated with age. Chris cleaned out the bottom of the engine and rebuilt the carburettor and it now runs sweetly. When I saw it, it was being prepared for its first test run on the road.

Alan Milbank retired from the motor trade in Surrey and moved to the Isle of Wight in 1996 where he wrote and published his motoring autobiography *Another Set of Wheels* in 2010. Previously in 1984 when on holiday on the Isle of Wight, he spotted a 1929 Rolls-Royce 20hp 'in an open fronted stable/coach house at the end of a private drive some 100 metres from the sea front'. After moving to the Island, he frequently checked that the car was still there, though it was not until 2009 that he was allowed to inspect it closely. At that time the elderly owner, Colin Peckham, had died but even so, the family did not want to sell.

In October 2015 they told Alan they had changed their mind and how should they go about selling it? Alan gave them the name of a few dealers and auction houses, but they did not really want to follow that route, they were keen for it to stay on the Island and asked Alan if he would like it. Alan was not sure if he wanted 'another set of wheels'. The family told him the car's history. 'The two children recall them being taken out in the Rolls, together with two large dogs and often bales of hay on the rear luggage rack to feed the horses.' They went on to tell Alan that it had been used to take the two of them to the local church for their weddings in 1978 and 1986. In the latter case it was discovered the car had a petrol problem and a Seagull outboard motor petrol tank was fixed up under the bonnet to supply the carburettor by gravity. Externally it looked in poor condition due to its exposure to sea air, but Alan took a risk and bought it.

Originally it was bodied by Connaught with a coupe body. The first owner was L.H. Crake of Plymouth. He sold the car in late 1934 to T.E. Metcalf of Wroughton in Wiltshire. At this time, it is thought that it was re-registered in Devon as OD 9816, presumably because the first owner wanted to keep the original number. By 1946 it was owned by D.A. Collis of London W8. In around 1956 it was purchased by Colin Peckham and soon taken to Yarmouth on the Isle of Wight. At some stage in its life, it was re-bodied with its present tourer body, four seats, plus two occasional seats. It is believed that this Hooper body had come from a 1929 Rolls-Royce 20/25. The body has a supplier's plate on it, Paddon Bros of London. We do not know when or why the body change took place.

Alan described the state of the car as purchased:

The tyres were almost flat. The starting handle was bent in attempts to turn over the seized engine. Rats had nested in the body and there were skeletons present. The Barker dipping headlight mechanism was seized. The leather of the seat squabs was split with horsehair protruding. The paintwork had lifted over areas of the aluminium body and there was powdered alloy corrosion over these areas. The hood was in tatters, hoops and mechanism were laying in the rear of the body.

The 1929 Rolls-Royce 20hp as purchased by Alan Milbank after years of storage in a seaside garage.

With friend John Elliott in attendance and Tony Lester with his Series 1 Land Rover, the car was towed the one mile to Alan's home where it stood next to his 1952 Bentley Mk VI. Apart from the two wedding outings, the car had been off the road for 63 years.

Alan carefully restored all the engine and the running gear to make the car legal. This had taken a considerable amount of time and money. At this point Alan felt he could not afford a Rolls-Royce quality respray. He carefully rubbed the existing paint with wet and dry, paying particular attention to the many 'powdered scabs' on the aluminium. When this was completed, he just lacquered the paintwork from an aerosol. Quite by accident he had produced an oily rag finish. At the few shows he has already attended, many people have urged him not to repaint the car! I think Alan is very glad he bought 'another set of wheels', but he does say that this one is the last – I wonder.

In an issue of *Hemmings Motor News*, the 'Find of the Day' was a 1926 20hp Rolls-Royce Shooting Brake. This car has had a chequered career. It was ordered new by A. Lloyd Roberts of London, who commissioned Hooper to build a limousine body. It was London registered YR 7058. The Rolls-Royce records show that by 1938 it was owned by a D. Leigh. Sometime during the period 1938 to 1967 it had been fitted with a shooting brake body, the builder of which is unknown, though it is recorded as having been with Rippon Brothers of Huddersfield, well known coachbuilders, and after the Second

'Many people have asked me not to repaint the car.'

World War were also retailers. I do not think Rippons built the body. During the Second World War many larger cars were requisitioned and turned into ambulances and NAAFI waggons. When the war ended, they needed to be re-bodied, steel was in short supply and wooden shooting brake bodies were one obvious answer.

In 1968 it was owned by my friend John Fasal, acknowledged expert on all things pre-war Rolls-Royce. John had bought it from T.A. Wilkinson of Hartley Witney for £325.10.6d. He told me what he had bought:

> We found a rather neglected and tatty example of a shooting brake which, however, suited my requirements. The test run revealed the sad condition of the engine with an external crack in the cylinder head and the temperature reaching 100c due to a worn impeller shaft on the water pump, a noisy gearbox and back axle and unoriginal exhaust system with holes … the 'back yard' body was in poor shape with woodworm and dry rot. Beneath the rear door valance on the near side was a bird's nest.

John did the repairs necessary for its use on the road and drove it for two years. He amused me by saying, 'Travelling in the shooting brake

The Graham family from Illinois stored the car for forty-four years.

John Fasal 'did the repairs necessary' and drove it for two years.

was greatly enhanced when I installed the latest 4-track stereo cartridge music system and acoustics.' John's meticulous record keeping showed that after D. Leigh it went to John Adams of Great Gidding, a well-known Rolls-Royce specialist and breaker, then to George Berry in Exmouth in August 1958, to Peter Calver of Chichester in January 1960, and quickly on to W.D. Watchurst of Romsey before being bought by T.A. Wilkinson. In 1971 the car was in the USA owned by eminent anesthesiologist Dr M. Shepherd in St. Petersburg in Florida. (After he sold the car in 1973 he was murdered in New Orleans.) Dale Power, a car collector and race driver, was the next owner. He kept it only a short while before selling to the Graham family of Illinois. It was then partly dismantled and stored for the next 44 years. In 2017 it was moved from the family home to be with the son in Madison in Alabama. Lance Smith of Rocket City Custom of Huntsville recently bought the car. He told me, 'I bought the car on its trailer and a Model T Ford from the family in a deal. I could not remove the car from the trailer as the rear wheels were not mounted.' Because of the fragile condition of the body Lance was advised, 'This car must be shipped in an enclosed trailer and will not leave this shop without one.'

Whilst we tend to call them all woodies these days, we must remember they were originally called estate cars and then shooting brakes. After the war when there was a shortage of steel, a number of pre-war cars were given a new lease of life with a Woodie body – wood and aluminium, unlike steel, not being rationed. This is what we think happened to a 1932 Rolls-Royce 20/25 first owned by A.S. Taylor who is thought to have been an MP. It was originally fitted with a limousine body by Hooper and registered YY 2988. This Woodie has recently been removed from possibly forty years of storage by Daniel Rapley of Brookfield, Connecticut, who has been telling me about it:

No idea who converted it. I purchased the car from the largest estate I have ever visited, up on Lake Erie. The car was in store in a garage, on flat tyres and dry as a bone. The previous owner was an iron ore magnate. According to his son, his father had purchased it in

1932 Rolls-Royce 20/25 as bought by Daniel Rapley.

Britain on a whim on a visit [c mid-1960s]. The car had an engine problem with the oil and the water mixing.

No other history is known. When I wrote about this car originally, I said, 'From the photographs it would appear that a removable spat had been fitted over the rear wheels to give a more modern appearance, possibly accomplished after it had arrived in America.' I am now convinced that this car was bodied in the early 1950s by a little known British coach builder, the Belgrave Engineering Company in a style they had called 'The Belgravia'. Rolls-Royce historian Tom Clarke has a brochure put out by this company and the illustration is almost identical.

In late 1924, Mr Bullwell Smith (later Sir), who was Chairman of Arsenal Football Club amongst other things, bought a 1924 Rolls-Royce Silver Ghost and registered it XT 209. In 1925 it went back to the factory and was modified by fitting

Subsequent research showed this to be a Belgravia conversion by a little known British coachbuilder, 'the Belgrave Engineering Company'.

XT 209 is the left-hand car in this group and was used in the film *The Man in the White Suit*.

front wheel brakes. The coachwork was a rather formal closed example by Windovers. There is no history known until 1951 when the car appeared in the film *The Man in the White Suit* starring Alec Guinness. A continuation logbook showed the car now belonged to Carr Brothers who offered cars for hire for filming as well as specialist vehicles for the film industry. Soon the Rolls-Royce was registered as 'Utility' and painted maroon and had

become a camera car with a special woody type body, coachbuilder unknown. Present owner Bob Vass told me:

> The body was designed with a strong roof section over the driver and bonnet and a ladder for a camera man to operate 'up top'. There are fitments between the front dumb irons for a camera platform in front of the radiator and a very substantial tube across for a safety harness.

In 1958 ownership changed to Professor George du Boulay, who undertook some repairs and additions and used it for family camping holidays. A few years later the car was pushed into the shed and left. Shortly before he died in 2007, he bequeathed the car to the Sir Henry Royce Memorial Foundation. The Foundation kept the car for a few years but knowing that it would never have enough funds to restore the car properly, offered it for sale. Hilary and Bob Vass bought it to save it from being sold to those who might take the body off and turn it into yet another tourer. They were determined to put it back into the form it

1924 Rolls-Royce Silver Ghost being removed from storage by Hilary & Bob Vass.

The car now restored to the condition it was in when owned by Carr Brothers film prop specialists.

was with the Carr Brothers. After a lot of work on body and engine, the car is now able to appear at shows. It has not been re-painted but a Du Boulay paint-over has been mainly removed as Bob said: 'A modern, high gloss re-spray would destroy a great deal of its character'.

This is not the first Rolls-Royce I have written about which has been pressed into service as a camera car. In 2002 in a Bonhams auction in Monaco they offered an immaculate Rolls-Royce Phantom 1 with reproduction open coachwork. The auction catalogue stated, 'In the 1960s, it had a rather undistinguished period serving as a movie camera platform at Pinewood Studios'. It may have been used to film *Thunderball* but certainly did appear in a short film entitled *A Child's Guide To Blowing Up A Motor Car*. This film starred Denis Norden and his young nephew visiting Silverstone (the racetrack being disguised as a main road) where some of the car stunts were being shot for

Rolls-Royce Phantom I in use as a camera car when making *Thunderball* at a disguised Silverstone circuit.

this movie. Included in the film are a number of shots of the Rolls-Royce in use as a camera car. It is quite obvious that it is being driven pretty hard. I suppose it had to be as it was filming scenes with James Bond's Aston Martin DB5.

# POSTSCRIPT

Thank you for reading this book, I hope you found it interesting. I have thoroughly enjoyed my forty years of writing about the so called 'barn find' and hope that I will be able to do so for a few more years.

One subject I have hardly touched on is values. It's interesting when a barn find car gets offered at auction, it often fetches more than you think it ought to, if you were to take into account the restoration costs. In many cases the buyer has been influenced by the background story to the car or just plain nostalgia. It may be that the car is so original that restoration may not be as complicated as you first thought. Having written many articles about cars that enthusiasts have restored I am not often shocked by the lengths they have taken to get a barn find back on the road. In the end it must be a most satisfying feeling of achievement and worth all those hundreds of hours in the garage, the financial reward however may be far less than the expenditure. Not everyone wants to restore to a concourse condition. Many people are happy just to have a good-looking car that will give them endless fun on the road or rally field. In recent years there has been a new type of restoration, the 'oily rag'. Here a car is worked on in such a way that its patina, warts and all are retained, whilst running gear and engine are rebuilt to a good working order. Some say 'oily rag' is just an excuse not to spend so much time or money on restoration; however, there are cars on which an 'oily rag' finish is actually more difficult to achieve than a restoration! I have not gone into much detail about restoration in these pages. It's a far more complicated process than many might think. It needs a book to itself. May I wish you great enjoyment in your hobby whether it's finding cars or restoring them.

Each year I think the supply of suitable barn find cars will dry up, but so far thank goodness it has not. If you think you have a story for me, I would love to hear from you; please contact me at waremichael29@gmail.com or write to me c/o the publishers Pen and Sword.

# ACKNOWLEDGEMENTS

I was delighted when Jools Holland said he would write the foreword for this book. He is one of a number of our top musicians who have an interest in, and collections of, historic motor cars. He often attends the September International Autojumble at Beaulieu as a guest of the Montagu family. Thank you Jools for your time and trouble.

I must thank *Classic and Sports Car* magazine, especially the editor Alastair Clements, for allowing me to base this book on articles which I have written in the last few years in my 'Lost and Found' column. Most of the stories and photographs have come from you, the enthusiast. I thank you most sincerely and have tried to acknowledge you or your club in the individual items. I am grateful for the time and trouble you have taken on my behalf. I must single out Jeroen Booij, a Dutch motoring journalist who has a nose for barn finds, some of his stories appear in my column and in the book.

The Library at the National Motor Museum has been 'as always' invaluable. Patrick Collins, the Search and Enquiries Officer, has been extremely helpful and has always pointed me in the right direction. He also kindly read the manuscript and offered a number of suggested alterations. In the preparation of the manuscript, I have been helped by Theresa Browning, who was previously my secretary when I worked at Beaulieu and who still helps me with my freelance work. Theresa loves typing – I do not. It's a good combination! Roger Beale kindly provided the cartoon which features on the Introduction page.

I thank John Scott-Morgan, Janet Brookes and the team at publishers Pen and Sword for having faith in an author of whom they had never heard and taking on this book project which covers a subject they had not contemplated covering before.